THE VERSO BOOK OF DISSENT

VERSO

THE VERSO BOOK OF DISSENT

From Spartacus to the Shoe-Thrower of Baghdad

Preface by Tariq Ali
Edited by Andrew Hsiao and Audrea Lim

VERSO
London • New York

First published by Verso 2010
Preface and selection © Verso 2010

All rights reserved

The moral rights of the author have been asserted

1 3 5 7 9 10 8 6 4 2

Verso
UK: 6 Meard Street, London W1F 0EG
US: 20 Jay Street, Suite 1010, Brooklyn, NY 11201
www.versobooks.com

Verso is the imprint of New Left Books

ISBN-13: 978-1-84467-448-0

British Library Cataloguing in Publication Data
A catalogue record for this book is available from the British Library

Library of Congress Cataloging-in-Publication Data
A catalog record for this book is available from the Library of Congress

Typeset in Bembo by Hewer Text UK Ltd, Edinburgh
Printed in the US by Quad/Graphics and in Sweden by Scandbook AB

PREFACE: IN PRAISE OF DISSENT

The big bee flies high,
The little bee makes the honey;
The black folks makes the cotton,
And the white folk gets the money.

Leadbelly

Dissenting voices and rebellions against existing authority—pagan, tribal, religious, civil, feudal, bourgeois and Communist—form a global pattern. They have always existed in some shape or another. It is sometimes automatically assumed that conflict in ancient times or the medieval period, and even the English, Dutch and French revolutions, lacked the clarity, insight and precision of twentieth-century upheavals. This was not always the case. There are good reasons why the slave rebellion led by Spartacus left such a deep mark on history and was to be forever remembered, especially by the European theorists and practitioners of revolution in the nineteenth and twentieth centuries. It was not accidental that the highly literate and cultivated German revolutionaries of the early twentieth century named their organization *Spartacusbund*, only to be crushed just as ruthlessly by the German state as the slaves who dared to free themselves were by its antique Roman predecessor.

Or take the example of 2 BCE Sparta; here, a huge class fissure developed in the two centuries following the Peloponnesian conflict, unusually for that city-state accustomed to all its male citizens carrying out similar military tasks. The gap between rich and poor grew so wide that a revolution from above, backed by the peasantry, became inevitable. The class divide precipitated a set of socio-politico-economic reforms that prefigured all the struggles in the modern world and created a city-state that was more politically advanced than, to take but one instance, contemporary Britain.

A triumvirate of three radical monarchs—Agis IV, Cleomenes III and Nabis—created a structure to help revive the state on a new basis: nobles were sent packing into exile; the dictatorship of magistrates was abolished, slaves were given their freedom, all citizens were allowed to vote and lands confiscated from the rich were distributed to the poor. The early Roman Republic, threatened by this example, sent its legions under Quintus Flaminius to crush Sparta. According to Livy, the great Roman historian of Antiquity, Nabis responded with a cold anger but great dignity:

> Do not demand that Sparta conform to your own laws and institutions . . . You select your cavalry and infantry by their property qualifications and desire that a few should excel in wealth and the common people be subject to them. Our lawgiver did not want the state to be in the hands of a few, whom you call the Senate, nor that any one class should have supremacy in the State. He believed that by equality of fortune and dignity there would be many to bear arms for their country.[1]

Had Charles I, Louis XVI and Abdulmecid I followed the example of the Spartan rulers, the history of Europe might have taken a different course. These episodes alone, properly contextualized and described in detail, could take up half a book, but all anthologies are notorious for their inability to satisfy every reader. That is the nature of the beast.

The Verso Book of Dissent is no exception, but there is a difference. Unlike its various predecessors in the Anglophone world, we have attempted to cover the entire globe. The book was compiled in our offices in New York and London with the help of authors and friends of Verso across every continent. To do proper justice to the subject, we would have needed several editors stationed in different parts of the world, unlimited time and resources to produce a three-volume encyclopedia on this theme. Logistical problems and material scarcity made this an impossible task. Speed was essential since the volume marks the fortieth anniversary of New Left Books/Verso, a publishing endeavor that has survived the fall of the Berlin Wall because it challenges the established verities of all the different worlds that existed in 1970 when it was founded: the United States and its satellites, the Soviet Union and its subordinates, with China and India, amongst others, also subjected

---

1 Quoted in Perry Anderson, *Passages from Antiquity to Feudalism*, New Left Books, 1974. This work cannot be too strongly recommended for its Gibbonsian-Marxist account of the rise and fall of the ancient empires of the European world.

to critical analyses. Entire thought-systems and state structures, economies capitalist and non-capitalist were analyzed and challenged by many of our authors. The contrast between the vision of socialism defended by Marx and the reality of the post-capitalist states was too stark to be ignored. Dissenting voices from Eastern Europe and China always found a place in Verso catalogues.

We were fortunate in that the group of people who founded New Left Books/Verso were, in the main, associated with the *New Left Review*. Intellectual affinities with *NLR* essayists were the foundation stone of New Left Books before it expanded and created Verso as its paperback arm in 1975: Perry Anderson did the books, Anthony Barnett did the first business plan with a handwritten cash flow in red and blue. More importantly, Barnett understood the crucial importance of a single-market strategy, retaining and re-taking rights to the US market that helped establish Verso as a transcontinental publishing house a good decade before many illustrious publishing names followed suit. The name "Verso"—the left-hand page—was Francis Mulhern's suggestion and only squeezed through the horse-race mechanism deployed by the *NLR* editorial committee, displacing more popular suggestions that included "October," "Salamander" and "Arcades." We owe a debt to Mulhern.

In 1970, the first book published by New Left Books was Ernest Mandel's *Europe versus America: The Contradictions of Imperialism*, a sharp polemical response to the French liberal politician Jean-Jacques Servan-Schreiber's *The American Challenge*: a plea in favor of Europe becoming America's permanent second fiddle and for France to break with all Gaullist ideas of independence. On this, Servan-Schreiber, we must regretfully acknowledge, appears to have been totally vindicated by history. In 2010, Perry Anderson revisited the subject in his *The New Old World*, which revealed the consequences of EU Atlanticism. A deep crisis confronted the European elites: a growing democratic deficit at home, the adoption of the economically disastrous Wall Street system and the support for American wars and policies in the world, in many cases against the expressed desires of European citizens.

The contents of this anthology, therefore, should not come as a surprise to those who read Verso books. We have concentrated on dissenters and rebels who have attempted to move mountains, to improve, change, transform the world since the earliest times. There are, of course, forms of dissent within established structures whose aim is to strengthen the existing order by preventing obvious errors that might lead to the most extreme form of dissent: revolutions . . . from below. These we have avoided even though temptations were strong. Take for instance, a letter written (but not dispatched) by Emperor Joseph II of Austria to his flighty sister Marie-Antoinette in her Versailles bunker, which is harsher in tone and far more insightful than the recent pseudo-feminist biographies of her that encourage gender-sympathy while ignoring the larger picture. Joseph knew his sister rather better than her present-day fan club and the letter is therefore worth quoting in some detail (a case of using the preface to cheat on the anthology):

> Let me, my dearest sister, address you with a frankness justified by my affection for you and my interest in your welfare. From what I hear, you are becoming involved in a great many matters that are no concern of yours, and of which you know nothing, led on by intrigue and flattery that excite in you not only self-conceit and a desire to shine but jealousy and ill-feeling. This conduct may well impair your happiness and sooner or later must provoke serious trouble between you and the King, which will detract from his affection and esteem for you, and cause you to fall into disfavor with the public . . . Why should you, my dear sister, employ yourself in removing ministers from their posts, in banishing one and giving office to another, in seeing that some friend of yours wins his lawsuit or in creating a new and expensive court appointment . . . Have you ever asked yourself what right you have to meddle in the affairs of the French Government or monarchy? What studies have you made, what knowledge have you acquired, that you believe your opinion of value, particularly in matters calling for such wide experience? You, a charming young woman, who think only of frivolity, of your *toilette*, of your amusements; who do not read books or listen to serious talk for more than ten minutes in a month; who never stop to reflect, or to give a thought to the consequences of what you say or do? . . . Listen to the advice of a friend, give up all these intrigues, have nothing what-ever to do with public affairs . . . For the rest, do some reading, improve your mind.

Some of the more complacent and visionless rulers of Europe as well as their accompaniments—Sarkozy-Bruno, Berlusconi and his prostitutes, for example—might ponder these sage words.

Had we more space and time we would have included an illustrated section with various covers from satirical magazines such as the old *Private Eye* and the young *Charlie Hebdo*, *Le Canard Enchaine*, *Titanic*, etc. Earlier this year, while in Zagreb, I spoke to young dissidents, some of whom had been involved with a satirical paper which I had not heard of before, the *Feral Tribune*, whose writers and designers challenged the narrow nationalism defended by state-controlled media, described war-crimes committed by their own soldiers, denounced Franjo Tudjman's ultra-nationalist views justifying the *Ustaše* collaboration with German fascism during Croatia's first experiment with controlled independence. Corruption, state-church relations, warmongering and xenophobia were the regular targets. The issue of *Feral Tribune* that is now a collector's item and impossible to locate was the cover depicting digitally altered images of Tudjman and Milošević as lovers in bed as Bosnia-Herzegovina is being divided.

In Sarajevo, most people regret the breakup of the country. Tito's portraits are visible in a number of places, and journalists, students and war veterans speak openly of the large-scale corruption and the fragility. In Serbia, I spoke to the courageous journalists of B92, a radio station that criticized its own government as well as the NATO jets dumping bombs on Belgrade and the bridge to Novi Sad. Dissent was alive and well in the former Yugoslavia. Many critics of what took place twenty years ago as well as the crisis of the present situation are beginning to cross frontiers and meet again at book fairs and film festivals, and there is talk of making the island of Korcula in Croatia a virtual Yugo-space where dissenters from the whole region can gather once a year to exchange ideas and experiences.

There is much that had to be left out of this volume to preserve a geographical and historical balance. In order to preempt some nit-picking criticism, let me explain the reasons for one of the absences. Were there dissenters in the early Stone Age? Despite the lack of any evidence, it's likely that primitive forms of dissent did exist (as they do in parts of the animal kingdom today). Disagreements before the emergence of language were expressed through gestures—still the case in Naples,

Lahore and elsewhere (as Sraffa pointed out to Wittgenstein in Cambridge after the latter claimed that all propositions have logical forms; Sraffa made a derogatory gesture in response and asked, "What is the logical form of this?")—or grunts, or in extreme cases, through violence, though probably far less frequently than in the agricultural civilizations that followed. Contrary to comic book clichés, there is nothing to suggest that early Stone Agers were either patriarchal or matriarchal. But since the emergence of a primitive alphabet was still several hundred centuries away and even cave art had not yet emerged it was, regretfully, not possible to include a single dissenting voice or image from those times in this anthology. If a reader demonstrates our ignorance here we will include the missing link in a subsequent edition.

Andrew Hsiao and Audrea Lim (Verso NY) have worked long and hard to prepare this volume, and to them and all those who helped, our thanks.

Tariq Ali
August 2010

ACKNOWLEDGMENTS

Let's begin with a quote:

> Did Malcolm X (or Alex Haley, with whose "assistance" his *Autobiography* was written) thank the brothers who'd helped him in his life and work? Did Philip Roth thank Portnoy's mother? Did Emily Brontë thank her sisters? Of course not. Maybe in those psychologically naïve days, authors weren't aware of how much the sometimes passive contributions of others helped them to pursue their dreams.[1]

Malcolm X, who appears in this book, does not seem to us to have been naïve, psychologically or otherwise. But perhaps he didn't have as much of a need to acknowledge others as we do, for *The Verso Book of Dissent* is truly the brainchild of many. This book is a testament to the community, global in scope, which Verso has built over its lifespan of forty years. The book was born on a conference call and was nurtured by virtually everyone at Verso—and many of our friends—through each stage of its rapid growth.

Tariq Ali shaped the book from its inception, and Jacob Stevens watched over it through final edits. Sebastian Budgen drew on his amazing knowledge of left theory and communism; Tom Penn helped with his precise view of English history; Tony Wood added expertise on Eastern Europe; Mark Martin, Tamar Shlaim and Rowan Wilson all made many contributions. Bob Bhamra presided with calm over an impossible schedule. Our interns kept us afloat: Rahel Aima; Anwyn Crawford with her trove of songs and poems; Puya Gerami, multi-linguist; John Kwiatkowski; Josh LeMorey; Marissa Solow; and Matt Turney with his diplomatic skills.

Friends contributed essential insight and expertise, not only in areas where we knew we were lacking but also where we thought we were informed: Gilbert Achcar's incisive understanding of the Middle Eastern left; Samar Al-Bulushi's grasp of African radicalism; Benedict Anderson's sweeping and unparalleled knowledge of Southeast Asian history; Charles Anderson's sharp sense of bottom-up history in the

---

1 Sara Nelson, *So Many Books, So Little Time*, Berkeley, 2004.

Middle East; Matthew Brown's thorough understanding of Latin America in the nineteenth century; Paul Buhle's encyclopedic knowledge of the American left, which helped produce his, Mari Jo Buhle's, and Dan Georgakas's *Encyclopedia of the American Left*—an indispensable resource; Mike Davis's memory of what has been forgotten; Adriana Diaz Enciso's useful critique and respect for Latin American history; Neil Faulker's vast knowledge of the British left; Bill Fletcher's insight into African social movements; Greg Grandin's broad view of imperialism in Latin America; Adam Hochschild's important recovery of African rebel voices; George Katsiaficas's knowledge of global radicalism, especially Korean social movements, which will soon deliver a book on South Korea, *Deliver Us From Evil*; Naveen Kishore's acumen about India; Heonik Kwon's understanding of Korean history; Peter Kwong's judicious sense of Chinese radicalism, reform, and reaction; Francis Mulhern's keen judgments about European history; Todd Muller's devotion to America's hidden histories; Vijay Prashad's encouraging support of the project from its beginning and his astonishing erudition about global radical history; John Saul's critical and productive views on left movements in Africa; Lorna Scott-Fox's insights on Latin American history; S. Shankar's knowledge—and translations—of Tamil writing; Christy Thornton's smart sense of Latin America; and Peter Zinoman's precise and deep comprehension of Vietnamese history. Two more books deserve acknowledgment: *The Vintage Book of Dissent*, edited by Michael Rosen and David Widgery, was an early inspiration, and *The Radical Reader: A Documentary History of the American Radical Tradition*, edited by Timothy Patrick McCarthy and John McMillian, is the best book of its kind and contains much fuller extracts than we have managed in this book.

Many others helped, including Anthony Arnove, Avita Bansee, Robert Barnett, Mamadou Bocoum, Patrick Bond, Jeff Chang, Fan Pan Chen, Lisa Chen, Jace Clayton, Joanna Dawson, Georgi Derluguian, Efrain Kristal, Max Elbaum, Mark Elvin, Sarah Fan, Ronald Fraser, Matthew Gandy, Javier Genao, Richard Gott, Eric Hazan, Christina Marie Sabio Hilo, Forrest Hylton, Esther Kaplan, Caglar Keyder, Shaun Lin, Gavan McCormack, Ying-Ying Ma, Iain Marlow, Tom Mertes, Frey Mortenssen, Tiarra Mukherjee, David Murphy, Amilcar Navarro, Jason Ng, Michael Parenti, Yoav Peled, Marcus Rediker,

Moss Roberts, Dennis Rodgers, David Roediger, Ann Sandhorst, Jacob Scheier, Alisa Solomon, Kasian Tejapira, Senait Tesfai, Jeffrey Treviño, Cihan Tugal, Achin Vanaik, Jeffrey Wasserstrom, Jason Wu, and Marilyn Young.

Two people deserve special mention. Through months of digging in libraries and many days of writing and research, Rafael Khachaturian and Blair Taylor—two young radical scholars who are destined for great things and, if we are lucky, will grace Verso's author list soon— played an essential role in the making of this book.

A heartfelt thanks to them and all of our comrades above.

Of course, all errors and especially omissions are our own, and diligent readers might notice the absence of many historically significant manifestoes, which we've guillotined because they don't make for great reading. But readers can make suggestions for future editions on our website, helping us to plug these holes.

Andrew Hsiao and Audrea Lim

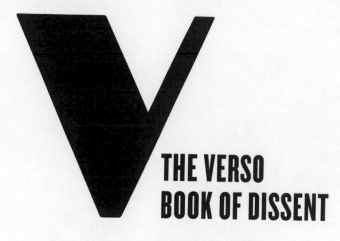

THE VERSO
BOOK OF DISSENT

From Spartacus to
the Shoe-Thrower
of Baghdad

"The Tale of the Eloquent Peasant"

Your heart is greedy, it does not become you. You despoil: this is not praiseworthy for you . . . The officers, who are set as a protection against injustice—a curse to the shameless are these officers, who are set as a bulwark against lies. Fear of you has not deterred me from supplicating you; if you think so, you have not known my heart. The Silent one, who turns to report to you his difficulties, is not afraid to present them to you . . . Do the truth for the sake of the Lord of Truth . . .

Does it then happen that the scales stand aslant? Or is it thinkable that the scales incline to one side? Behold, if I come not, if another comes, then you host opportunity to speak as one who answers, as one who addresses the silent, as one who responds to him who has not spoken to you . . . You have not fled, you have not departed. But you have not yet granted me any reply to this beautiful word which comes from the mouth of the sun-god himself: "Speak the truth; do the truth: for it is great, it is mighty, it is everlasting. It will obtain for you merit, and will lead you to veneration." For does the scale stand aslant? It is their scale-pans that bear the objects, and in just scales there is no . . . wanting.

"The Tale of the Eloquent Peasant" tells of an Egyptian who was tricked into letting his donkey eat a noble's grain, after which the overseer of the noble's land took the donkey and beat the peasant. The peasant's subsequent appeals were so persuasive that his case was eventually brought to the Pharoah, who asked that his petition be put into writing. This is his petition. The Pharoah ordered the noble to transfer all of his property to the peasant; the peasant's donkey was also returned.

ca. 700 BCE   **HESIOD**

Works and Days

For the gods keep hidden from men the means of life [crops]. Else you would easily do work enough in a day to supply you for a full year even without working; soon would you put away your rudder over the smoke, and the fields worked by ox and sturdy mule would run to waste. But Zeus in the anger of his heart hid it, because Prometheus the crafty deceived him; therefore he planned sorrow and mischief against men. He hid fire; but that the noble son of Iapetos stole again for men from Zeus the counselor in a hollow fennel-stalk, so that Zeus who delights in thunder did not see it. But afterwards Zeus who gathers the clouds said to him in anger: "Son of Iapetos, surpassing all in cunning, you are glad that you have outwitted me and stolen fire—a great plague to you yourself and to men that shall be. But I will give men as the price for fire an evil thing in which they may all be glad of heart while they embrace their own destruction." So said the father of men and gods, and laughed aloud.

Hesiod's Works and Days *is a didactic poem on the necessity of human labor. While Hesiod's early account of the Prometheus myth portrays him as a harmful figure for invoking Zeus's wrath, in modern times Prometheus has become a symbol of human ambition and defiance in the face of the gods.*

SAPPHO ## ca. 590 BCE

"Supreme Sight on the Black Earth"

Some say cavalry and others claim
infantry or a fleet of long oars
is the supreme sight on the black earth.
I say it is
the one you love. And easily proved.
Didn't Helen, who far surpassed all
mortals in beauty, desert the best
of men, her king,
and sail off to Troy and forget
her daughter and her dear parents? Merely
Aphrodite's gaze made her readily bend
and led her far
from her path. These tales remind me now
of Anaktoria who isn't here,
yet I
for one
would rather see her warm supple step
and the sparkle in her face than watch all
the chariots in Lydia and foot soldiers armored
in glittering bronze.

*Sappho hailed from the Greek island of Lesbos. The lack of information about
her life, coupled with the romantic and homoerotic subject matter of her surviving work, has led to much speculation about whether her poetry was
autobiographical in nature.*

ca. 522 BCE HERODOTUS

Otanes's Speech

Then Otanes, whose proposal to give the Persians equality was defeated, spoke thus among them all: "Fellow partisans, it is plain that one of us must be made king (whether by lot, or entrusted with the office by the choice of the Persians, or in some other way), but I shall not compete with you; I desire neither to rule nor to be ruled; but if I waive my claim to be king, I make this condition, that neither I nor any of my descendants shall be subject to any one of you." To these terms the six others agreed; Otanes took no part in the contest but stood aside; and to this day his house (and no other in Persia) remains free, and is ruled only so far as it is willing to be, so long as it does not transgress Persian law.

Herodotus recounts Persian nobleman Otanes's speech during a debate between the Persian conspirators who overthrew the Magian usurper Gaumata. By asking neither to rule nor to be ruled, Otanes invokes the Greek idea of isonomía—roughly, equality under the law.

ca. 415 BCE THUCYDIDES

The Melian Dialogue

Melians: But we know that the fortune of war is sometimes more impartial than the disproportion of numbers might lead one to suppose; to submit is to give ourselves over to despair, while action still preserves for us a hope that we may stand erect . . . You may be sure that we are as well aware as you of the difficulty of contending against your power and fortune, unless the terms be equal. But we trust that the gods may grant us fortune as good as yours, since we are just men fighting against unjust.

The twenty-seven-year-long conflict between Athens and Sparta documented by Thucydides drew in other Greek city-states. The people of Melos first wished to remain neutral—but, facing a superior Athenian force and urged to surrender, they refused to yield and took up arms instead. Despite fighting bravely, the Melians finally succumbed, after which their men were put to death and their women and children enslaved.

PLATO   # 399 BCE

The Apology of Socrates

And now, Athenians, I am not going to argue for my own sake, as you may think, but for yours, that you may not sin against the God, or lightly reject his boon by condemning me. For if you kill me you will not easily find another like me, who, if I may use such a ludicrous figure of speech, am a sort of gadfly, given to the state by the God; and the state is like a great and noble steed who is tardy in his motions owing to his very size, and requires to be stirred into life. I am that gadfly which God has given the state and all day long and in all places am always fastening upon you, arousing and persuading and reproaching you. And as you will not easily find another like me, I would advise you to spare me. I dare say that you may feel irritated at being suddenly awakened when you are caught napping; and you may think that if you were to strike me dead, as Anytus advises, which you easily might, then you would sleep on for the remainder of your lives, unless God in his care of you gives you another gadfly. And that I am given to you by God is proved by this: that if I had been like other men, I should not have neglected all my own concerns, or patiently seen the neglect of them during all these years, and have been doing yours, coming to you individually, like a father or elder brother, exhorting you to regard virtue; this, I say, would not be like human nature. And had I gained anything, or if my exhortations had been paid, there would have been some sense in that: but now, as you will perceive, not even the impudence of my accusers dares to say that I have ever exacted or sought pay of anyone; they have no witness of that. And I have a witness of the truth of what I say; my poverty is a sufficient witness.

After citizens' charges were brought against Socrates for being a man "who corrupted the young, refused to worship the gods, and created new deities," he was given the chance to defend himself against the accusations. Found guilty and condemned to death, he drank hemlock.

ca. 300 BCE   QU YUAN

"The Lament"

I marvel at the folly of the king,
So heedless of his people's suffering.
They envied me my mothlike eyebrows fine,
And so my name his damsels did malign.
Truly to craft alone their praise they paid,
The square in measuring they disobeyed;
The use of common rules they held debased;
With confidence their crooked lines they traced.
In sadness plunged and sunk in deepest gloom,
Alone I drove on to my dreary doom.
In exile rather would I meet my end,
Than to the baseness of their ways descend.

Qu Yuan, scholar and minister in the state of Chu during China's Warring States Period, is said to have waded into the Miluo River holding a big rock after hearing that the Chu capital had been captured by the state of Qin. The villagers tried to save him but couldn't find his body, and the act of racing boats to find his body became the Dragon Boat Festival, which remains a Chinese tradition to this day. "The Lament," one of his most famous poems, was written in exile, after having rebuked the Chu king for his corruption and complicity with the Qin.

ca. 200 BCE   THIRUVALLUVAR

"Thirukkural"

Harsher than a killer's cruelty is the cruel reign of an oppressive king.

Thiruvalluvar's "Thirukkural" is a classic of Tamil poetry, and the first work on ethics in Dravidian literature. This is Kural (couplet) 560.

Pattinappaalai

Like the Tiger cub with its sharp claws and its curved stripes growing (strong) within the cage, his strength came to maturity (like wood in grain) while he was in the bondage of his enemies. As the large-trunked elephant pulls down the banks of the pit, and joins its mate, even so after deep and careful consideration, he drew his sword, effected his escape by overpowering the strong guard and attained his glorious heritage in due course.

The Pattinappaalai *was an epic Tamil poem from the Sangam period chronicling the tale of Karikala Chola—the "elephant slayer"—and his dramatic escape from bondage to become a "just and able" Tamil ruler.*

Letter to Jen An

It was in consequence of my speaking out that I met disaster in the first place; were I to make myself doubly a laughing stock in my native place, to the disgrace of my forebears, how could I ever have the face again to visit the grave of my father and my mother? Even after a hundred generations my shame will but be the more. This is what makes my bowels burn within me nine times a day, so that at home I sit in a daze and lost, abroad I know not where I am going. Whenever I think of this shame the sweat drenches the clothes on my back. I am fit only to be a slave guarding the women's apartments: better that I should hide away in the farthest depths of the mountains. Instead I go on as best I can, putting up with whatever treatment is meted out to me, and so complete my degradation . . .

When the Chinese General Li Ling was blamed by Emperor Wu of the Han Dynasty and all the court officials for the military defeat by the Xiongnu nomads, the great court historian Sima Qian was the only person that came to his defense. As punishment, Sima Qian was given the choice of paying a fine or being castrated; he had no money, so he chose the latter.

63 BCE SALLUST

"On the Corrupting Power of Wealth"

As soon as riches came to be held in honour, and brought glory, imperium, and power, virtue began to grow dull; poverty was seen as disgraceful, innocence as malevolence. Therefore because of wealth, our youths were seized by luxury, greed and pride; they stole and squandered; reckoning their own property of little worth, they coveted other peoples'; contemptuous of modesty and chastity, of everything divine or human, they were without thought or restraint.

The politician and historian Sallust held that the defeat of Carthage, Rome's rival, led to a rapid decline in Roman morals. A supporter of Julius Caesar and opponent of Cicero, Sallust rose from plebian origins to join the Roman Senate, where he sided with the popular against the aristocratic party. In retirement, he consistently portrayed a nation corrupted by wealth; yet as governor of North Africa he had bled the region dry.

ca. 83 CE TACITUS

Calgacus's Speech

To us who dwell on the uttermost confines of the earth and of freedom, this remote sanctuary of Britain's glory has up to this time been a defense. Now, however, the farthest limits of Britain are thrown open, and the unknown always passes for the marvelous. But there are no tribes beyond us, nothing indeed but waves and rocks, and the yet more terrible Romans, from whose oppression escape is vainly sought by obedience and submission. Robbers of the world, having by their universal plunder exhausted the land, they rifle the deep. If the enemy be rich, they are rapacious; if he be poor, they lust for dominion; neither the east nor the west has been able to satisfy them. Alone among men they covet with equal eagerness poverty and riches. To robbery, slaughter, plunder, they give the lying name of empire; they make a solitude and call it peace.

According to the Roman historian Tacitus, Calgacus was a Caledonian chieftain who gave a rousing speech urging resistance against the encroaching Roman armies. Since there is little historical evidence about his existence, Calgacus could have been a literary creation of Tacitus.

SPARTACUS   ca. 150

Slave Uprising

At the same time Spartacus, a Thracian by birth, who had once served as a soldier with the Romans, but had since been a prisoner and sold for a gladiator, and was in the gladiatorial training-school at Capua, persuaded about seventy of his comrades to strike for their own freedom rather than for the amusement of spectators. They overcame the guards and ran away, arming themselves with clubs and daggers that they took from people on the roads, and took refuge on Mount Vesuvius. There many fugitive slaves and even some freemen from the fields joined Spartacus, and he plundered the neighboring country, having for subordinate officers two gladiators named Oenomaus and Crixus. As he divided the plunder impartially he soon had plenty of men. Varinius Glaber was first sent against him and afterwards Publius Valerius, not with regular armies, but with forces picked up in haste and at random, for the Romans did not consider this a war yet, but a raid, something like an attack of robbery. They attacked Spartacus and were beaten. Spartacus even captured the horse of Varinius; so narrowly did the very general of the Romans escape being captured by a gladiator.

Appian (Appianus of Alexandria), the author of this excerpt, was a Roman historian of Greek background whose Roman History *consists of twenty-four books. Spartacus's slave rebellion took place between 73 and 71 BCE, and is known as the Third Servile War. Roman forces eventually routed the slaves in southern Italy, and Spartacus is thought to have perished in battle.*

300s

BASIL OF CAESARIA
"Which Things Are Yours?"

Which things, tell me, are yours? Whence have you brought your goods into life? You are like one occupying a place in a theater, who should prohibit others from entering, treating that as his own which was designed for the common use of all. Such are the rich. Because they preoccupy common goods, they take these goods as their own. If each one would take that which is sufficient for his needs, leaving what is superfluous to those in distress, no one would be rich, no one poor . . . The rich man is a thief.

Basil of Caesaria was the bishop of Caesaria Mazaca in Cappadocia, Asia Minor (modern-day Turkey). He was sainted in both the Western and Eastern traditions of Christianity. He gave away his family inheritance to help the poor.

869

ALI IBN MUHAMMAD
Zanj Slave Uprising

A man who claimed to be Ali ibn Muhammad appeared in Furat al-Basrah. He assembled his forces from among the Zanj, who labored in removing the nitrous topsoil of the marshland districts . . .

In the early morning of Saturday, the 28th of Ramadan . . . some slaves of one of the Shurajiyyin known as al-'Attar met him as they were setting about their business. Ali ordered them to be seized, along with their agent, who was placed in fetters. They numbered in all some fifty slaves.

Ali next proceeded to a place where al-Sana'i worked, and there around five hundred slaves were seized, among them one known as Abu Hudayd. Their agent was likewise bound with fetters and taken along as well . . .

Ali proceeded next to a place belonging to al-Sirafi and captured there another 150 slaves . . . Ali continued to operate in this fashion all day until he had amassed a large number of the Shurajiyyin slaves.

Assembling them together, Ali rose and addressed them, raising their spirits by promising to lead and command them and to give them possession of property. He swore a solemn oath to them that he would neither deceive nor betray them and they would experience only kind treatment from him. Ali then summoned their masters and said to them: "I wanted to behead you all for the way you have treated these slaves, with arrogance and coercion and, indeed, in ways that Allah has forbidden, driving them beyond endurance. But my companions have spoken to me about you, and now I have decided to set you free." . . .

Ali ordered their slaves to bring whips of palm branches and, while their masters and agents were prostrated on the ground, each one was given 500 lashes.

He continued efforts to gather blacks to his camp right up to the time of the prayer breaking the fast of Ramadan. On the day of the celebration of the feast he summoned his followers to assemble for prayer . . . Ali said that he wanted to improve their condition, giving them slaves, money, and homes to possess for themselves, and that by them they could achieve the greatest things . . .

In the 600s, and possibly even earlier, the Zanj—"Land of the Black," a term used by medieval Arab geographers to refer to Africans on the East Coast—were being shipped as slaves to all the Arab countries bordering the Indian Ocean. From 869 to 883, a series of revolts took place in Basra, involving around half a million slaves. One of these revolts was led by Ali ibn Muhammad, who was captured and executed by the Abbasid dynasty in 881. This account is taken from the famous history of Ibn Jarir Al-Tabari, available in English today in thirty-nine volumes. Al-Tabari was a Persian historian who lived from 838–923.

CIVAVAKKIYAR   900s

Aphorisms on Shiva

Suckled milk never returns to the udder. Churned butter never dissolves back into milk.

The sound of the conch does not return to the broken shell, nor life to the broken body.

The unfurled blossom, the fallen fruit do not reappear on the tree.
And the dead are never, never, never reborn.

*Civavakkiyar is held by legend to have been a Tamil Brahmin who took a
low-caste wife. Like other siddhas (yogis with supernatural powers) he argued
against the institutionalization of religion, the efficacy of ritual, and the reality
of caste.*

ca. 1000   ABU ALA AL-MA'ARI

"None to Lead but Reason"

You've had your way a long, long time,
You kings and tyrants,
And still you work injustice hour by hour.
What ails you that do not tread a path of glory?
A man may take the field, although he love the bower.
But some hope a divine leader with prophetic voice
Will rise amid the gazing silent ranks.
An idle thought! There's none to lead but reason,
To point the morning and the evening ways.

*Al-Ma'ari, a philosopher, poet and writer born just outside Aleppo in what is
now northern Syria, was a controversial figure of his time: a constant champion
of reason against superstition, authority and tradition.*

1198   MANJOK

Speech to Fellow Slaves

Are generals and ministers born to these glories? No! For when the
time is auspicious anyone can hold such office. Why then should we
work ourselves to the bone and suffer under the whip? . . . If each
individual [*nobi*] kills his master and burns records of his status, thus
ending the *nobi* system in our country, then each of us will be able to
become a minister or general.

Manjok, a hereditary slave (nobi) in Korea, organized a slave revolt that would become known as the Manjok Slave Rebellion. The plot was discovered before it could be carried out, and Manjok was thrown into the river.

ANONYMOUS　　　**1300s**

"Judgments of Karakash"

A certain rich old miser was subject to fainting fits, which tantalized two nephews who desired his death; for, though constantly falling down lifeless, he always got up again. Unable to bear the strain any longer, they took him in one of his fits and prepared him for burial.

They called in the professional layer-out, who took off the miser's clothes which, by ancient custom, were his perquisite, bound up his jaws, performed the usual ablutions upon the body, stuffed the nostrils, ears and other apertures with cotton wool against the entrance of demons, sprinkled the wool with a mixture of water, pounded camphor, and dried and pounded leaves of the lotus-tree, and also with rose-water; bound the feet together by a bandage round the ankles, and disposed the hands upon the breast.

All this took time, and before the operator had quite finished, the miser revived; but he was so frightened at what was going on, that he fainted again; and his nephews were able to get the funeral procession under way.

They had performed half the road to the cemetery when the miser was again brought to life by the jolting of the bier, caused by the constant change of the bearers, who incessantly pressed forward to relieve one another in the meritorious act of carrying a true believer to the grave. Lifting the loose lid, he sat up, and roared for help. To his relief he saw Karakash, the impartial judge, coming down the path the procession was mounting, and appealed to him by name. The judge at once stopped the procession, and, confronting the nephews, asked:

"Is your uncle dead or alive?" "Quite dead, my lord." He turned to the hired mourners. "Is this corpse dead or alive?" "Quite dead, my lord," came the answer from a hundred throats. "But you can see for yourself that I am alive!" cried the miser wildly. Karakash looked him

13

sternly in the eyes. "Allah forbid," said he, "that I should allow the evidence of my poor senses, and your bare word, to weigh against this crowd of witnesses. Am I not the impartial judge? Proceed with the funeral!" At this the old man once more fainted away, and in that state was peacefully buried.

"This is one of the judgments of Karakash" was a commonly-used saying in Palestine through to the 1900s, meant to indicate that a decision or judgment was hopelessly absurd, despite having been arrived at on the basis of strict evidence. Karakash was a real judge; these are satirical indictments of the institution of law.

1381   JOHN BALL

Sermon

When Adam delved and Eve span,
Who was then the gentleman?

Called "the mad priest of Kent" by the medieval chronicler Jean Froissart, John Ball was an English priest who took a prominent role in the Peasants' Revolt of 1381 by giving voice to the rebels' complaints through his speeches and sermons. When the revolt was crushed, Ball was ordered drawn and quartered by Richard II.

1400s   PATTIRAKIRIYAR

Lamentations for True Knowledge

Oh when will come the day when we shall live without caste distinctions?

Pattirakiriyar is said to have been a king who, after being converted to siddhism, renounced his kingdom, became a mendicant, and composed the Lamentations for True Knowledge.

LE LOI

The Elephant and the Grasshopper

Today it is a case of the grasshopper pitted against the elephant. But tomorrow the elephant will have its guts ripped out.

From 1407–28, Vietnam was ruled by the Chinese Ming Dynasty. After ten years of rebellion led by the aristocrat Le Loi, Vietnam achieved its independence again. This saying, later made famous to the rest of the world by Ho Chi Minh, who predicted victory over Vietnam's French colonialists with great confidence, is from Le's victory speech.

SKANDERBEG

Resistance to the Ottoman Empire

The bravest adventurers of France and Germany were allured by his fame and retained in his service: his standing militia consisted of 8,000 horse and 7,000 foot; the horses were small, the men were active: but he viewed with a discerning eye the difficulties and resources of the mountains; and, at the blaze of the beacons, the whole nation was distributed in the strongest posts. With such unequal arms, Skanderbeg resisted twenty-three years the powers of the Ottoman empire; and two conquerors, Amurath the Second, and his greater son, were repeatedly baffled by a rebel whom they pursued with seeming contempt and implacable resentment . . . The Albanian prince may justly be praised as a firm and able champion of his national independence.

Considered a national hero of Albania, Skanderbeg was initially an Ottoman officer. After rebelling against the empire in 1443, he waged a guerrilla war that managed to hold off annual Ottoman campaigns of conquest for twenty-four years. Skanderbeg fell ill and died in 1468; ten years later, the Ottomans crushed the final Albanian resistance.

1450   JACK CADE

"The Complaint of the Poor Commons of Kent"

Item. They say that the commons of England would first destroy the king's friends and afterward himself, and then bring the Duke of York to be king so that by their false means and lies they may make him to hate and destroy his friends, and cherish his false traitors. They call themselves his friends, and if there were no more reason in the world to know, he may know they be not his friends by their covetousness.

Item. They say that it were great reproof to the king to take again what he has given, so that they will not suffer him to have his own good, nor land, nor forfeiture, nor any other good but they ask it from him, or else they take bribes of others to get it for him.

Jack Cade was the nom-de-guerre of the anonymous leader of a popular revolt against King Henry VI. After organizing about 5,000 peasant rebels, Cade led the group through London, capturing and beheading the king's associates. After promising to fulfill the listed demands, of which a small extract is included here, the government set out to capture Cade, killing him in battle.

1511   HATUEY

Speech to the Taínos

Here is the God the Spaniards worship. For these they fight and kill; for these they persecute us and that is why we have to throw them into the sea . . . They tell us, these tyrants, that they adore a God of peace and equality, and yet they usurp our land and make us their slaves. They speak to us of an immortal soul and of their eternal rewards and punishments, and yet they rob our belongings, seduce our women, violate our daughters. Incapable of matching us in valor, these cowards cover themselves with iron that our weapons cannot break.

Hatuey, the legendary Taíno chief who headed a native guerrilla resistance against Spanish colonists, led a siege against the Spanish fort at Baracoa, Cuba, pinning the Spanish in the fort for months. Hatuey was eventually captured and burned alive at the stake and is considered the first hero in the struggle for Cuban independence. He was holding out a basket of gold and jewels as he gave this speech.

MARTIN LUTHER   1517

Disputation of Doctor Martin Luther on the Power and Efficacy of Indulgences

28. It is certain that when the penny jingles into the money-box, gain and avarice can be increased, but the result of the intercession of the Church is in the power of God alone.

. . .

45. Christians are to be taught that he who sees a man in need, and passes him by, and gives [his money] for pardons, purchases not the indulgences of the pope, but the indignation of God.

Written to protest the Catholic Church's sale of indulgences, German priest and theologian Luther's Ninety-Five Theses quickly spread across Europe and provided one of the sparks for the Protestant Reformation.

THOMAS MÜNTZER   1524

"Sermon to the Princes"

One sees now how prettily the eels and snakes copulate together in a heap. The priests and all the evil clergy are the snakes, as John the Baptist calls them, and the temporal lords and rulers are the eels, as is symbolized by the fish in Leviticus 11. For the devil's empire has painted its face with clay.

Oh, you beloved lords, how well the Lord will smash down the old pots of clay [ecclesiastical authorities] with his rod of iron. Therefore, you most true and beloved regents, learn your knowledge directly from the mouth of God and do not let yourselves be seduced by your flattering priests and restrained by false patience and indulgence. For the stone [Christ's spirit] torn from the mountain without human touch has become great. The poor laity and the peasants see it much more clearly than you do.

Now, should you want to be true rulers, then you must begin government at the roots, as Christ commanded. Drive his enemies away from the elect, for that is your appointed task. Beloved ones, do not offer us any stale posturing about how the power of God should do it without your application of the sword. Otherwise, may the sword rust away in its scabbard on you. May God grant this!

A German theologian who became a leader in the Peasants' War of 1524–26, Müntzer's radicalism superseded Martin Luther's. In his "Sermon to the Princes," said to have been delivered to Duke John of Saxony, he presented himself as a visionary capable of seeing the eventual kingdom of God on earth. Captured during the following year, Müntzer confessed under torture that he believed "omnia sunt communia"—all things are in common.

1532   FRANÇOIS RABELAIS

Pantagruel

I want to tell you how Panurge treated his prisoner [the king] Anarche . . . [O]ne day he dressed up his said king in a fine little linen doublet, all slashed like an Albian's cap, and nice sailor's breeches, without shoes (for, he said, they would spoil his vision), and a little blue cap with one big capon's feather—I'm wrong, I think he had two—and a handsome blue and green belt, saying that this livery served him well, seeing that he had been perverse [a pun on the French words for blue and green]. In this state he brought him before Pantagruel and said to him:

"Do you recognize this clown?"

"No, indeed," said Pantagruel.

"It's Milord the pluperfect king; I want to make a good man of him. These devils the kings are nothing but dumb calves; they know nothing and they're good for nothing, except to do harm to their poor subjects, and trouble the whole world by making war, for their wicked and detestable pleasure. I want to set him to a trade, and make him a hawker of green sauce [made of onions]. So now start shouting: 'Don't you need some green sauce?'"

And the poor devil shouted.

"That's too soft," said Panurge; and he took him by the ear and said: "Sing louder, in the key of G. So, you poor devil! You have a strong throat, you've never been so lucky as not to be king any more."

Pantagruel was the French writer Rabelais' first published work, which, by way of the adventures of two giants, Gargantua and Pantagruel, explores and subverts the Renaissance social order.

ÉTIENNE DE LA BOÉTIE   1548

Discourse on Voluntary Servitude

A people enslaves itself, cuts its own throat, when, having a choice between being vassals and being free men, it deserts its liberties and takes on the yoke, gives consent to its own misery, or, rather, apparently welcomes it. If it cost the people anything to recover its freedom, I should not urge action to this end, although there is nothing a human should hold more dear than the restoration of his own natural right, to change himself from a beast of burden back to a man, so to speak. I do not demand of him so much boldness; let him prefer the doubtful security of living wretchedly to the uncertain hope of living as he pleases.

He who thus domineers over you has only two eyes, only two hands, only one body, no more than is possessed by the least man among the infinite numbers dwelling in your cities; he has indeed nothing more than the power that you confer upon him to destroy you. Where has he acquired enough eyes to spy upon you, if you do not provide them yourselves? How can he have so many arms to beat you with, if he does not borrow them from you? The feet that trample down your cities, where does he get them if they are not your own? How does he have any power over you except through you? How would he dare assail you if he had no cooperation from you? What could he do to you if you yourselves did not connive with the thief

19

who plunders you, if you were not accomplices of the murderer who kills you, if you were not traitors to yourselves? . . . From all these indignities, such as the very beasts of the field would not endure, you can deliver yourselves if you try, not by taking action, but merely by willing to be free. Resolve to serve no more, and you are at once freed. I do not ask that you place hands upon the tyrant to topple him over, but simply that you support him no longer; then you will behold him, like a great Colossus whose pedestal has been pulled away, fall of his own weight and break in pieces.

A French poet, political philosopher, and judge, Étienne de La Boétie wrote the Discourse on Voluntary Servitude *when he was just twenty-two years old. La Boétie's argument that the exercise of power requires the cooperation of the governed provides a foundation for civil disobedience and non-violent resistance.*

1579   STEPHEN JUNIUS BRUTUS

"A Defense of Liberty Against Tyrants"

Briefly, for so much as none were ever born with crowns on their heads and scepters in their hands, and that no man can be a king by himself nor reign without people; whereas on the contrary, the people might subsist of themselves, and were long before they had any kings, it must of necessity follow that kings were at the first constituted by the people . . .

If, therefore, any offer either by fraud or force to violate this law, we are all bound to resist him, because he wrongs that society to which we owe all that we have, and would ruin our country, to the preservation whereof all men by nature, by law and by solemn oath, are strictly obliged . . . the meanest private man may resist and lawfully oppose such an intruding tyrant.

Stephen Junius Brutus was a pseudonym for a French writer widely thought to have been Hubert Languet. Languet belonged to a loose group of Huguenot diplomats and philosophers today referred to as the Monarchomachs, meaning "those who fight against monarchs." They argued for the legitimacy of tyrannicide in cases where the implicit agreement between the sovereign ruler and the people had been violated.

FAKHR AL-DIN II

1613

Message to the People

Having set before our eyes a goal toward which we shall unswervingly move—the goal being full independence of our country and its complete sovereignty—we are resolved that no promise of reward or threat of punishment shall in the least dissuade us.

Fakhr al-Din was a Druze ruler in Mount Lebanon, where he fought to unite the families to fight for independence from the Ottoman Empire. In 1613 the Empire moved against al-Din with 50,000 troops and a sixty-galley fleet; he escaped and wrote this message. In 1635 he was executed along with three of his children, and today is considered one of Lebanon's first freedom fighters.

GUAMAN POMA DE AYALA

1615

Letter to King Phillip III of Spain

Your Majesty, in your great goodness you have always charged your viceroys and prelates, when they came to Peru, to look after our Indians and show favor to them, but once they disembark from their ships and set foot on land, they forget your commands and turn against us. Our ancient idolatry and heresy was due only to our ignorance of the true path. Our Indians, who may have been barbarous but were still good creatures, wept for their idols when these were broken up at the time of the conquest. But it is the Christians who still adore property, gold and silver as their idols.

Guaman Poma de Ayala was a Quechua Peruvian noble who sent an illustrated 1,189-page letter to King Phillip III of Spain, criticizing Spanish colonialism and advocating self-rule by Indians. Never read by its intended recipient, the letter was essentially forgotten until unearthed in 1908 in a Danish archive.

1647

THE LEVELLERS

Agreement of the People

Having by our late labors and hazards made it appear to the world at how high a rate we value our just freedom, and God having so far owned our cause as to deliver the enemies thereof into our hands, we do now hold ourselves bound in mutual duty to each other to take the best care we can for the future to avoid both the danger of returning into a slavish condition and the chargeable remedy of another war; for, as it cannot be imagined that so many of our countrymen would have opposed us in this quarrel if they had understood their own good, so may we safely promise to ourselves that, when our common rights and liberties shall be cleared, their endeavors will be disappointed that seek to make themselves our masters.

Emerging during the English Civil War (1642–51), the Levellers called for the expansion of suffrage, religious toleration, and sweeping political reforms. The Agreement of the People *was discussed in the Putney Debates in 1647.*

1647

LAURENCE CLARKSON

A General Charge

For who are the oppressors, but the nobility and gentry; and who are oppressed, if not the yeoman, the farmer, the tradesman, and the labourer? Then consider, have you not chosen oppressors to redeem you from oppression? . . . It is naturally inbred in the major part of the nobility and gentry . . . to judge the poor but fools, and themselves wise, and therefore when you the commonalty call a parliament, they are confident such must be chosen that are noblest and richest . . . but . . . reason affirms . . . these are not your equals, neither are these sensible of the burden that lies upon you; for indeed . . . your slavery is their liberty, your poverty is their prosperity.

English tailor Clarkson was a leading Ranter (see p. 24) and the author of a number of radical works. He rejected the concept of sin, stating it was "invented by the ruling class to keep the poor in order."

THOMAS RAINSBOROUGH 1647

The Putney Debates

I desired that those that had engaged in it [might vote]. For I really think that the poorest he that is in England hath a life to live, as the greatest he; and therefore truly, sir, I think it's clear that every man that is to live under a government ought first by his own counsel to put himself under that government; and I do think the poorest man in England is nor at all bound in a strict sense to that government that he hath not had a voice to put himself under . . .

. . . I do not find anything in the Law of God, that a lord shall choose twenty burgesses, and a gentleman but two, or a poor man choose one; I found no such things in the law of nature, nor in the law of nations. But I do find that all Englishmen must be subject to English laws, and I do verily believe that there is no man but will say that the foundation of all law lies in

Colonel Rainsborough was the highest-ranking supporter of the Levellers in the New Model Army during the English Revolution, and argued for universal male suffrage at the Putney Debates.

GERRARD WINSTANLEY 1649

"Declaration from the Poor Oppressed People Of England"

We are resolved to be cheated no longer, nor be held under the slavish fear of you no longer, seeing the Earth was made for us, as well as for you. And if the Common Land belongs to us who are the poor oppressed, surely the woods that grow upon the Commons belong to us likewise: therefore we are resolved to try the uttermost in the light of reason, to know whether we shall be free men, or slaves. If we lie still, and let you steale away our Birthrights, we perish; and if we Petition we perish also, though we have paid taxes, given free quarter, and ventured our lives to preserve the Nation's freedom as much as you, and therefore by the law of contract with you, freedom in the land is our portion as well as yours, equal with you: and if we strive for freedom, and your murdering, governing Laws destroy us, we can but perish.

Winstanley was one of the founders of the Diggers, a radical egalitarian group in England that sought to implement a social order with no property or wages. Occupying common land to put these ideas into practice, such as at St. George's Hill in Surrey, they were initially tolerated by the New Model Army but later suppressed by landowners.

1650
THE RANTERS

Christmas Carol

They prate of God; believe it, fellow-creatures,
There's no such bugbear; all was made by Nature.
We know all came of nothing, and shall pass
Into the same condition once it was,
By Nature's power; and that they grossly lie
That say there's hope of immortality.
Let them but tell us what a soul is, then
We will adhere to these mad brain-sick men.

One of the most radical sects to emerge during the English Revolution (1640–60), the Ranters, believing that God resided in all things, denied the authority of churches, priests, and holy writ. Their religiously inspired assertion of the freedom of the human spirit was a threat to power, property, and privilege.

JAMES NAYLOR 1660

Final Statement

There is a spirit which I feel that delights to do no evil, nor to revenge any wrong, but delights to endure all things, in hope to enjoy its own in the end. Its hope is to outlive all wrath and contention, and to weary out all exaltation and cruelty, or whatever is of a nature contrary to itself. It sees to the end of all temptations. As it bears no evil in itself, so it conceives none in thoughts to any other. If it be betrayed, it bears it, for its ground and spring is the mercies and forgiveness of God. Its crown is meekness, its life is everlasting love unfeigned; it takes its kingdom with entreaty and not with contention, and keeps it by lowliness of mind . . . I found it alone, being forsaken. I have fellowship therein with them who lived in dens and desolate places in the earth, who through death obtained this resurrection and eternal holy life.

Naylor was a radical English Quaker who was arrested for blasphemy in 1656. He was whipped, branded, pilloried, pierced through the tongue with a red-hot iron, and imprisoned for two years with hard labor. Radical Quakers were closely aligned with the Ranters (see p. 24) in the 1650s.

BENEDICT SPINOZA 1670

Theological-Political Treatise

The ultimate aim of government is not to rule, or restrain, by fear, nor to exact obedience, but contrariwise, to free every man from fear, that he may live in all possible security; in other words, to strengthen his natural right to exist and work without injury to himself or others.

No, the object of government is not to change men from rational beings into beasts or puppets, but to enable them to develop their minds and bodies in security, and to employ their reason unshackled; neither showing hatred, anger, or deceit, nor watched with the eyes of jealousy and injustice. In fact, the true aim of government is liberty.

Exiled for heresy from Amsterdam's Jewish community at the age of twenty-three, Spinoza eventually became a central figure in the history of Western philosophy, referred to by French Marxist philosopher Louis Althusser as the first materialist thinker. His Theological–Political Treatise *is an early defense of secular government and a criticism of religious intolerance and superstition.*

1674

JOHN MILTON

Paradise Lost

> The mind is its own place, and in it self
> Can make a Heav'n of Hell, a Hell of Heav'n.
> What matter where, if I be still the same,
> And what I should be, all but less then he
> Whom Thunder hath made greater? Here at least
> We shall be free; th' Almighty hath not built
> Here for his envy, will not drive us hence:
> Here we may reign secure, and in my choyce
> To reign is worth ambition though in Hell:
> Better to reign in Hell, then serve in Heav'n.
> But wherefore let we then our faithful friends,
> Th' associates and copartners of our loss
> Lye thus astonisht on th' oblivious Pool,
> And call them not to share with us their part
> In this unhappy Mansion, or once more
> With rallied Arms to try what may be yet
> Regaind in Heav'n, or what more lost in Hell?

Telling the Biblical story of humankind's expulsion from the Garden of Eden, Milton's aim in Paradise Lost *was to "justify the ways of God to men." The excerpt above is spoken by the fallen angel Lucifer upon his exile from Heaven, as he plots his revenge against God.*

ANDREW MARVELL   1677

An Account of the Growth of Popery and Arbitrary Government in England

Popery is such a thing as cannot, but for want of a word to express it, be called a religion; nor is it to be mentioned with that civility which is otherwise decent to be used in speaking about the differences of human opinion about divine matters.

. . .

There has now for divers years a design been carried on, to change the lawful government of England into an absolute tyranny, and to convert the established Protestant religion into downright Popery.

An English poet and parliamentarian during the tumultuous years of the Anglo-Dutch Wars, Marvell wrote numerous tracts against the corruption of the English court, criticizing censorship and defending the individual rights of Puritan dissenters. An Account of the Growth of Popery *is his last known work.*

JUANA INÉS DE LA CRUZ   1681

"Reply to Sor Filotea"

If my crime lies in the "Letter Worthy of Athena," was that anything more than a simple report of my opinion, with all the indulgences granted me by our Holy Mother Church? For if She, with her most holy authority, does not forbid my writing, why must others forbid it? Is it bold of me to oppose Vieira, yet not so for that Reverend Father to oppose the three holy Fathers of the Church? Is my mind, such as it is, less free than his, though it derives from the same source? Is his opinion to be taken as one of the principles of the Holy Faith made manifest, that we must believe it blindly?

Mexican writer, scholar, and poet of the Baroque school, Sor (Sister) Juana, a 1600s nun of the Order of St Jerome, defended the right of women to study. As a result, she was often censured by her church superiors and finally forbidden from studying. Sor Filotea was the pseudonym used by the Bishop of Puebla to publicly reprimand her for refuting a sermon by Portuguese Jesuit Antonio de Vieyra.

1773

PETER BESTES ET AL.

Slave Petition for Freedom

Sir, The efforts made by the legislative of this province in their last sessions to free themselves from slavery, gave us, who are in that deplorable state, a high degree of satisfaction. We expect great things from men who have made such a noble stand against the designs of their fellow men to enslave them. We cannot but wish and hope Sir, that you will have the same grand object, we mean civil and religious liberty, in view in your next session. The divine spirit of freedom, seems to fire every human breast on this continent, except such as are bribed to assist in executing the execrable plan.

This letter, signed by African American slaves Peter Bestes, Sambo Freeman, Felix Holbrook, and Chester Joie "in behalf of our fellow slaves in this province, and by order of their Committee," was submitted to the provincial legislature in Massachusetts on April 20, 1773.

1775

PATRICK HENRY

Speech at the Second Virginia Convention

They tell us, sir, that we are weak; unable to cope with so formidable an adversary. But when shall we be stronger? Will it be the next week, or the next year? Will it be when we are totally disarmed, and when a British guard shall be stationed in every house? Shall we gather strength by irresolution and inaction? Shall we acquire the means of effectual resistance, by lying supinely on our backs, and hugging the delusive phantom of hope, until our enemies shall have bound us hand and foot? Sir, we are not weak, if we make a proper use of the means which the God of nature hath placed in our power. Three millions of people, armed in the holy cause of liberty, and in such a country as that which we possess, are invincible by any force which our enemy can send against us . . . Besides, sir, we have no election. If we were base enough to desire it, it is now too late to retire from the contest. There is no retreat, but in submission and slavery! Our chains are forged! Their clanking may be heard on the plains of Boston! The war is inevitable—and let it come! I repeat it, sir, let it come!

It is in vain, sir, to extenuate the matter. Gentlemen may cry peace, peace—but there is no peace. The war is actually begun! The next gale that sweeps from the north will bring to our ears the clash of resounding arms! Our brethren are already in the field! Why stand we here idle? What is it that gentlemen wish? What would they have? Is life so dear, or peace so sweet, as to be purchased at the price of chains and slavery? Forbid it, Almighty God! I know not what course others may take: but as for me, give me liberty, or give me death!

Henry became the first post-colonial Governor of Virginia, and would later be a staunch anti-federalist opponent of the US constitution. This famous speech, given in Saint John's Church in Richmond, Virginia, was reconstructed by his first biographer, William Wirt, in 1816. Henry was also known to have stoked fears of Indian and slave revolts to encourage insurgency against the British.

ABIGAIL ADAMS **1776**

Letter to John Adams

I feel a gaieti de Coar to which before I was a stranger. I think the Sun looks brighter, the Birds sing more melodiously, and Nature puts on a more chearfull countanance. We feel a temporary peace, and the poor fugitives are returning to their deserted habitations. Tho we felicitate ourselves, we sympathize with those who are trembling least the Lot of Boston should be theirs. But they cannot be in similar circumstances unless pusilanimity and cowardise should take possession of them. They have time and warning given them to see the Evil and shun it—I long to hear that you have declared an independancy—and by the way in the new Code of Laws which I suppose it will be necessary for you to make I desire you would Remember the Ladies, and be more generous and favorable to them than your ancestors. Do not put such unlimited power into the hands of the Husbands. Remember all Men would be tyrants if they could. If perticuliar care and attention is not paid to the Laidies we are determined to foment a Rebelion, and will not hold ourselves bound by any Laws in which we have no voice, or Representation.

That your Sex are Naturally Tyrannical is a Truth so thoroughly established as to admit of no dispute, but such of you as wish to be happy willingly give up the harsh title of Master for the more tender and endearing one of Friend.

In another letter written to her husband John in the same month as this famous missive, Adams—an ardent abolitionist—doubted most Virginians had quite the "passion for Liberty" they claimed, since they had been used to "depriving their fellow Creatures" of freedom. When John Adams was elected president, opponents dubbed Abigail Adams "Mrs President" because of her political activism—and after her support for the repressive Alien and Sedition Acts, "Her Majesty."

1776   JOHN HANCOCK ET AL.

"Declaration of Independence"

We hold these truths to be self-evident, that all men are created equal, that they are endowed by their Creator with certain unalienable Rights, that among these are Life, Liberty and the pursuit of Happiness.—That to secure these rights, Governments are instituted among Men, deriving their just powers from the consent of the governed.— That whenever any Form of Government becomes destructive of these ends, it is the Right of the People to alter or to abolish it, and to institute new Government, laying its foundation on such principles and organizing its powers in such form, as to them shall seem most likely to effect their Safety and Happiness.

Thomas Jefferson drafted the Declaration on behalf of a committee that also included John Adams, Benjamin Franklin, Robert Livingston, and Roger Sherman. Jefferson included in his initial draft a strongly worded denunciation of Britain's role in the slave trade, which was removed at the behest of delegates from southern states.

TUPAC AMARU II   1781

Last Words to General José Antonio de Areche

There are no accomplices here but you and I. You the oppressor, and I the liberator. Both of us deserve to die.

Tupac Amaru II was a Quechua leader and grandson of Tupac Amaru, the last member of the royal Inca family. He led a legendary indigenous uprising against the Spanish in Peru.

TUPAC KATARI   1781

Last Words

You kill me now, but I will return, and then I will be millions.

The Aymaran indigenous leader raised an army of 40,000 and laid siege to La Paz, Bolivia, against the Spanish colonialists for 184 days. He was betrayed, captured and subsequently quartered, and has been revived as an icon of the contemporary indigenous struggle in Bolivia.

PLOUGH JOGGER   1786

"No More Courts, Nor Sheriffs"

I have been greatly abused, have been obliged to do more than my part in the war; been loaded with class rates, town rates, province rates, Continental rates and all rates . . . been pulled and hauled by sheriffs, constables and collectors, and had my cattle sold for less than they were worth . . . The great men are going to get all we have and I think it is time for us to rise and put a stop to it, and have no more courts, nor sheriffs, nor collectors nor lawyers.

From 1786–7, poor farmers crushed by debt and taxes rose in armed rebellion in Massachusetts, led by Daniel Shay; the incident is known as Shay's Rebellion. Plough Jogger was one such farmer, speaking here at an illegal convention opposing the Massachusetts legislature.

1787

THOMAS JEFFERSON

Letter to William Smith

God forbid we should ever be 20 years without such a rebellion. The people cannot be all, & always well informed. The part which is wrong will be discontented in proportion to the importance of the facts they misconceive. If they remain quiet under such misconceptions it is a lethargy, the forerunner of death to the public liberty. We have had 13 states independent 11 years. There has been one rebellion. That comes to one rebellion in a century & a half for each state. What country before ever existed a century & a half without a rebellion? & what country can preserve its liberties if their rulers are not warned from time to time that their people preserve the spirit of resistance? Let them take arms. The remedy is to set them right as to facts, pardon & pacify them. What signify a few lives lost in a century or two? The tree of liberty must be refreshed from time to time with the blood of patriots & tyrants. It is its natural manure.

Despite having authored the Declaration of Independence, Jefferson was a slaveholder and a proponent of the view that black people were inferior to whites in both body and mind. These famous words appeared in a letter to William Smith. Jefferson was also the inventor of the coat hanger, the dumbwaiter and the hideaway bed.

1789

NATIONAL CONSTITUENT ASSEMBLY

"Declaration of the Rights of Man and of the Citizen"

1. Men are born and remain free and equal in rights. Social distinctions may be founded only upon the general good.

2. The aim of all political association is the preservation of the natural and imprescriptible rights of man. These rights are liberty, property, security, and resistance to oppression.

3. The principle of all sovereignty resides essentially in the nation. No body nor individual may exercise any authority which does not proceed directly from the nation.

4. Liberty consists in the freedom to do everything which injures no one else; hence the exercise of the natural rights of each man has no limits except those which assure to the other members of the society the enjoyment of the same rights. These limits can only be determined by law.

Prepared and proposed by the Marquis de Lafayette, the Declaration was adopted by the National Constituent Assembly on August 26, 1789. Nicolas de Condorcet, Etta Palm d'Aelders and then Olympe de Gouges called for these rights to be extended to women; Vincent Ogé, followed by the Haitian Revolution of 1791–1804, attempted to extend them to men of color and then to slaves.

OLYMPE DE GOUGES   1792

"Declaration of the Rights of Woman and the Female Citizen"

Mothers, daughters, sisters [and] representatives of the nation demand to be constituted into a national assembly. Believing that ignorance, omission, or scorn for the rights of woman are the only causes of public misfortunes and of the corruption of governments, [the women] have resolved to set forth in a solemn declaration the natural, inalienable, and sacred rights of woman in order that this declaration, constantly exposed before all the members of the society, will ceaselessly remind them of their rights and duties; in order that the authoritative acts of women and the authoritative acts of men may be at any moment compared with and respectful of the purpose of all political institutions; and in order that citizens' demands, henceforth based on simple and incontestable principles, will always support the constitution, good morals, and the happiness of all.

Consequently, the sex that is as superior in beauty as it is in courage during the sufferings of maternity recognizes and declares in the presence and under the auspices of the Supreme Being, the following Rights of Woman and of Female Citizens.

Articles:

1. Woman is born free and lives equal to man in her rights. Social distinctions can be based only on the common utility.

2. The purpose of any political association is the conservation of the natural and imprescriptible rights of woman and man; these rights are liberty, property, security, and especially resistance to oppression.

3. The principle of all sovereignty rests essentially with the nation, which is nothing but the union of woman and man; no body and no individual can exercise any authority which does not come expressly from it.

4. Liberty and justice consist of restoring all that belongs to others; thus, the only limits on the exercise of the natural rights of woman are perpetual male tyranny; these limits are to be reformed by the laws of nature and reason.

French playwright, novelist, and pamphleteer, de Gouges was an anti-slavery activist as well as women's rights advocate. She was executed in 1793 during the Reign of Terror—officially for "opposition to the death penalty," unofficially for her association with the Girondists and for attacking the regime of Robespierre.

1792   MAXIMILIEN ROBESPIERRE

"On the Trial of the King"

When a nation has been forced to resort to the right of insurrection, it returns to the state of nature in relation to the tyrant. How can the tyrant invoke the social pact? He has annihilated it. The nation can still keep it, if it thinks fit, for everything concerning relations between citizens; but the effect of tyranny and insurrection is to break it entirely where the tyrant is concerned; it places them reciprocally in a state of war. Courts and legal proceedings are only for members of the same side.

The right to punish the tyrant and the right to dethrone him are the same thing; both include the same forms. The tyrant's trial is the insurrection; the verdict, the collapse of his power; the sentence, whatever the liberty of the people requires.

Peoples do not judge in the same way as courts of law; they do not hand down sentences, they throw thunderbolts; they do not condemn kings, they drop them back into the void; and this justice is worth just as much as that of the courts. If it is for their salvation that they take arms against their oppressors, how can they be made to adopt a way of punishing them that would pose a new danger to themselves?

Early in his career, Robespierre resigned a judgeship to avoid pronouncing a sentence of death. Soon after giving this speech in December 1792, he became a driving force of the Reign of Terror. He met the guillotine in 1794.

THOMAS PAINE   1793

The Age of Reason, Part I

All national institutions of churches, whether Jewish, Christian, or Turkish, appear to me no other than human inventions set up to terrify and enslave mankind, and monopolize power and profit.

Born in England, Paine emigrated to the American colonies in 1774 to take part in the Revolution. Two years later he published Common Sense, *in which he encouraged the colonies to declare their independence. A participant in the French Revolution too, he nevertheless argued against the execution of Louis XVI as a member of the French National Convention, drawing the distrust of Robespierre and his followers. Jailed in Paris, Paine wrote the first part of* The Age of Reason *while awaiting execution, which he only narrowly escaped.*

1794   LOUIS ANTOINE DE SAINT-JUST

Speech to the National Convention

Dare! This word contains all the politics of our revolution.

Saint-Just was executed alongside his close friend and ally Robespierre five months after making this speech. Albert Camus wrote that Saint-Just "introduced Rousseau's ideas into the pages of history."

1795   MARQUIS DE SADE

Philosophy in the Bedroom

No act of possession can be exercised on a free being; it is as unjust to own a wife monogamously as it is to own slaves. All men are born free, all are equal before the law; we must never lose sight of these principles. Hence, no sex is granted the legitimate right to seize the other sex exclusively, and never can any sex or any class possess the other arbitrarily.

Donatien-Alfonse-François, Marquis de Sade, lived as a libertine but drafted his first works in prison, after a series of scandals led his mother-in-law to secure his arrest. In this speech by the fictional libertine Dolmancé, French republicans are urged to overturn existing religions, laws and morals, in favor of liberty and equality. Philosophy in the Bedroom *was published anonymously during a single decade of freedom, before Sade was committed to the asylum where he died at age seventy-four.*

1796   WOLFE TONE

Declaration

To subvert the tyranny of our execrable government, to break the connection with England, the never failing source of all our political evils, and to assert the independence of my country—these were my objects. To unite the whole people of Ireland, to abolish the memory of all past dissensions, and to substitute the common name of Irishman, in the place of the denominations of Protestant, Catholic, and Dissenter—these were my means.

If the men of property will not support us, they must fall. Our strength shall come from that great and respectable class, the men of no property.

Called the father of Irish republicanism, Wolfe Tone sought to unite Irish Catholics and Protestants under a common opposition to English rule. Jailed and sentenced to death for collaborating with the French during the Irish Rebellion of 1798, he took his own life.

SYLVAIN MARÉCHAL   1796

"Manifesto of the Equals"

People of France!

For fifteen centuries you lived as a slave and, consequently, unhappy. For the last six years you barely breathe, waiting for independence, freedom and equality.

. . . we'll have this real equality, at whatever price. Unhappy will be those who stand between it and us! Unhappy will be those who resist a wish so firmly expressed.

The French Revolution was nothing but a precursor of another revolution, one that will be bigger, more solemn, and which will be the last.

The people marched over the bodies of kings and priests who were in league against it: it will do the same to the new tyrants, the new political Tartuffes seated in the place of the old.

What do we need besides equality of rights?

We need not only that equality of rights written into the Declaration of the Rights of Man and the Citizen; we want it in our midst, under the roofs of our houses. We consent to everything for it, *to make a clean slate so that we hold to it alone*. Let all the arts perish, if need be, as long as real equality remains!

Maréchal, a French poet and philosopher, and an early proponent of utopian socialism, wrote this manifesto in support of François-Noel Babeuf—known as

Gracchus Babeuf—a leader of the Conspiracy of the Equals against the Directory. Babeuf was guillotined the following year.

1796

THOMAS SPENCE

"The Rights of Infants"

Is not this earth our common also, as well as it is the common of brutes? May we not eat herbs, berries, or nuts as well as other creatures? Have we not a right to hunt and prowl for prey with she-wolves? And have we not a right to fish with she-otters? Or may we not dig coals or cut wood for fuel? Nay, does nature provide a luxuriant and abundant feast for all her numerous tribes of animals except us? As if sorrow were our portion alone, and as if we and our helpless babes came into this world only to weep over each other?

Spence, an English radical and advocate of the common ownership of land, was twice jailed for his pamphleteering.

1797

TOUSSAINT L'OUVERTURE

Address to Soldiers for the Universal Destruction of Slavery

Let the sacred flame of liberty that we have won lead all our acts . . . Let us go forth to plant the tree of liberty, breaking the chains of those of our brothers still held captive under the shameful yoke of slavery. Let us bring them under the compass of our rights, the imprescriptible and inalienable rights of free men. [Let us overcome] the barriers that separate nations, and unite the human species into a single brotherhood. We seek only to bring to men the liberty that [God] has given them, and that other men have taken from them only by transgressing His immutable will.

Toussaint, a slave to the age of 33, became the leader of the Haitian Revolution, the only slave revolt against European colonialists that successfully achieved an independent state. Napoleon dispatched a force that restored French control of the island in 1802, and Toussaint died in a French dungeon.

"The Petition of the Sharks of Africa"

Showeth,

That your petitioners are a numerous body, and at present in a very flourishing situation, owing chiefly to the constant visitation of the shipping of your island.

That by hovering round these floating dungeons, your petitioners are supplied with large quantities of their most favorite food—human flesh.

That your petitioners are sustained, not only by the carcasses of those who have fallen by distempers, but are frequently gratified with rich repasts from the bodies of living negroes who voluntarily plunge into the abodes of your petitioners, preferring instant destruction by their jaws, to the imaginary horrors of a lingering slavery.

That among the enormous breakers and surfs which roll on the shores of your petitioners, numbers of English boats are destroyed, the crews of which usually fall to their lot, and afford them many a delicious meal, but, above all, that large vessels crowded with negroes, are sometimes dashed on the rocks and shoals which abound in the regions of your petitioners, whereby hundreds of human beings, both black and white, are at once precipitated into their element, where the gnawing of human flesh, and the crashing of bones, afford to your petitioners the highest gratification which their natures are capable of enjoying.

Thus benefited, as your petitioners are, by this widely extended traffic, a traffic which has never before been molested, it is with the utmost indignation they hear that there are in Britain men, who under the specious plea of humanity, are endeavoring to accomplish its abolition. But your petitioners trust that this attempt at innovation, this flourishing of the trumpet of liberty, by which "more is meant than meets the ear," will be effectually frustrated.

Your petitioners know, that the truly benevolent will ever be consistent—that they will not sacrifice one part of animated nature to the preservation of another, that they will not suffer sharks to starve in order that negroes may be happy [and] hope to evince, that the sustenance of sharks, and the best interests of your Lordships, are intimately connected with the traffic in human flesh.

Tytler, a Scottish physician, poet, composer, and editor of the Encyclopedia Britannica, *was arrested and charged with sedition for his radicalism, only to flee to Ireland, then to Salem, Massachusetts, where he died in 1804. He was also Britain's first hot-air balloonist.*

1798   IRISH SAYING

"Irish Prophecy for 1798"

A wet winter, a dry spring,
A bloody summer, and no king.

The Irish Rebellion of 1798 was an uprising organized by the United Irishmen, a republican group influenced by the American and French Revolutions seeking Irish independence from England. The outbreak, which was eventually crushed by the British, lasted for three months and caused the death of some 30,000 people.

ca. 1800   HO XUAN HUONG

"On Sharing a Husband"

Screw the fate that makes you share a man.
One cuddles under cotton blankets; the other's cold.

Every now and then, well, maybe or maybe not.
Once or twice a month, oh, it's like nothing.

You try to stick to it like a fly on rice
but the rice is rotten. You slave like the maid,

but without pay. If I had known how it would go
I think I would have lived alone.

The Vietnamese poet Ho was the daughter of a concubine and at one time essentially a concubine herself—which she described as being "like a maid, but without the pay." She wrote erudite, satirical and quasi-pornographic poetry dissenting against social norms and patriarchy. Celebrated in her own time, she wrote in Vietnamese, unlike the majority of Vietnamese writers, who wrote in classical Chinese.

CHARLES FOURIER 1808

The Theory of the Four Movements and of the General Destinies

The extension of women's rights is the basic principle of all social progress.

The French utopian socialist Fourier is credited with originating the term "feminism." He imagined a future in which the seas would lose their salt and turn into oceans of lemonade, and, with the spread of his ideas overseas, utopian communities—based around the cooperative buildings he called Phalanstaires—were started in the US, including half a dozen in New York state.

MIGUEL HIDALGO 1810

"Cry of Dolores"

My children: a new dispensation comes to us today. Will you receive it? Will you free yourselves? Will you recover the lands stolen three hundred years ago from your forefathers by the hated Spaniards? We must act at once . . . Will you defend your religion and your rights as true patriots? Long live Our Lady of Guadalupe! Death to bad government! Death to the *gachupines*!

Hidalgo, a Mexican priest now considered the "father of the nation," led a group of indigenous and mestizo peasants in revolt against the Spanish colonialists, which would spark the Mexican War of Independence. After his capture and execution, his head was placed on public display for ten years as a warning to other insurgents.

1811   **TECUMSEH**

Address to William Henry Harrison

The only way to stop this evil is for all the red men to unite in claiming an equal right in the land. That is how it was at first, and should be still, for the land never was divided, but was for the use of everyone. Any tribe could go to an empty land and make a home there. And if they left, another tribe could come there and make a home. No groups among us have a right to sell, even to one another, and surely not to outsiders who want all, and will not do with less. Sell a country! Why not sell the air, the clouds, and the Great Sea, as well as the earth? Did not the Great Good Spirit make them all for the use of his children?

Faced with hostile settlers who pushed his people off their land, the leader of the Shawnee confederacy, Tecumseh, confronted Harrison, the governor of the Indiana Territory. Harrison had negotiated the Treaty of Fort Wayne, in which Indians ceded 3 million acres of land to the United States. In 1813, Tecumseh was killed in battle while fighting Harrison's forces at the Battle of the Thames in modern-day Ontario. Harrison was elected president in 1840.

ca. 1812   **LUDDITES**

"General Ludd's Triumph"

The guilty man fears but not vengeance he aims
At the honest man's life or Estate,
His wrath is entirely confined to wide frames
And to those that old prices abate.
This Engine of mischief were sentenced to die
By unanimous vote of the Trade
And Ludd who can opposition defy
Was the Grand Executioner made.

He may censure great Ludd's disrespect for the Laws
Who ne'er for a moment reflects

That foul Imposition alone was the cause
Which produced these unhappy effects.
Let the haughty no longer the humble oppress
Then shall Ludd sheath his conquering sword,
His grievances instantly meet with redress
Then peace will be quickly restored.

Let the wise and the great lend their aid and advice
Nor e'er their assistance withdraw
Till full-fashioned work at the old-fashioned price
Is established by Custom and Law.
Then the Trade when this arduous contest is o'er
Shall raise in full splendor its head,
And colting and cutting and squaring no more
Shall deprive honest workmen of bread.

Ned Ludd was a legendary English weaver from the late eighteenth century, who was later adopted as the imaginary leader of the Luddites—artisans whose livelihoods were threatened by mechanization during the Industrial Revolution. Organizing themselves to carry out acts of sabotage and intimidation, the Luddites claimed to act under the orders of "Captain Ludd," "General Ludd," or "King Ludd."

SIMÓN BOLÍVAR

1813

"Decree of War to the Death"

We are sent to destroy the Spaniards, to protect the Americans, and to re-establish the republican governments that once formed the Confederation of Venezuela. The states defended by our arms are again governed by their former constitutions and tribunals, in full enjoyment of their liberty and independence, for our mission is designed only to break the chains of servitude which still shackle some of our towns, and not to impose laws or exercise acts of dominion to which the rules of war might entitle us.

Moved by your misfortunes, we have been unable to observe with indifference the afflictions you were forced to experience by the barbarous Spaniards, who have ravished you, plundered you, and brought you death and destruction. They have violated the sacred rights of nations. They have broken the most solemn agreements and treaties. In fact, they have committed every manner of crime, reducing the Republic of Venezuela to the most frightful desolation. Justice therefore demands vengeance, and necessity compels us to exact it. Let the monsters who infest Colombian soil, who have drenched it in blood, be cast out forever; may their punishment be equal to the enormity of their perfidy, so that we may eradicate the stain of our ignominy and demonstrate to the nations of the world that the sons of America cannot be offended with impunity.

Despite our just resentment toward the iniquitous Spaniards, our magnanimous heart still commands us to open to them for the last time a path to reconciliation and friendship; they are invited to live peacefully among us, if they will abjure their crimes, honestly change their ways, and cooperate with us in destroying the intruding Spanish government and in the re-establishment of the Republic of Venezuela . . .

Spaniards and Canary Islanders, you will die, though you be neutral, unless you actively espouse the cause of America's liberation. Americans, you will live, even if you have trespassed.

Known throughout Latin America as El Libertador, Bolívar led Bolivia, Colombia, Ecuador, Panama, Peru and his native Venezuela to independence from Spain. His counterpart in the southern part of South America, José de San Martín, successfully vanquished the Royalist forces in Chile with his Army of the Andes. A year after Peruvian Independence was declared in 1821, Bolívar took over the leadership of the Independence campaign and San Martín retired from political life.

1815

LORD BYRON

"Ode (From the French)"

The chief has fallen, but not by you,
Vanquishers of Waterloo!
When the soldier-citizen

Sway'd not o'er his fellow men—
Save in deeds that led them on
Where Glory smiled on Freedom's son—
Who, of all the despots banded,
With that youthful chief competed?
Who could boast o'er France defeated,
Till lone tyranny commanded?
Till, goaded by ambition's sting,
The hero sunk into the King?
Then her fell:—so perish all,
Who would men by man enthrall!

Byron, like fellow English Romantics Keats and Shelley, was radicalized by the French Revolution and its subsequent betrayal by Napoleon, and later participated in the Italian Carbonari insurgency against Austrian Rule. "Ode (From the French)" initially appeared in the Morning Chronicle *and was jokingly attributed to Chateaubriand—a French poet who had written a pamphlet against Napoleon in 1814—upon Byron's suggestion.*

PERCY BYSSHE SHELLEY

1819

"Song to the Men of England"

Men of England, wherefore plough
For the lords who lay ye low?
Wherefore weave with toil and care
The rich robes your tyrants wear?

Wherefore feed and clothe and save,
From the cradle to the grave,
Those ungrateful drones who would
Drain your sweat—nay, drink your blood?

Men of England, wherefore plough
For the lords who lay ye low?
Wherefore weave with toil and care
The rich robes your tyrants wear?

Wherefore feed and clothe and save,
From the cradle to the grave,
Those ungrateful drones who would
Drain your sweat—nay, drink your blood?

Sow seed—but let no tyrant reap;
Find wealth—let no imposter heap;
Weave robes—let not the idle wear;
Forge arms—in your defence to bear.

Shelley, the English poet who was much maligned in his lifetime for his radical views, famously wrote in "The Masque of Anarchy": "Rise like Lions after slumber / In unvanquishable number / Shake your chains to earth like dew / Which in sleep had fallen on you— / Ye are many—they are few."

1829

GEORGE HENRY EVANS

"Working Men's Party Declaration of Independence"

"We hold these truths to be self-evident, that all men are *created equal*; that they are endowed by their creator with certain unalienable rights; that among these are *life, liberty*, and the *pursuit of happiness*; that to secure these rights" against the undue influence of other classes of society, prudence, as well as the claims of self-defense, dictates the necessity of the organization of a party, who shall, by their representatives, prevent dangerous combinations to subvert these indefeasible and fundamental privileges.

. . .

Therefore, we, the working class of society, of the city of New York, "appealing to the supreme judge of the world," and to the reason, and consciences of the impartial of all parties, "for the rectitude of our intentions, do, in the spirit, and by the authority," of that political liberty which has been promised to us equally with our fellow men, solemnly publish and declare, and invite all under like pecuniary circumstances, together with every liberal mind, to join us in the declaration, "that we are, & of right ought to be," entitled to EQUAL MEANS to obtain equal moral happiness, and social enjoyment, and that all lawful and constitutional measures ought to be adopted to the attainment of those objects. "And for the support of this declaration, we mutually pledge to each other" our faithful aid to the end of our lives.

The "Father of the Homestead Act," Evans was also the publisher of "The Man," "The Radical," and "Young America," among other broadsides. He was a founder of the National Reform Association, which pushed the US government to grant free public land to homesteaders—often on land recently emptied of Native Americans.

DAVID WALKER   1829
"An Appeal to the Colored Citizens of the World"

The whites want slaves, and want us for their slaves, but some of them will curse the day they ever saw us. As true as the sun ever shone in its meridian splendor, my color will root some of them out of the very face of the earth. They shall have enough of making slaves of, and butchering, and murdering us in the manner which they have.

. . .

I aver, that when I look over these United States of America, and the world, and see the ignorant deceptions and consequent wretchedness of my brethren, I am brought oftimes solemnly to a stand, and in the midst of my reflections I exclaim to my God, "Lord didst thou make us to be slaves to our brethren, the whites?" But when I reflect that God is just, and that millions of my wretched brethren would meet death with glory—yea, more, would plunge into the very mouths of cannons and be torn into particles as minute as the atoms which compose the elements of the earth, in preference to a mean submission to the lash of tyrants, I am with streaming eyes, compelled to shrink back into nothingness before my Maker, and exclaim again, thy will be done, O Lord God Almighty.

Walker, a contributor to Freedom's Journal, *the first African American newspaper, was also the author of the incendiary* Walker's Appeal, *which prompted southern plantation owners to put a $3,000 bounty on his head.*

1830

Address to Young Mechanics

Whatever may be the *conceived advantages* of college education, it is but rarely that a bold intellect or a sound judgment issues from the walls of privileged, and but too often useless and superannuated learning; while, on the other hand, what are the *real disadvantages* of the neglected child of labor, he is saved from the conceit of pedantry, and the jargon of sophistry, and thus remains free to profit by whatever lessons experience may bring, and to distinguish simple truth whenever it may meet his ears.

I have made human kind my study, from my youth up; the American community I have considered with most especial attention; and I can truly say that, wherever the same are not absolutely pressed down by labor and want, I have invariably found, not only the best feelings, but the soundest sense among the operative classes of society. I am satisfied, and that by extensive observation, that, with few exceptions, the whole sterling talent of the American community lies (latent indeed, and requiring the stimulus of circumstance for its development) among that large body who draw their subsistence from the labor of their hands.

Speaking out both in opposition to slavery and for the rights of workers, Frances "Fanny" Wright was an early proponent of free education, and attacked the greed of businessmen and the exploitation of manual laborers. In 1825, she founded the Nashoba Commune to educate freed slaves.

1831

"Liberty, that Nightingale"

Liberty, that nightingale with the voice of a giant, rouses the most profound sleepers . . . How is it possible to think of anything today except to fight for or against freedom? Those who cannot love humanity can still be as great as tyrants. But how can one be indifferent?

Boerne, a German writer, published a series of satirical letters, Briefe aus Paris, *a landmark in German journalism.*

WILLIAM LLOYD GARRISON   **1831**

Opening Editorial of *The Liberator*

Assenting to the "self-evident truth" maintained in the American Declaration of Independence, "that all men are created equal, and endowed by their Creator with certain inalienable rights—among which are life, liberty and the pursuit of happiness," I shall strenuously contend for the immediate enfranchisement of our slave population. In Park-Street Church, on the Fourth of July, 1829, in an address on slavery, I unreflectingly assented to the popular but pernicious doctrine of gradual abolition. I seize this opportunity to make a full and unequivocal recantation, and thus publicly to ask pardon of my God, of my country, and of my brethren the poor slaves, for having uttered a sentiment so full of timidity, injustice and absurdity. A similar recantation, from my pen, was published in the Genius of Universal Emancipation at Baltimore, in September, 1829. My conscience is now satisfied.

I am aware, that many object to the severity of my language; but is there not cause for severity? I will be as harsh as truth, and as uncompromising as justice. On this subject, I do not wish to think, or speak, or write, with moderation. No! no! Tell a man whose house is on fire, to give a moderate alarm; tell him to moderately rescue his wife from the hands of the ravisher; tell the mother to gradually extricate her babe from the fire into which it has fallen;—but urge me not to use moderation in a cause like the present. I am in earnest—I will not equivocate—I will not excuse—I will not retreat a single inch—AND I WILL BE HEARD. The apathy of the people is enough to make every statue leap from its pedestal, and to hasten the resurrection of the dead.

Editor of the abolitionist newspaper The Liberator *and one of the founders of the American Anti-Slavery Society, Garrison once burned a copy of the US Constitution on July 4th, calling it a pro-slavery document.*

1831

NAT TURNER

The Confessions of Nat Turner

Question: Do you not find yourself mistaken now?
Answer: Was not Christ crucified?

. . . I saluted them on coming up, and asked Will how came he there, he answered, his life was worth no more than others, and his liberty as dear to him. I asked him if he thought to obtain it? He said he would, or lose his life. This was enough to put him in full confidence. Jack, I knew, was only a tool in the hands of Hark, it was quickly agreed we should commence at home (Mr J. Travis) on that night, and until we had armed and equipped ourselves, and gathered sufficient force, neither age nor sex was to be spared (which was invariably adhered to). We remained at the feast, until about two hours in the night, when we went to the house and found Austin; they all went to the cider press and drank, except myself. On returning to the house, Hark went to the door with an axe, for the purpose of breaking it open, as we knew we were strong enough to murder the family, if they were awaked by the noise; but reflecting that it might create an alarm in the neighborhood, we determined to enter the house secretly, and murder them whilst sleeping. Hark got a ladder and set it against the chimney, on which I ascended, and hoisting a window, entered and came down stairs, unbarred the door, and removed the guns from their places. It was then observed that I must spill the first blood. On which, armed with a hatchet, and accompanied by Will, I entered my master's chamber, it being dark, I could not give a death blow, the hatchet glanced from his head, he sprang from the bed and called his wife, it was his last word, Will laid him dead, with a blow of his axe, and Mrs Travis shared the same fate, as she lay in bed. The murder of this family, five in number, was the work of a moment, not one of them awoke; there was a little infant sleeping in a cradle, that was forgotten, until we had left the house and gone some distance, when Henry and Will returned and killed it; we got here, four guns that would shoot, and several old muskets, with a pound or two of powder. We remained some time at

50

the barn, where we paraded; I formed them in a line as soldiers, and after carrying them through all the maneuvers I was master of marched them off to Mr Salathul Francis', about six hundred yards distant. Sam and Will went to the door and knocked. Mr Francis asked who was there, Sam replied it was him, and he had a letter for him, on which he got up and came to the door; they immediately seized him, and dragging him out a little from the door, he was dispatched by repeated blows on the head; there was no other white person in the family. We started from there for Mrs Reese's, maintaining the most perfect silence on our march, where finding the door unlocked, we entered, and murdered Mrs Reese in her bed, while sleeping; her son awoke, but it was only to sleep the sleep of death, he had only time to say who is that, and he was no more.

Turner's slave rebellion in Virginia was put down in two days—though he eluded capture for two months—but the rebels killed fifty-six whites, the most to die in a single uprising in the antebellum US. His lawyer published The Confessions of Nat Turner, *based in part on jailhouse interviews, before Turner was hanged, flayed, beheaded, and quartered on November 11, 1831.*

LOUIS-AUGUSTE BLANQUI   1832

Defense Speech at the Trial of the Fifteen

The Prosecuting Attorney has, so to speak, summoned before your imaginations a revolt of the slaves, in order, by fear, to excite your hatred: "You see," he says, "it is the war of the poor against the rich; all those who have property must repel the invasion. We bring you your enemies; strike them now, before they become any more fearsome!"

Yes, Messrs, this is the war between the rich and the poor: the rich wanted it thus, because they are the aggressors. Only they find it evil that the poor fight back; they would readily say in speaking of the people, "This animal is so ferocious that it defends itself when attacked."
. . .
It is not the first time that executioners take on the air of victims. Who are they, these robbers worthy of so much of hatred and torment?

Thirty million French people who pay to the tax department a billion and half, and about an equal amount to the privileged classes. And the people of property who live off the labors of the whole society, they are two or three hundred thousand idlers who peacefully devour the billion paid by these "robbers." It seems to me that it is here, in a new form, and between other adversaries, that we find the war of the feudal barons against the merchants they robbed on the highways.

. . .

You confiscated the rifles of July. Yes; but the bullets have taken off. Every bullet of the Parisian workers is on its way around the world: they strike without cease; they will continue to strike until not a single enemy of the happiness of the people and of freedom is left standing.

The trial at which Blanqui made this speech, in which fifteen leaders of the French Society of the Friends of the People were tried, led to one of many prison terms for the French revolutionary in a lifetime of agitation. He spent half his life in prison, and died in 1881.

1832   **SAMUEL SHARPE**

Last Words

I would rather die upon yonder gallows than live in slavery.

A Baptist preacher, Sharpe became a leader of the Great Jamaican Slave Revolt, which mobilized 60,000 of Jamaica's roughly 300,000 slaves. The unconditional emancipation of chattel slaves was achieved two years after Sharpe's execution.

1835   **ABD AL-QADIR AL-JAZA'IRI**

"They Betrayed Us"

. . . God said in the Qur'an: "O Believers! Fight the infidels who are near you . . . " We made a treaty with these people, and they violated it. We trusted them, and they betrayed us; we were patient with them, and they were impatient. If we leave them alone, they will assault us. They have already subdued the Dawa'ir and the Zmalah and other weaklings of the Faith. What prevents us from opposing and resisting them? We have been promised that we will prevail over our enemies. So come, O Muslims, to the jihad! Anyone of you who dies, will die a martyr; those who survive will gain glory and live happily.

After the French invaded Algeria in 1830, a confederation of tribes banded together and fought the colonizers for a decade, led by Abd al-Qadir, a Sufi and Muslim scholar, scoring numerous victories over their French foes. Known for his personal bravery, Abd al-Qadir is venerated as Algeria's first anticolonial leader.

MARIA STEWART   **1835**
"Productions"

It appears to me that America has become like the great city of Babylon, for she has boasted in her heart, "I sit a queen, and am no widow, and shall see no sorrow." She is indeed a seller of slaves and the souls of men; she has made the Africans drunk with the wine of her fornication; she has put them completely beneath her feet, and she means to keep them there; her right hand supports the reins of government, and her left hand the wheel of power, and she is determined not to let go her grasp. But many powerful sons and daughters of Africa will shortly arise, who will put down vice and immorality among us, and declare by Him that sitteth upon the throne, that they will have their rights; and if refused, I am afraid they will spread horror and devastation around. I believe that the oppression of injured Africa has come up before the Majesty of Heaven; and when our cries shall have reached the ears of the Most High, it will be a tremendous day for the people of this land; for strong is the arm of the Lord God Almighty.

The first American woman to lecture publicly on political themes, Stewart, a black woman, was born free but orphaned at five and worked as a maid. She later wrote for the abolitionist paper The Liberator.

1836

WILLIAM APESS

"An Indian's Looking-Glass for the White Man"

Can you charge the Indians with robbing a nation almost of their whole continent, and murdering their women and children, and then depriving the remainder of their lawful rights, that nature and God require them to have? And to cap the climax, rob another nation to till their grounds and welter out their days under the lash with hunger and fatigue under the scorching rays of a burning sun? I should look at all the skins, and I know that when I cast my eye upon that white skin, and if I saw those crimes written upon it, I should enter my protest against it immediately and cleave to that which is more honorable. And I can tell you that I am satisfied with the manner of my creation, fully—whether others are or not . . .

A preacher, writer, and politician, Apess was the first Native American to publish a book. A Son of the Forest *was written partly in reaction to advocates for Indian removal, including president-to-be Andrew Jackson, whose ethnic cleansing policies were cornerstones of his election campaigns of 1824 and 1828.*

1836

ANGELINA GRIMKE

An Appeal to the Christian Women of the South

But perhaps you will be ready to query, why appeal to women on this subject? We do not make the laws which perpetuate slavery. No legislative power is vested in us; we can do nothing to overthrow the system, even if we wished to do so. To this I reply, I know you do not make the laws, but I also know that you are the wives and mothers, the sisters and daughters of those who do; and if you really suppose you can do nothing to overthrow slavery, you are greatly mistaken. You can do much in every way: four things I will name. 1st. You can read on this subject. 2d. You can pray over this subject. 3d. You can speak on this subject. 4th. You can act on this subject. I have not placed reading before praying because I regard it more important, but because, in order to pray aright, we must understand what we are praying for; it is only then we can "pray with the understanding and the spirit also."

. . .

4. Act on this subject. Some of you own slaves yourselves. If you believe slavery is sinful, set them at liberty, "undo the heavy burdens and let the oppressed go free." If they wish to remain with you, pay them wages, if not let them leave you.

Grimke, along with her older sister Sarah, was a prominent abolitionist from the south. The Appeal *was distributed by the American Anti-Slave Society and met with wide support from radical abolitionists.*

SARAH GRIMKE   1838

Letters on the Equality of Sexes

During the early part of my life, my lot was cast among the butterflies of the fashionable world; and of this class of women, I am constrained to say, both from experience and observation, that their education is miserably deficient; that they are taught to regard marriage as the one thing needful, the only avenue to distinction; hence to attract the notice and win the attentions of men, by their external charms, is the chief business of fashionable girls.

. . .

There is another and much more numerous class in this country, who are withdrawn by education or circumstances from the circle of fashionable amusements, but who are brought up with the dangerous and absurd idea, that marriage is a kind of preferment; and that to be able to keep their husband's house, and render his situation comfortable, is the end of her being. Much that she does and says and thinks is done in reference to this situation; and to be married is too often held up to the view of girls as the sine qua non of human happiness and human existence.

. . .

There is another class of women in this country, to whom I cannot refer, without feelings of the deepest shame and sorrow. I allude to our female slaves. Our southern cities are whelmed beneath a tide of pollution; the virtue of female slaves is wholly at the mercy of irresponsible tyrants, and women are bought and sold in our slave markets, to gratify the brutal lust of those who bear the name of Christians.

. . .

Can any American woman look at these scenes of shocking licentiousness and cruelty, and fold her hands in apathy, and say, "I have nothing to do with slavery"? She cannot and be guiltless.

. . .

Our brethren may reject my doctrine, because it runs counter to common opinions, and because it wounds their pride; but I believe they would be "partakers of the benefit" resulting from the Equality of the Sexes, and would find that woman, as their equal, was unspeakably more valuable than woman as their inferior, both as a moral and an intellectual being.

Born to a rich slaveholding family, Grimke, with her sister Angelina, became a staunch abolitionist and women's rights activist.

1838   THE CHARTISTS

"The People's Charter and Petition"

The energies of a mighty kingdom have been wasted in building up the power of selfish and ignorant men, and its resources squandered for their aggrandisement.

The good of a party has been advanced to the sacrifice of the good of the nation; the few have governed for the interest of the few, while the interest of the many has been neglected, or insolently and tyrannously trampled upon . . .

Our slavery has been exchanged for an apprenticeship to liberty, which has aggravated the painful feeling of our social degradation, by adding to it the sickening of still deferred hope . . .

When the State calls for defenders, when it calls for money, no consideration of poverty or ignorance can be pleaded, in refusal or delay of the call. Required, as we are universally, to support and obey the laws, nature and reason entitle us to demand that in the making of the laws, the universal voice shall be implicitly listened to. We perform the duties of freemen; we must have the privileges of freemen. Therefore, we demand universal suffrage. The suffrage, to be exempt from the corruption of the wealthy and the violence of the powerful, must be secret.

The Chartists were the first mass working-class movement in Europe: subsequent petitions were signed by millions and presented to the British parliament. Although the Chartists later split over whether to stage an uprising, all but their demand for annual parliaments would eventually become law.

PIERRE-JOSEPH PROUDHON   1840

What Is Property?

If I were asked to answer the following question: *What is slavery?* and I should answer in one word, *It is murder*, my meaning would be understood at once. No extended argument would be required to show that the power to take from a man his thought, his will, his personality, is a power of life and death; and that to enslave a man is to kill him. Why, then, to this other question: *What is property!* may I not likewise answer, *It is theft*, without the certainty of being misunderstood; the second proposition being no other than a transformation of the first . . . ?

The French revolutionary Proudhon was the first person to call himself an anarchist. In What is Property? *he defined anarchy as "the absence of a master, of a sovereign." He was a printer and later a member of parliament, a friend and then a foe of Marx, and he participated in the French Revolution of 1848.*

LOUIS BLANC   1840

"The Organization of Labor"

What does competition mean to working men? It is the distribution of work to the highest bidder. A contractor needs a laborer: three apply. "How much do you ask for your work?" "Three francs, I have a wife and children." "Good, and you?" "Two and a half francs, I have no children, but a wife." "So much the better, and you?" "Two francs will do for me; I am single." "You shall have the work." With this the affair is settled, the bargain is closed. What will become now of the other two proletarians? They will starve, it is to be hoped. But what if they become thieves? Never mind, why have we our police? Or murderers? Well, for them we have the gallows. And the fortunate one of the three; even his victory is only temporary. Let a fourth laborer appear, strong enough to fast one out of every two days; the desire to cut down the wages will be exerted to its fullest extent. A new pariah, perhaps a new recruit for the galleys . . .

French socialist Blanc was a member of the provisional government following the Revolution of 1848. Forced into exile, he completed a twelve-volume History of the French Revolution of 1789. *After the fall of the Second Empire he became a member of the National Assembly, and his last important act was to win amnesty for the Paris Communards.*

1844

HEINRICH HEINE

Germany: A Winter's Tale

Ye fools, so closely to search my trunk!
Ye will find in it really nothing:
My contraband goods I carry about
In my head, not hid in my clothing.
Point lace is there that's finer far.

A German-Jewish poet best known for writing, "Where they burn books, they will eventually burn people," Heine was also very vocal in his criticism of nationalist sentiments in the German provinces in the nineteenth century. Germany: A Winter's Tale *was prompted by a visit to his homeland from Paris, where he had been living.*

The Condition of the Working Class in England

Having . . . ample opportunity to watch the middle-classes, your opponents, I soon came to the conclusion that you are right, perfectly right in expecting no support whatever from them. Their interest is diametrically opposed to yours, though they always will try to maintain the contrary and to make you believe in their most hearty sympathy with your fates. Their doings give them the lie. I hope to have collected more than sufficient evidence of the fact, that—be their words what they please—the middle-classes intend in reality nothing else but to enrich themselves by your labor while they can sell its produce, and to abandon you to starvation as soon as they cannot make a profit by this indirect trade in human flesh. What have they done to prove their professed good-will towards you? Have they ever paid any serious attention to your grievances? Have they done more than paying the expenses of half-a-dozen commissions of inquiry, whose voluminous reports are damned to everlasting slumber among heaps of waste paper on the shelves of the Home Office? Not they indeed, those are things they do not like to speak of—they have left it to a foreigner to inform the civilized world of the degrading situation you have to live in.

Engels spent several years of his youth in Manchester, the world's first industrial city, where his family owned a textile mill. Originally written for a German audience, his analysis of the working class in Manchester marked his radicalization and brought him into contact with Karl Marx: the beginning of a lifelong political and intellectual partnership.

1848   KARL MARX AND FRIEDRICH ENGELS

The Communist Manifesto

A specter is haunting Europe—the specter of communism. All the powers of old Europe have entered into a holy alliance to exorcise this specter: Pope and Tsar, Metternich and Guizot, French Radicals and German police-spies.

. . .

The history of all hitherto existing society is the history of class struggles. Freeman and slave, patrician and plebeian, lord and serf, guild-master and journeyman, in a word, oppressor and oppressed, stood in constant opposition to one another, carried on an uninterrupted, now hidden, now open fight, a fight that each time ended, either in a revolutionary reconstitution of society at large, or in the common ruin of the contending classes. In the earlier epochs of history, we find almost everywhere a complicated arrangement of society into various orders, a manifold gradation of social rank. In ancient Rome we have patricians, knights, plebeians, slaves; in the Middle Ages, feudal lords, vassals, guild-masters, journeymen, apprentices, serfs; in almost all of these classes, again, subordinate gradations. The modern bourgeois society that has sprouted from the ruins of feudal society has not done away with class antagonisms. It has but established new classes, new conditions of oppression, new forms of struggle in place of the old ones. Our epoch, the epoch of the bourgeoisie, possesses, however, this distinct feature: it has simplified class antagonisms. Society as a whole is more and more splitting up into two great hostile camps, into two great classes directly facing each other—Bourgeoisie and Proletariat.

. . .

Each step in the development of the bourgeoisie was accompanied by a corresponding political advance of that class. An oppressed class under the sway of the feudal nobility, an armed and self-governing association in the medieval commune: here independent urban republic (as in Italy and Germany); there taxable "third estate" of the monarchy (as in France); afterwards, in the period of manufacturing proper, serving either the semi-feudal or the absolute monarchy as a counterpoise against the nobility, and, in fact, cornerstone of the great monarchies in general, the bourgeoisie has at last, since the establishment of Modern Industry and of the world market, conquered for itself, in the modern representative State, exclusive political sway. The executive of the modern state is but a committee for managing the common affairs of the whole bourgeoisie.

The bourgeoisie, historically, has played a most revolutionary part.

The bourgeoisie, wherever it has got the upper hand, has put an end to all feudal, patriarchal, idyllic relations. It has pitilessly torn asunder the motley feudal ties that bound man to his "natural superiors," and has left remaining no other nexus between man and man than naked self-interest, than callous "cash payment." It has drowned the most heavenly ecstasies of religious fervor, of chivalrous enthusiasm, of philistine sentimentalism, in the icy water of egotistical calculation. It has resolved personal worth into exchange value, and in place of the numberless indefeasible chartered freedoms, has set up that single, unconscionable freedom—Free Trade. In one word, for exploitation veiled by religious and political illusions, it has substituted naked, shameless, direct, brutal exploitation.

The bourgeoisie has stripped of its halo every occupation hitherto honored and looked up to with reverent awe. It has converted the physician, the lawyer, the priest, the poet, the man of science, into its paid wage-laborers.

The bourgeoisie has torn away from the family its sentimental veil, and has reduced the family relation to a mere money relation.

The bourgeoisie has disclosed how it came to pass that the brutal display of vigor in the Middle Ages, which reactionaries so much admire, found its fitting complement in the most slothful indolence. It has been the first to show what man's activity can bring about. It has accomplished wonders far surpassing Egyptian pyramids, Roman aqueducts, and Gothic cathedrals; it has conducted expeditions that put in the shade all former Exoduses of nations and crusades.

The bourgeoisie cannot exist without constantly revolutionizing the instruments of production, and thereby the relations of production, and with them the whole relations of society. Conservation of the old modes of production in unaltered form, was, on the contrary, the first condition of existence for all earlier industrial classes. Constant revolutionizing of production, uninterrupted disturbance of all social conditions, everlasting uncertainty and agitation distinguish the bourgeois epoch from all earlier ones. All fixed, fast-frozen relations, with their train of ancient and venerable prejudices and opinions, are swept away, all new-formed ones become antiquated before they can ossify. All that is solid melts into air, all that is holy is profaned, and man is at last compelled to face with sober senses his real conditions of life, and his relations with his kind.

. . .

Of all the classes that stand face to face with the bourgeoisie today, the proletariat alone is a really revolutionary class. The other classes decay and finally disappear in the face of Modern Industry; the proletariat is its special and essential product. In the condition of the proletariat, those of old society at large are already virtually swamped. The proletarian is without property; his relation to his wife and children has no longer anything in common with the bourgeois family relations; modern industry labor, modern subjection to capital, the same in England as in France, in America as in Germany, has stripped him of every trace of national character. Law, morality, religion, are to him so many bourgeois prejudices, behind which lurk in ambush just as many bourgeois interests. All the preceding classes that got the upper hand sought to fortify their already acquired status by subjecting society at large to their conditions of appropriation. The proletarians cannot become masters of the productive forces of society, except by abolishing their own previous mode of appropriation, and thereby also every other previous mode of appropriation. They have nothing of their own to secure and to fortify; their mission is to destroy all previous securities for, and insurances of, individual property. All previous historical movements were movements of minorities, or in the interest of minorities. The proletarian movement is the self-conscious, independent movement of the immense majority, in the interest of the immense majority. The proletariat, the lowest stratum of our present society, cannot stir, cannot raise itself up, without the whole superincumbent strata of official society being sprung into the air.

. . .

The essential conditions for the existence and for the sway of the bourgeois class is the formation and augmentation of capital; the condition for capital is wage-labor. Wage-labor rests exclusively on competition between the laborers. The advance of industry, whose involuntary promoter is the bourgeoisie, replaces the isolation of the laborers, due to competition, by the revolutionary combination, due to association. The development of Modern Industry, therefore, cuts from under its feet the very foundation on which the bourgeoisie produces and appropriates products. What the bourgeoisie therefore produces, above all, are its own grave-diggers. Its fall and the victory of the proletariat are equally inevitable.

. . .

Communists fight for the attainment of the immediate aims, for the enforcement of the momentary interests of the working class; but in the movement of the present, they also represent and take care of the future of that movement . . . The Communists disdain to conceal their views and aims. They openly declare that their ends can be attained only by the forcible overthrow of all existing social conditions. Let the ruling classes tremble at a Communistic revolution. The proletarians have nothing to lose but their chains. They have a world to win.

Marx was thirty and Engels twenty-eight when they collaborated on the Manifesto, which was published by the League of Communists in London shortly before the outbreak of the revolutions of 1848. Although in his youth he was pulled out of the University of Bonn for his poor grades, Marx would go on to become the London correspondent for the New York Tribune, a council member of the First International, and the founder of the New Rhenish Newspaper in Cologne, which was quickly suppressed, forcing Marx into exile.

HENRY DAVID THOREAU   1849

Civil Disobedience

Under a government which imprisons any unjustly, the true place for a just man is also a prison. The proper place today, the only place which Massachusetts has provided for her freer and less desponding spirits, is in her prisons, to be put out and locked out of the State by her own act, as they have already put themselves out by their principles. It is there that the fugitive slave, and the Mexican prisoner on parole, and the Indian come to plead the wrongs of his race, should find them; on that separate, but more free and honorable ground, where the State places those who are not with her but against her—the only house in a slave-state in which a free man can abide with honor.

Thoreau refused to pay his poll tax in 1843 and spent a night in jail (one of his aunts paid the bill, to his chagrin). "If the government requires you to be the agent of injustice to another," he wrote after his home state of Massachusetts voted to return escaped slaves, "then, I say, break the law . . . What I have to do is to see, at any rate, that I do not lend myself to the wrong which I condemn." The essay was originally published as Resistance to Civil Government.

1850   ALEXANDER HERZEN

From the Other Shore

The world will not know liberty until all that is religious, political, is transformed into something simple and human, is made susceptible to criticism and denial. Logic when it comes of age detests canonized truths . . . it thinks nothing sacrosanct, and if the republic arrogates to itself the same rights as the monarchy, it will despise it as much, nay, more . . . It is not enough to despise the crown—one must not be filled with awe before the Phrygian Cap; it is not enough to consider *lèse-majesté* a crime: one must look on *salus populi* as being one.

Herzen, the father of Russian socialism and a key figure in the rise of populism, was also Russia's first independent political publisher. He fought against serfdom and advocated for socialism and individualism; Tolstoy said he had never met a man "with so rare a combination of scintillating brilliance and depth."

"Song for Certain Congressmen"

Principle—Freedom!—Fiddlesticks!
We know not where they're found.
Rights of the masses—Progress!—Bah!
Words that tickle and sound;
But claiming to rule o'er "practical men"
Is very different ground.

Beyond all such we know a term
Charming to ears and eyes,
With it we'll stab young Freedom,
And do it in disguise;
Speak soft, ye wily Dough-Faces—
That term is "compromise."

In the Compromise of 1850, thirty-five Northern US politicians agreed to implement tougher fugitive slave laws to appease Southerners, some of whom were mooting secession. "Dough-face" was a contemptuous reference to those in the North who favored slavery. Whitman is widely assumed to have been homosexual or bisexual, and his great collection Leaves of Grass *was criticized for being sexually obscene, leading to his firing from the Department of the Interior following its first publication.*

"Ain't I a Woman?"

I want to say a few words about this matter. I am a woman's rights. I have as much muscle as any man, and can do as much work as any man. I have plowed and reaped and husked and chopped and mowed, and can any man do more than that? I have heard much about the sexes being equal. I can carry as much as any man, and can eat as much too, if I can get it. I am as strong as any man that is now. As for intellect, all I can say is, if a woman have a pint, and a man a quart—why can't she have her little pint full? You need not be afraid to give us our rights for fear we will take too much—for we can't take more than our pint'll hold. The poor men seems to be all in confusion, and don't know what to do. Why children, if you have woman's rights, give it to her and you will feel better. You will have your own rights, and they won't be so much trouble. I can't read, but I can hear. I have heard the Bible and have learned that Eve caused man to sin. Well, if woman upset the world, do give her a chance to set it right side up again.

Truth, the nom de guerre of Isabella Baumfree, delivered this impromptu speech at the Women's Rights Convention in Akron, Ohio. She campaigned for abolition, women's rights, prison reform, and against capital punishment.

1852　　FREDERICK DOUGLASS

"The Meaning of July Fourth for the Negro"

What, to the American slave, is your 4th of July? I answer: a day that reveals to him, more than all other days in the year, the gross injustice and cruelty to which he is the constant victim. To him, your celebration is a sham; your boasted liberty, an unholy license; your national great-ness, swelling vanity; your sounds of rejoicing are empty and heartless; your denunciations of tyrants, brass-fronted impudence; your shouts of liberty and equality, hollow mockery; your prayers and hymns, your sermons and thanksgivings, with all your religious parade and solemnity, are, to him, mere bombast, fraud, deception, impiety, and hypocrisy—a thin veil to cover up crimes which would disgrace a nation of savages. There is not a nation on the earth guilty of practices more shocking and bloody than are the people of the United States, at this very hour.

Go where you may, search where you will, roam through all the monarchies and despotisms of the Old World, travel through South America, search out every abuse, and when you have found the last, lay your facts by the side of the everyday practices of this nation, and you will say with me, that, for revolting barbarity and shameless hypocrisy, America reigns without a rival . . .

"The arm of the Lord is not shortened," and the doom of slavery is certain. I, therefore, leave off where I began, with hope. While drawing encouragement from "the Declaration of Independence," the great principles it contains, and the genius of American Institutions, my spirit is also cheered by the obvious tendencies of the age. Nations do not now stand in the same relation to each other that they did ages ago. No nation can now shut itself up from the surrounding world and trot round in the same old path of its fathers without interference. The time was when such could be done. Long-established customs of hurtful character could formerly fence themselves in, and do their evil work with social impunity. Knowledge was then confined and enjoyed by the privileged few, and the multitude walked on in mental darkness. But a change has now come over the affairs of mankind. Walled cities and empires have become unfashionable. The arm of commerce has borne away the gates of the strong city. Intelligence is penetrating the darkest corners of the globe. It makes its pathway over and under the sea, as well as on the earth. Wind, steam, and lightning are its chartered agents. Oceans no longer divide, but link nations together. From Boston to London is now a holiday excursion. Space is comparatively annihilated. Thoughts expressed on one side of the Atlantic are distinctly heard on the other.

The far-off and almost fabulous Pacific rolls in grandeur at our feet. The Celestial Empire, the mystery of ages, is being solved. The fiat of the Almighty, "Let there be Light," has not yet spent its force. No abuse, no outrage whether in taste, sport or avarice, can now hide itself from the all-pervading light. The iron shoe, and crippled foot of China must be seen in contrast with nature. Africa must rise and put on her yet unwoven garment. "Ethiopia shall stretch out her hand unto God." In the fervent aspirations of William Lloyd Garrison, I say, and let every heart join in saying it:

> God speed the year of jubilee
> The wide world o'er!
> When from their galling chains set free,
> Th' oppress'd shall vilely bend the knee,
> And wear the yoke of tyranny
> Like brutes no more.

That year will come, and freedom's reign
To man his plundered rights again
Restore.

Douglass became a famous American author and orator while still unfree—he had escaped from his owner at the age of twenty, and wrote his Narrative of the Life of Frederick Douglass *before British friends purchased his freedom. Douglass made common cause with feminists, becoming the only African American to attend the Seneca Falls convention of 1848. He split with his early collaborator William Lloyd Garrison over the US Constitution—Douglass believed it was an anti-slavery document; Garrison did not. Douglass was later appointed a US envoy, among other government positions.*

1852

ELIZABETH OAKES SMITH

Address to the Woman's Rights Convention at Syracuse, NY

Do we fully understand that we aim at nothing less than an entire subversion of the existing order of society, a dissolution of the whole existing social compact? Do we see that it is not an error of to-day, nor of yesterday, against which we are lifting up the voice of dissent; but it is against hoary-headed error of all times; error borne onward from the first footprints of the first pair ejected from Paradise—intermingled in every aspect of civilization, down to our own times?

Smith, a prolific poet, novelist, and newspaperwoman, was nominated to be president of the convention where she gave this speech, but was rejected when she showed up in a dress baring her neck and arms. She wrote a series of feminist articles for Horace Greeley's New York Tribune, *just before Karl Marx became the London correspondent for the paper.*

SANTHAL REBELLION 1855

Battle Cry

Death to the money-lenders, the police, the civil court officers and the landlords!

The Santhal rebellion swept across the tribal regions of the Bengal Presidency (now the Indian state of Jharkhand) as peasants took up arms against the British Raj as well as landlords and exploitative traders. The rebels—led by two brothers, Sidu and Kanu of Bhagnadihi—were joined by the poor and landless peasants of other lower castes. They defeated the British in several skirmishes, but were eventually crushed by British troops, with as many as 10,000 bow-and-arrow-armed rebels perishing.

MUKTABAI 1855

"On the Griefs of the Mangs and Mahars"

If one attempts to refute, on the basis of the Vedas, the argument of these brahmins, the great gluttons, who consider themselves to be superior to us and hate us, they counter that the Vedas are their own property. Now obviously, if the Vedas are only for the brahmins, they are absolutely not for us. Teach us, O Lord, thy true religion so that we all can lead our lives according to it. Let that religion, where only one person is privileged and the rest are deprived, perish from the earth and let it never enter our minds to be proud of such a religion!

Muktabai, a Dalit woman educated at the school of Savitribai and Jyotirao Phule, published this essay against the injustices of caste in an Ahmednagar periodical when she was fourteen years old.

1856

Wall Poster

Those local officials are all ruffians!
They extort fortunes,
They fleece sums of money,
They turn nice scenery into hell.
Alongside of extracting the land tax,
They scrape from the earth even its skin.

Du Wenxiu was the leader of a separatist movement of the Muslim Hui people in China, called the Panthay Rebellion, against the Qing dynasty. These verses were posted in public places in Dali, Yunnan, and quickly became a sensation. One month later, the rebels captured Dali and drove away the foreigners and local officials.

1858

TANYUS SHAHIN

Letter to a Maronite Emir in the Service of the Ottoman Government

Because you are Christian, and because your intentions [are in alliance with] the Druzes, we are warning you without haughtiness: if you desire [to fight], we are more eager than you, and we are not afraid, because the death of a youth in his prime is like his wedding.

In 1858, the Maronite peasants in Lebanon, led by the peasant Shahin, rebelled against the Ottoman agrarian order and high taxation. The peasants set up their own state after driving the Druze sheikhs out of the province, but an armed uprising in 1859–60 ended with their defeat and the massacre of between 7,000 and 11,000 Maronites.

Letter of Proclamation

God has created you for the destruction of the destroyers of your creed . . . but it is evident to all men that these English are perverters of all men's religion . . . Various endeavors have they made to contaminate our creed . . . The Europeans deprive us of our thrones and wealth . . . They have forced the prisoners to eat their bread . . . they powdered bones and mixed them with flour, sugar, etc., and exposed it for sale . . . they ordered the Brahmins and others attached to the army to bite greased cartridges . . . I conjure the Hindoos in the name of Gunga, Tollsee and Salikram, and the Mahomedans in the name of God and the Koran, and entreat them to join us in destroying the English for their mutual welfare . . . Let not this opportunity pass away. Know oh people! You will never have such another.

Rani Lakshmibai, the Queen of Jhansi and one of the leaders of the 1857 Indian Rebellion, became a symbol of resistance against British rule. This rebellion became known as the First Indian War of Independence, and erupted in various places throughout India. Here she calls for an alliance of Hindus and Muslims against the British.

Speech to His Soldiers

To arms, then, all of you! All of you! And the oppressors and the mighty shall disappear like dust. You, too, women, cast away all the cowards from your embraces; they will give you only cowards for children, and you who are the daughters of the land of beauty must bear children who are noble and brave. Let timid doctrinaires depart from among us to carry their servility and their miserable fears elsewhere. This people is its own master. It wishes to be the brother of other peoples, but to look on the insolent with a proud glance, not to grovel before them imploring its own freedom. It will no longer follow in the trail of men whose hearts are foul. No! No! No!

Credited with making the unification of Italy possible, Garibaldi also offered to command the Union forces in the American Civil War if Lincoln would declare abolition of slavery as the war's objective (Lincoln declined). Late in life he formed the League of Democracy, which advocated universal suffrage, the emancipation of women, and abolition of ecclesiastical property.

1865

IRA STEWARD

The Eight Hour Movement

Think carefully of the difference between the operative and mechanic leaving his work at half-past seven (after dark, the most of the year), and that of the more leisurely walk home at half-past four p.m., or three hours earlier. Remember also that there is a vast difference in the strength and feelings of those who commence labor at half-past four in the morning, and those who commence two hours and a half later, or at seven o'clock. It is the hard practical necessary differences between the two systems which control the daily habits and thoughts of all who are living under them. You can hardly dwell too long upon this point, for upon it turns this whole question of social science—poverty and wealth—vice and virtue—ignorance and knowledge.

Known today as the father of the eight-hour day, Steward was a machinist from Boston whose activism was crucial in pushing the National Union of Machinists and Blacksmiths to pass a resolution approving the reduction of working hours.

1866

MIKHAIL BAKUNIN

"Revolutionary Catechism"

VIII. The political and economic organization of social life must not, as at present, be directed from the summit to the base—the center to the circumference—imposing unity through forced centralization. On the contrary, it must be reorganized to issue *from the base to the summit*—

from the circumference to the center—according to the principles of free association and federation.

IX. *Political organization.* It is impossible to determine a concrete, universal, and obligatory norm for the internal development and political organization of every nation. The life of each nation is subordinated to a plethora of different historical, geographical, and economic conditions, making it impossible to establish a model of organization equally valid for all. Any such attempt would be absolutely impractical. It would smother the richness and spontaneity of life which flourishes only in infinite diversity and, what is more, contradict the most fundamental principles of freedom. However, without certain *absolutely essential conditions* the practical realization of freedom will be forever impossible.

Russian revolutionary and theorist of collectivist anarchism, Bakunin was condemned to death in Saxony, lost his teeth in a Russian prison, survived exile in Siberia, and helped lead insurrections in Lyon, Dresden, and Czechoslovakia. He was expelled from the Marx-led First International in 1872, and became a fierce critic of authoritarian socialism, about which he declared, "If you took the most ardent revolutionary, vested him in absolute power, within a year he would be worse than the Tsar himself."

SITTING BULL   1867

Fort Union Interview

I have killed, robbed, and injured too many white men to believe in a good peace. They are medicine, and I would eventually die a lingering death. I had rather die on the field of battle.

Hunkpapa Lakota Sioux holy man Sitting Bull, or Thatháŋka Íyotake in Lakota, commanded Indian forces at the Battle of the Little Bighorn—site of Lt Col George Custer's last stand in what is now Montana. After the victory, Sitting Bull was forced to flee to exile in Canada, where he remained for many years. He eventually returned to a Dakota reservation, where he was killed by Indian agency police.

1870

JULIA WARD HOWE

"Mother's Day Proclamation"

Arise, all women who have hearts, whether your baptism be of water or of tears! Say firmly: "We will not have questions answered by irrelevant agencies. Our husbands will not come to us, reeking with carnage, for caresses and applause. Our sons shall not be taken from us to unlearn all that we have been able to teach them of charity, mercy and patience. We, the women of one country, will be too tender of those of another country, to allow our sons to be trained to injure theirs." From the bosom of a devastated Earth a voice goes up with our own. It says: "Disarm, disarm! The sword of murder is not the balance of justice." Blood does not wipe out dishonor, nor violence indicate possession. As men have often forsaken the plow and the anvil at the summons of war, let women now leave all that may be left of home for a great and earnest day of counsel.

Howe, American poet and activist, was the author of the abolitionist "Battle Hymn of the Republic." She campaigned for pacifism and women's suffrage.

1871

PARIS COMMUNARDS

"Declaration by the Central Committee of the National Guard"

It is the same old story: the criminals are trying to escape punishment by committing one last crime that will terrify the people into silence . . .

Workers, make no mistake—this is all-out war, a war between parasites and workers, exploiters and producers. If you are tired of vegetating in ignorance and poverty; if you want your children to grow up to enjoy the fruits of their labor rather than be some sort of animal reared for the factory or the battlefield, increasing some exploiter's fortune by the sweat of their brow or shedding their blood for a tyrant; if you no longer want your daughters, whom you cannot raise and care for as you wish, to be instruments of pleasure for the aristocracy of money; if you no longer want poverty and debauchery to drive men into the police force and women into prostitution; finally if you want justice to reign, workers use your intelligence, arise! Let your strong hands crush the loathsome forces of reaction! ...

The Central Committee is convinced that the heroic population of Paris will win immortal fame and regenerate the world.

Karl Marx argued in The Civil War in France *that after the Paris Commune "the form was at last discovered" for the emancipation of the proletariat. A plethora of radical measures were enacted by a participatory workers' democracy during the brief two-month existence of the Commune, from separation of church and state to the abolition of night work in bakeries. The Army of Versailles savagely crushed the Commune during April and May that year; tens of thousands were executed, and many thousands more were imprisoned and exiled.*

PARIS COMMUNARDS   1871

Speech in a Women's Club

Marriage, *citoyennes*, is the greatest error of ancient humanity. To be married is to be a slave ... Marriage, therefore, cannot be tolerated any longer in a free city. It ought to be considered a crime, and suppressed by the most severe measures. Nobody has the right to sell his liberty, and thereby set a bad example to his fellow citizens ... Therefore, I propose to this assembly, that it should get the Paris Commune to modify the decree which assures pensions to the legitimate or illegitimate companions of the National Guards, killed in the defense of our municipal rights. No half measures. We, the illegitimate companions, will no longer suffer the legitimate wives to usurp rights they no longer possess, and which they ought never to have had at all. Let the decree be modified. All for the free women, none for the slaves!

This speech was made in the Church of Saint-Eustache by a now unknown woman, and according to a contemporary report was greeted by "thunders of applause." A Women's Union was active in the Commune, and included figures like Nathalie Lemel, a socialist bookbinder who created a cooperative restaurant that served free food to the poor, and who later fought on the barricades during the Bloody Week.

1871

VICTORIA WOODHULL

"And the Truth Shall Make You Free"

Yes, I am a Free Lover. I have an inalienable, constitutional and natural right to love whom I may, to love as long or as short a period as I can; to change that love every day if I please, and with that right neither you nor any law you can frame have any right to interfere. And I have the further right to demand a free and unrestricted exercise of that right, and it is your duty not only to accord it, but, as a community, to see that I am protected in it. I trust that I am fully understood, for I mean just that, and nothing less!

Woodhull, suffragist, free love advocate, labor reformer, and spiritualist, was the first American woman to operate a brokerage firm, which she opened with her sister, Tennessee. They made a fortune on Wall Street and were dubbed the "Bewitching Brokers." With their profits, they founded a newspaper, which published the first English edition of the Communist Manifesto. *She ran for president in 1872, with Frederick Douglass as her running mate, on behalf of the Equal Rights Party.*

1875

SIOUX WARRIORS

Song

The Black Hills is my land and I love it
And whoever interferes
Will hear this gun.

In September, Senator William Allison arrived in Sioux country to negotiate a land lease agreement with the Native Americans that would have allowed the United States government to mine the area for gold. His proposal was met with 300 mounted warriors, led by Little Big Man, who chanted the above song in response.

SUSAN B. ANTHONY

1876

"Declaration of Rights for Women"

Woman has not been a heedless spectator of the events of this century, nor a dull listener to the grand arguments for the equal rights of humanity. From the earliest history of our country woman has shown equal devotion with man to the cause of freedom, and has stood firmly by his side in its defense. Together, they have made this country what it is. Woman's wealth, thought and labor have cemented the stones of every monument man has reared to liberty.

Read by Anthony on July 4—the centennial of the United States—the "Declaration of Rights for Women" scolded the "aristocracy of sex" that had developed in the country since its founding. She had been arrested four years before for voting in the presidential election. Anthony fought to unite the abolitionist, labor, and women's movements.

WENYA BOATMAN

1876

Address to Henry Stanley's Expedition

Go back Wasambywe you are bad!
Wasambywe are bad, bad, bad! The river is deep,
Wasambywe . . . You have not wings, Wasambywe.
Go back, Wasambywe.

Stanley's expedition up the River Congo was one of the inspirations for Joseph Conrad's Heart of Darkness. *His first encounter with a local tribe of "natives" was with the Wenya tribe.*

1877

"The Great Uprising"

The strikers mounted a passing loaded coal train, put on the brakes, stopped the train and pushed back the caboose and several loaded cars, thus virtually blockading the down track. One of the eight-ton cars was dumped on the rails. At ten minutes after four o'clock, July 25th, the down express train came along slowly on the other track. The strikers were led by a large man wearing a dark shirt and dark pants. His hair looked as if it had been recently shaved from his head.

Fully two hundred strikers would rush right up squarely to the front of the approaching locomotive, wave their hands, shake their clenched fists, and by many devices intimidate and threaten the engine driver and train employees. An up freight train was compelled to go back, and the crew made to desert the cars . . .

At a quarter after eleven o'clock, the night of the 25th, the strikers had torn down the watch boxes at the street corners, and proceeded down the road to tear up the tracks. They signalized their departure by a perfect hurricane of yells and cheering, as they proceeded in their onward march of ruin and destruction. The city had become turbulent again, and the outlook indicated desperate work. The cry among the men was, "Wages and revenge" . . .

The Great Railroad Strike of 1877 pitted thousands of railway workers across the United States against state militias and national guardsmen summoned to break it. As the strike spread to various states, Dacus, the editor of the St Louis Republican, *described what was happening in his own city.*

1879

"An Indian's View of Indian Affairs"

The earth was created by the assistance of the sun, and it should be left as it was . . . The Country was made without lines of demarcation and it is no man's business to divide it . . . I see the whites all over the country gaining wealth and see their desire to give us lands which are worthless. The earth and myself are of one mind. The measure of land and the measure of our bodies are the same. Say it to us if you can say it, that you were sent by Creative Power to talk to us. Perhaps you think the creator sent you here to dispose of us as you see fit. If I thought you were sent by the creator I might be induced to think you had a right to dispose of me. Do not misunderstand me, but understand me fully with reference to my affection for the land. I never said the land was mine to do with as I chose. The one who has a right to dispose of it is the one who has created it. I claim a right to live on my land, and accord you the privilege to live on yours.

Heinmot Tooyalaket, also known as Chief Joseph, was a leader of the Nez Percé tribe. In 1877, after refusing to accept the US government's forced relocation of the tribe from their native land in the Pacific Northwest to Idaho, he led the Nez Percé in a legendary three-month fighting flight to Canada, but they didn't make it, and Chief Joseph surrendered, proclaiming, "From where the sun now stands, I will fight no more forever."

ROBERT INGERSOLL **1880**

Some Mistakes of Moses

Whoever produces anything by weary labor, does not need a revelation from heaven to teach him that he has a right to the thing produced.

Walt Whitman considered Ingersoll the greatest orator in 1800s America, when oratory was popular entertainment. Ingersoll delivered Whitman's eulogy. Fellow Illinois Republicans wanted him to run for governor, but he refused to conceal his agnosticism—he was a famous freethinker.

TARABAI SHINDE

A Comparison Between Men and Women

Oh, you idiots, women are shy, delicate and foolish in their very natures. And you, what lords you are, naturally so bold, courageous, strong, learned—so there you are calling women all these names, even before your lips have touched the nectar from your mother's golden breast. But just because you happen to be strong, does that make it right? You label women with all sorts of insulting names, calling them utterly feeble, stupid, bold, thoughtless—you beat out the sound of their names in shame. You shut them up endlessly in the prison of the home, while you go about building up your own importance, becoming Mr, Sir and so on . . . Starting from your childhood you collect all rights in your own hands and womankind you just push in a dark corner far from the real world, shut up in purdah, frightened, sat on, dominated as if she was a female slave. And all the while you go about dazzling us all with the light of your own virtue. Learning isn't for women, nor can they come and go as they please . . . In fact, we women don't even need someone like the Rani of Jhansi to show us how: just take four or five hundred women who are free from attachments, put bayonets in their hands, then see what a time they'd give you. You wouldn't even find a place to hide near the stove.

Shinde's forty-page essay appeared in response to a Pune, India, newspaper article about the conviction of a young widow who had killed her newborn illegitimate child, out of fear of ostracism. She worked with the activists Jyotirao and Savitribai Phule and was a member of their Satyashodak Samaj ("Truth Finding Community") organization. The Phules started the first school for Dalit girls in 1848, as well as a shelter for upper-caste widows (who were forbidden from remarrying) in 1854.

"To Tramps"

Next winter when the cold blasts are creeping through the rents in your seedy garments, when the frost is biting your feet through the holes in your worn-out shoes, and when all wretchedness seems to have centered in and upon you, when misery has marked you for her own and life has become a burden and existence a mockery, when you have walked the streets by day and slept upon hard boards by night, and at last determine by your own hand to take your life—for you would rather go out into utter nothingness than to longer endure an existence which has become such a burden—so, perchance, you determine to dash yourself into the cold embrace of the lake rather than longer suffer thus. But halt, before you commit this last tragic act in the drama of your simple existence. Stop! Is there nothing you can do to insure those whom you are about to orphan, against a like fate? The waves will only dash over you in mockery of your rash act; but stroll you down the avenues of the rich and look through the magnificent plate windows into their voluptuous homes, and here you will discover the *very identical robbers* who have despoiled you and yours. Then let your tragedy be enacted *here!* Awaken them from their wanton sport at your expense! Send forth your petition and let them read it by the red glare of destruction. Thus when you cast "one long lingering look behind" you can be assured that you have spoken to these robbers in the only language which they have ever been able to understand, for they have never yet deigned to notice any petition from their slaves that they were not *compelled* to read by the red glare bursting from the cannons' mouths, or that was not handed to them upon the point of the sword. You need no organization when you make up your mind to present this kind of petition. In fact, an organization would be a detriment to you; but each of you hungry tramps who read these lines, avail yourselves of those little methods of warfare which Science has placed in the hands of the poor man, and you will become a power in this or any other land.

Learn the use of explosives!

Parsons was likely born a slave in Texas to parents of Native American, black, and Mexican heritage. She and her fellow-anarchist husband Albert Parsons had to flee Texas for Chicago because of their interracial marriage. Albert was executed as a Haymarket conspirator; Lucy went on to participate in the founding of the IWW and many other radical causes, and was once described by the Chicago police as "more dangerous than a thousand rioters."

1880s

NGUYEN QUANG BICH

Letter to the French

As long as you continue to boast about your strength, your skills, we will continue to refuse to give up our failures, our weaknesses. Then, if we happen to win, to live, we will be the court's righteous men. If we are unlucky enough to lose and die, we will still be supernatural devils for killing bandits. Better to endure punishment from you than ever think of punishment from our monarch. Better to be sentenced once than be sentenced for eternity.

The Can Vuong (Aid the King) movement was a widespread Vietnamese insurgency from 1885–89 against French colonial rule. Nguyen was appointed to coordinate resistance in North Vietnam.

1885

LOUIS RIEL

"Final Statement to Jury"

I am glad that the Crown have proved that I am the leader of the half-breeds in the North-West. I will perhaps be one day acknowledged as more than a leader of the half-breeds, and if I am I will have an opportunity of being acknowledged as a leader of good in this great country . . .

Riel was one of the founders of Saskatchewan province in Canada, who led the Métis (mixed French and First Nations) people of the prairies in the Red River Rebellion of 1869 and the Northwest Rebellion of 1885. Fighting against the Dominion of Canada, Riel sought the preservation of Métis territory and way of life; Riel was captured in 1885, found guilty, and hanged.

ANNA JULIA COOPER 1886
"Womanhood A Vital Element"

Not even the senseless vegetable is content to be a mere reservoir. Receiving without giving is an anomaly in nature. Nature's cells are all little workshops for manufacturing sunbeams, the product to be given out to earth's inhabitants in warmth, energy, thought, action. Inanimate creation always pays back an equivalent.

Born to a slave woman, Cooper became a famous proponent of black feminism and one of the first African American women to earn a doctoral degree—which she received at age sixty-five.

JOSÉ RIZAL 1887
Epigraph to *Noli Me Tangere*

TO MY COUNTRY:

Recorded in the history of human suffering are cancers of such malignant character that even minor contact aggravates them, engendering overwhelming pain. How often, in the midst of modern civilizations have I wanted to bring you into the discussion, sometimes to recall those memories, sometimes to compare you to other countries, so often that your beloved image became to me like a social cancer.

Therefore, because I desire your good health, which is indeed all of ours, and because I seek better stewardship for you, I will do with you what the ancients did with their infirmed: they placed them on the steps of their temples so that each in his own way could invoke a divinity that might offer a cure.

With that in mind, I will try to reproduce your current condition faithfully, without prejudice; I will lift the veil hiding your ills, and sacrifice everything to truth, even my own pride, since, as your son, I, too, suffer your defects and shortcomings.

Noli Me Tangere is Filipino nationalist revolutionary and writer Rizal's first novel, a tragic love story set against the brutal realities of European colonialism in the Philippines. Rizal was executed by the Spanish on charges of rebellion, sedition and conspiracy.

1887

LOUIS LINGG

Trial Speech

I do not recognize your law, jumbled together as it is by the nobodies of bygone centuries, and I do not recognize the decision of the court. My own counsel have conclusively proven from the decisions of equally high courts that a new trial must be granted us. The State's attorney quotes three times as many decisions from perhaps still higher courts to prove the opposite, and I am convinced that if, in another trial, these decisions should be supported by twenty-five volumes, they will adduce one hundred in support of the contrary, if it is Anarchists who are to be tried. And not even under such a law, a law that a schoolboy must despise, not even by such methods have they been able to "legally" convict us. They have suborned perjury to boot.

I repeat that I am the enemy of the "order" of today, and I repeat that, with all my powers, so long as breath remains in me, I shall combat it. I declare again, frankly and openly, that I am in favor of using force. I have told Captain Schaack, and I stand by it, "If you cannonade us, we shall dynamite you." You laugh! Perhaps you think, "You'll throw no more bombs"; but let me assure you that I die happy on the gallows, so confident am I that the hundreds and thousands to whom I have spoken will remember my words; and when you shall have hanged us, then, mark my words, they will do the bomb throwing! In this hope I say to you: I despise you. I despise your order, your laws, your force-propped authority. Hang me for it!

A German immigrant, Lingg was one of eight anarchists tried for murder in the aftermath of the Haymarket Square bombing in Chicago in 1886. Despite an almost complete lack of evidence, Lingg and four others were convicted and sentenced to death. On the eve of his execution, he took a small bomb that had been smuggled into his jail cell, and killed himself by igniting it in his mouth.

WONG CHIN FOO 1887

"Why Am I a Heathen?"

The more I read the Bible the more afraid I was to become a Christian. The idea of coming into daily or hourly contact with cold-blooded murderers, cut-throats, and other human scourges, who had had but a few moments of repentance before roaming around heaven, was abhorrent. And suppose, to this horde of shrewd, "civilized" criminals should be added the fanatic thugs of India, the pirates of China, the slavers, the cannibals, et al. Well, this was enough to shock and dismay any mild, decent soul not schooled in eccentric Christianity.

The difference between the heathen and the Christian is that the heathen does good for the sake of doing good. With the Christian, what little good he does he does it for immediate honor and for future reward; he lends to the Lord and wants compound interest. In fact, the Christian is the worthy heir of his religious ancestors. The heathen does much and says little about it; the Christian does little good, but when he does he wants it in the papers and on his tombstone.

Publisher of the first Chinese American newspaper, and rebel in China and the US, Wong was known in San Francisco and New York for his outspoken personality, once challenging anti-Chinese working-class champion Denis Kearney to a duel, giving Kearney a choice of weapons: "chopsticks, Irish potatoes, or Krupp guns."

ANONYMOUS 1888

Congolese Folksong

O mother, how unfortunate we are! . . .
But the sun will kill the white man,
But the moon will kill the white man,
But the sorcerer will kill the white man,
But the tiger will kill the white man,

85

But the crocodile will kill the white man,
But the elephant will kill the white man,
But the river will kill the white man.

When the Belgian government began opening up the interior of the Congo, they impressed local "natives" to carry their things for them as they trudged ahead. As a result, many of the lower Congolese tribes developed an intense hatred against the white man for the grueling work they were forced to perform.

1890

ANTONIO MACEO

Oath

Whoever tries to conquer Cuba will gain nothing but the dust of her blood-soaked soil—if he doesn't perish in the struggle first!

Maceo, an Afro-Cuban leader known as the Bronze Titan, was a guerrilla fighter for a free Cuba, rising to the rank of Lieutenant General in the Cuban Army of Independence, also known as the Mambi Army. He died in battle against the Spanish in 1896.

1890

JACOB RIIS

How the Other Half Lives

The sea of a mighty population, held in galling fetters, heaves uneasily in the tenements. Once already our city, to which have come the duties and responsibilities of metropolitan greatness before it was able to fairly measure its task, has felt the swell of its resistless flood. If it rise once more, no human power may avail to check it. The gap between the classes in which it surges, unseen, unsuspected by the thoughtless, is widening day by day. No tardy enactment of law, no political expedient, can close it. Against all other dangers our system of government may offer defense and shelter; against this not. I know of but one bridge that will carry us over safe, a bridge founded upon justice and built of human hearts. I believe that the danger of such conditions as are fast growing up around us is greater for the very freedom which they mock.

Riis, muckraking journalist, pioneered the art of photojournalism with How the Other Half Lives, *which exposed New York City's tenements and sweatshops, where immigrants—Riis himself had immigrated to the US—endured conditions of squalor.*

OSCAR WILDE   1891

The Soul of Man Under Socialism

Just as the worst slave-owners were those who were kind to their slaves, and so prevented the horror of the system being realized by those who suffered from it, and understood by those who contemplated it, so, in the present state of things in England, the people who do most harm are the people who try to do most good; and at last we have had the spectacle of men who have really studied the problem and know the life—educated men who live in the East End—coming forward and imploring the community to restrain its altruistic impulses of charity, benevolence, and the like. They do so on the ground that such charity degrades and demoralizes. They are perfectly right. Charity creates a multitude of sins.

Man should not be ready to show that he can live like a badly fed animal. He should decline to live like that, and should either steal or go on the rates, which is considered by many to be a form of stealing . . . As for the virtuous poor, one can pity them, of course, but one cannot possibly admire them. They have made private terms with the enemy, and sold their birthright for very bad pottage. They must also be extraordinarily stupid. I can quite understand a man accepting laws that protect private property, and admit of its accumulation, as long as he himself is able under those conditions to realize some form of beautiful and intellectual life. But it is almost incredible to me how a man whose life is marred and made hideous by such laws can possibly acquiesce in their continuance.

Written after Wilde's encounter with the anarchist writings of Peter Kropotkin, The Soul of Man Under Socialism *imagines the aesthetic and individualist benefits of socialist politics. In 1895, Wilde, who was homosexual, was convicted on charges of sodomy and gross indecency in a high-profile trial that stirred up mass hysteria, and was subsequently imprisoned for two years.*

1891

JOSÉ MARTÍ

"Our America"

A cloud of ideas is a thing no armored prow can smash through. A vital idea set ablaze before the world at the right moment can, like the mystic banner of the last judgment, stop a fleet of battleships. Hometowns that are still strangers to one another must hurry to become acquainted, like men who are about to do battle together. Those who shake their fists at each other like jealous brothers quarreling over a piece of land or the owner of a small house who envies the man with a better one must join hands and interlace them until their two hands are as one. Those who, shielded by a criminal tradition, mutilate, with swords smeared in the same blood that flows though their own veins, the land of a conquered brother whose punishment far exceeds his crimes, must return that land to their brother if they do not wish to be known as a nation of plunderers . . . We can no longer be a nation of fluttering leaves, spending our lives in the air, our treetop crowned in flowers, humming or creaking, caressed by the caprices of sunlight or thrashed and felled by tempests. The trees must form ranks to block the seven-league giant! It is the hour of reckoning and of marching in unison, and we must move in lines as compact as the veins of silver that lie at the roots of the Andes.

Poet, essayist, journalist, revolutionary philosopher, political theorist, professor, publisher, and translator—he spoke English, French, Italian, Latin and ancient Greek—Martí is known as the "Apostle of Cuban Independence." He played a pivotal role in planning and executing the War of Independence, first from abroad in several countries, though mainly in New York and as an exile in Spain, then in actual warfare in Cuba. He was shot by the Spaniards in a skirmish at Dos Ríos.

MARY ELIZABETH LEASE

1891

"Raise Hell"

What you farmers need to do is raise less corn and more Hell.

Lease was an American activist in the Farmers' Alliance and the Knights of Labor, famed for this apocryphal remark, which was said to have been delivered during a long stump speech in Halstead, Kansas.

OHASHI GENZABURO

1892

"The Rain Still Falls"

An alliance for freedom,
taken with the idea of freedom:
it all becomes clear
in the small mirror of sincerity.
Yet while we lament, asking
why our insignificant selves
were oppressed,
the rain still falls
heavily on the people.

Ohashi was an uneducated farmer and Japanese Liberal Party member who had participated in the Kabasan Incident of 1884, a small-scale insurrection that attempted to overthrow the government. This poem was written while he was in prison; he died shortly thereafter.

1892

IDA B. WELLS-BARNETT

"Southern Horrors: Lynch Law in All Its Phases"

The lesson this teaches and which every Afro-American should ponder well, is that a Winchester rifle should have a place of honor in every black home, and it should be used for that protection which the law refuses to give. When the white man who is always the aggressor knows he runs as great a risk of biting the dust every time his Afro-American victim does, he will have greater respect for Afro-American life. The more the Afro-American yields and cringes and begs, the more he has to do so, the more he is insulted, outraged and lynched.

African American journalist and pioneering civil rights activist Wells-Barnett refused to give up her seat on a segregated train seventy years before Rosa Parks, and in the end had to be dragged out of the car by three men. Having lost many friends to KKK lynching mobs, Wells-Barnett became a documentarian of the practice of lynching throughout the United States.

1894

WILLIAM MORRIS

"How I Became a Socialist"

It must be remembered that civilization has reduced the workman to such a skinny and pitiful existence, that he scarcely knows how to frame a desire for any life much better than that which he now endures perforce. It is the province of art to set the true ideal of a full and reasonable life before him, a life to which the perception and creation of beauty, the enjoyment of real pleasure that is, shall be felt to be as necessary to man as his daily bread, and that no man, and no set of men, can be deprived of this except by mere opposition, which should be resisted to the utmost.

A member of the Pre-Raphaelite Brotherhood and founder of the Arts and Crafts Movement, Morris was an English designer, craftsman, artist, poet, novelist, essayist, and libertarian socialist. He founded the Socialist League in

1884, and the journal Commonweal *the following year, which published* News from Nowhere *in serial form; in it he looked forward to a creative and fulfilling economy that worked in harmony with nature.*

DONGHAK REBELLION

1894

Proclamation

The people are the root of the nation. If the root withers, the nation will be enfeebled. Heedless of their responsibility for sustaining the state and providing for its people, the officials build lavish residences in the countryside, scheming to ensure their own well-being at the expense of the resources of the nation. How can this be viewed as proper? We are wretched village people far from the capital, yet we feed and clothe ourselves with the bounty from the sovereign's land. We cannot sit by and watch our nation perish. The whole nation is as one, its multitudes united in their determination to raise the righteous standard of revolt, and to pledge their lives to sustain the state and provide for the livelihood of the people. However startling the action we take today may seem, you must not be troubled by it. For as we felicitously live out the tranquil years ahead, each man secure in his occupation, when all the people can enjoy the blessings of benevolent kingly rule, how immeasurably joyful will we be!

The Donghak Rebellion, an anti-government, anti-establishment and anti-Yangban (upper-class scholar officials) Korean peasant uprising, initially began as a protest against political corruption in local government. It was eventually quashed only with the help of foreign troops. "Donghak"—meaning "Eastern Thought"—was a cosmology and religion that emphasized "the equality of all human beings."

1894

Homogenic Love

It has become clear that the number of individuals affected with "sexual inversion" in some degree or other is very great—much greater than is generally supposed to be the case. It is however very difficult or perhaps impossible to arrive at satisfactory figures on the subject, for the simple reasons that the proportions vary so greatly among different peoples and even in different sections of society and in different localities, and because of course there are all possible grades of sexual inversion to deal with, from that in which the instinct is *quite exclusively* directed towards the same sex, to the other extreme in which it is normally towards the opposite sex but capable occasionally and under exceptional attractions, of inversions towards its own—this last condition being probably among some peoples very widespread, if not universal.

Although known primarily for his pioneering views on homosexuality, the English poet and philosopher Carpenter rethought almost every aspect of Victorian life: from literature and politics to food production and animal welfare. The first to propose in a pamphlet—Homogenic Love—that human sexuality lies on a spectrum between heterosexuality and homosexuality, Carpenter also pioneered early ideas of prison reform and sustainable living.

1894

BAHTA HAGOS

"Black Snake, White Snake"

Once a white snake has bitten you, you will find no cure for it.

In 1894, Bahta led 1,600 men in revolt against Ethiopia's Italian colonizers, leading to the Battle of Adwa, in which Ethiopian troops defeated the Italians. Ethiopia subsequently became a symbol of African resistance in the face of European colonialism throughout Africa. This is one of his most well-known sayings. Bahta was killed during the revolt and is now regarded as a martyr and hero.

1894

Statement to the American Railway Union

Pullman, both the man and the town, is an ulcer on the body politic. He owns the houses, the schoolhouses, and churches of God in the town he gave his once humble name. The revenue he derives from these, the wages he pays out with one hand—the Pullman Palace Car Company, he takes back with the other—the Pullman Land Association. He is able by this to bid under any contract car shop in this country. His competitors in business, to meet this, must reduce the wages of their men. This gives him the excuse to reduce ours to conform to the market. His business rivals must in turn scale down; so must he. And thus the merry war—the dance of skeletons bathed in human tears—goes on, and it will go on, brothers, forever, unless you, the American Railway Union, stop it; end it; crush it out.

In 1894, 3,000 employees of the Pullman Palace Car Company struck in response to a lowering of their wages. At its peak, their number grew to 250,000 and involved twenty-seven states. Eugene Debs, the leader of the American Railway Union, called for a national boycott of Pullman. The strike was crushed by federal troops sent in by President Grover Cleveland, just over a month after it began.

CLARA ZETKIN   **1896**

"Only in Conjunction With the Proletarian Woman Will Socialism Be Victorious"

The proletarian woman has become enmeshed in the mechanism of the economic life of our period and has been driven into the workshop and to the machines. She went out into economic life in order to aid her husband in making a living, but the capitalist mode of production transformed her into an unfair competitor. She wanted to bring prosperity to her family, but instead misery descended upon it. The proletarian woman obtained her own employment because she wanted to create a more sunny and pleasant life for her children, but instead she became almost entirely separated from them. She became an equal of the man as a worker; the machine rendered muscular force superfluous and everywhere women's work showed the same results in production as men's work. And since women constitute a cheap labor force and above all a submissive one that only in the rarest of cases dares to kick against the thorns of capitalist exploitation, the capitalists multiply the possibilities of women's work in industry . . . The proletarian woman has gained her economic independence, but neither as a human being nor as a woman or wife has she had the possibility to develop her individuality. For her task as a wife and a mother, there remain only the breadcrumbs which capitalist production drops from the table.

Therefore the liberation struggle of the proletarian woman cannot be similar to the struggle that the bourgeois woman wages against the male of her class. On the contrary, it must be a joint struggle with the male of her class against the entire class of capitalists . . . new barriers need to be erected against the exploitation of the proletarian woman. Her rights as wife and mother need to be restored and permanently secured. Her final aim is not free competition with the man, but the achievement of the political rule of the proletariat . . . She also agrees with the demands of the bourgeois women's movement, but she regards the fulfillment of these demands simply as a means to enable that movement to enter the battle, equipped with the same weapons, alongside the proletariat.

A close friend of Rosa Luxemburg, Zetkin established the first international women's day and co-founded the Spartacist League, which evolved into the Communist Party of Germany (KPD). For thirteen years she represented the KPD in the Reichstag, and in 1932, as the chairwoman of the Reichstag, she called on Germans to resist the Nazis. The next year Hitler's party banned the KPD, and Zetkin died in exile in the Soviet Union.

ÉMILE ZOLA

"J'Accuse . . . !"

They have dared to do this. Very well, then, I shall dare too. I shall tell the truth, for I pledged that I would tell it, if our judicial system, once the matter was brought before it through the normal channels, did not tell the truth, the whole truth. It is my duty to speak up; I will not be an accessory to the fact. If I were, my nights would be haunted by the specter of that innocent man so far away, suffering the worst kind of torture as he pays for a crime he did not commit . . .

Where, oh where is a strong and wisely patriotic ministry that will be bold enough to overhaul the whole system and make a fresh start? I know many people who tremble with alarm at the thought of a possible war, knowing what hands our national defense is in! And what a den of sneaking intrigue, rumor-mongering and back-biting that sacred chapel has become—yet that is where the fate of our country is decided! People take fright at the appalling light that has just been shed on it all by the Dreyfus Affair, that tale of human sacrifice! Yes, an unfortunate, a "dirty Jew" has been sacrificed. Yes, what an accumulation of madness, stupidity, unbridled imagination, low police tactics, inquisitorial and tyrannical methods this handful of officers have got away with! They have crushed the nation under their boots, stuffing its calls for truth and justice down its throat on the fallacious and sacrilegious pretext that they are acting for the good of the country! . . .

As for the persons I have accused, I do not know them; I have never seen them; I feel no rancor or hatred towards them. To me, they are mere entities, mere embodiments of social malfeasance. And the action I am taking here is merely a revolutionary means to hasten the revelation of truth and justice.

I have but one goal: that light be shed, in the name of mankind which has suffered so much and has the right to happiness. My ardent protest is merely a cry from my very soul. Let them dare to summon me before a court of law! Let the inquiry be held in broad daylight!

I am waiting.

By then already the author of more than two dozen novels, Zola risked his career, and possibly his life, with his front-page article accusing the French military of smearing a Jewish army engineer. The anti-Semitic army wanted to deflect suspicion of espionage from another officer and chose Alfred Dreyfus as its scapegoat, sending him to prison in French Guiana. Zola's intervention divided French opinion, but the novelist was convicted of libel and had to flee the country. Dreyfus was not exonerated until 1906.

1898   QUEEN LILI'UOKALANI

Hawaii's Story by Hawaii's Queen

Oh, honest Americans, as Christians hear me for my downtrodden people! Their form of government is as dear to them as yours is precious to you. Quite as warmly as you love your country, so they love theirs. With all your goodly possessions, covering a territory so immense that there yet remain parts unexplored, possessing islands that, although new at hand, had to be neutral ground in time of war, do not covet the little vineyard of Naboth's, so far from your shores, lest the punishment of Ahab fall upon you, if not in your day, in that of your children, for "be not deceived, God is not mocked." The people to whom your fathers told of the living God, and taught to call "Father," and now whom the sons now seek to despoil and destroy, are crying aloud to Him in their time of trouble; and He will keep His promise, and will listen to the voices of His Hawaiian children lamenting for their homes.

Hawaii's last monarch Lili'uokalani sought to draft a new constitution that would restore power to the monarchy and voting rights to Native Americans and Asians, which the 1887 Bayonet Constitution, written by white anti-monarchists, had taken away. Feeling threatened, American and European businessmen organized against her, eventually leading to the overthrow of the monarchy and the annexation of Hawaii to the United States.

JOSEPH CONRAD   1898

Heart of Darkness

The conquest of the earth, which mostly means the taking it away from those who have a different complexion or slightly flatter noses than ourselves, is not a pretty thing when you look into it too much.

Conrad's great novel, set in a place much like the Congo, is often seen as a withering indictment of the European exploitation of Africa; though the Nigerian writer Chinua Achebe called the book racist, saying it dehumanized Africans. Conrad himself was repulsed by socialism and once said, "I have no taste for democracy."

BAL GANGADHAR TILAK   1898

Slogan

Swaraj [self-rule] is my birthright, and I shall have it!

This motto was adopted by the first popular leader of the Indian Independence Movement, following his release from imprisonment for "incitement to murder." Tilak had written in an editorial that no one could be blamed for killing an oppressor, so long as there was no reward.

BOXERS ("RIGHTEOUS FISTS OF HARMONY")   1899

Wall Poster

Their men are all immoral;
Their women truly vile.
For the Devils it's mother–son sex
That serves as the breeding style.

No rain comes from Heaven,
The earth is parched and dry.
And all because the churches
Have bottled up the sky.

When at last all the Foreign Devils
Are expelled to the very last man,
The Great Qing, united, together,
Will bring peace to this our land.

The Boxer Rebellion was a Chinese anti-colonial uprising organized by the "Righteous Fists of Harmony Society," or "Boxers," largely in response to European opium trading, political and economic manipulation, and missionary evangelism. The Boxers numbered in the hundreds of thousands. This poem was widely circulated and posted in many public places.

1900s   KANNO SUGA

"Women Are Slaves"

For us women, the most urgent task at hand is to develop our self-awareness. In accordance with long-standing customs, we are seen as a form of property. Women in Japan are in a state of slavery.

Kanno was a Japanese socialist-anarchist activist who fought to achieve equality for women and was condemned to death at the age of thirty. This quote was taken from one of her many newspaper articles.

e. 1900s   ANONYMOUS

Colombian Folk Song

Rattler, little rattler
Wandering in the cane
Bite the boss's foot
Which stepped on my rosebush.

When they spotted planters or administrators approaching their fields, peasant men would sing songs warning the women not to be caught alone in the house, where they might be subject to their master's sexual depredations. These songs often invoked the protection of indigenous spirits.

HERERO MAN   e. 1900s

Words to a German Settler

The missionary says that we are the children of God like our white brothers . . . but look at us. Dogs, slaves, worse than baboons on rocks . . . that is how you treat us.

From 1904–7, the people of the Herero tribe rose up against their German rulers in what is now Namibia. Although the numbers are disputed, some say that the Herero population decreased from 80,000 to 8,000 through systematic violence, persecution and deportation.

JOHN MUIR   1901

"The Destruction of the Redwoods"

Our magnificent redwoods and much of the sugar-pine forests of the Sierra Nevada [have] been absorbed by foreign and resident capitalists. Uncle Sam is not often called a fool in business matters, yet he has sold millions of acres of timber land at two dollars and a half an acre on which a single tree was worth more than a hundred dollars. But this priceless land has been patented, and nothing can be done now about the crazy bargain. According to the everlasting law of righteousness, even the fraudulent buyers at less than one per cent of its value are making little or nothing, on account of fierce competition. The trees are felled, and about half of each giant is left on the ground to be converted into choice lumber and sold to citizens of the United States or to foreigners: thus robbing the country of its glory and impoverishing it without right benefit to anybody—a bad, black business from beginning to end.

A founder of conservationism, the Scottish-born American Muir wrote more than 300 articles and twelve books, co-founded the Sierra Club, and helped preserve Yosemite Valley in California. Many of his most revolutionary pronouncements remained unpublished until long after his death—including his rejection of Christianity and his scorn for capitalism; but he was known during his life as a strong opponent of commercial logging. He inspired radical environmentalism.

1903

ZOU RONG

The Revolutionary Army

You possess government, run it yourselves; you have laws, guard them yourselves; you have industries, administer them yourselves; you possess armed forces, order them yourselves; you possess lands, watch over them yourselves; you have inexhaustible resources, exploit them yourselves. You are qualified in every way for revolutionary independence.

Zou, an eighteen-year-old student when he published the slim book, The Revolutionary Army, *was one of the most articulate voices of the anti–Qing Dynasty movement in China. He called for the establishment of a parliament, equal rights for women, freedom of speech and freedom of the press, and died in prison at the age of twenty-one.*

1904

R. A. KARTINI

Letter to Etty Waworuntu

We wanted to establish a position for our sex on the basis of which they could become fully conscious of their role in this life. We wanted to seek their cooperation, which in fact they must contribute, to improve the welfare of the people. We wanted to provide education for women, wherever they have come to feel the need for becoming educated, to bring about an improvement in the moral state of the people, to shape them as a powerful force in general. How else would our struggle ever achieve a good result? . . .

Besides my sisters I know others who could work to this end. But I know also that no matter how much they would perhaps like to in their hearts, they would not dare take up this work, because, as you know, our task is that of pioneers, isn't it, and that does not suggest to them a very rose-colored future . . .

Kartini, a Javanese high aristocrat, became famous when a Dutchman published a selection (albeit bowdlerized) of her letters, all written in Dutch and mostly addressed to her Dutch women friends—although this one is addressed to an Indonesian friend. One of Indonesia's earliest proponents of women's rights, Kartini died very young, giving birth to a first child by a husband she had been forced by her parents to marry.

INDUSTRIAL WORKERS OF THE WORLD 1905
Preamble to the IWW Constitution

The working class and the employing class have nothing in common. There can be no peace so long as hunger and want are found among millions of working people and the few, who make up the employing class, have all the good things of life.

Between these two classes a struggle must go on until the workers of the world organize as a class, take possession of the earth and the machinery of production, and abolish the wage system.

Instead of the conservative motto, "A fair day's wage for a fair day's work," we must inscribe on our banner the revolutionary watchword, "Abolition of the wage system."

It is the historic mission of the working class to do away with capitalism. The army of production must be organized, not only for everyday struggle with capitalists, but also to carry on production when capitalism shall have been overthrown. By organizing industrially we are forming the structure of the new society within the shell of the old.

Delegates to the IWW, or the "Wobblies," founding convention in Chicago included Eugene Debs, Big Bill Haywood, Mother Jones, and Daniel De Leon, head of the Socialist Labor Party. Based on the principles of Marxist class conflict and the American philosophy of industrial unionism, the IWW sought to recruit immigrants, women, non-whites, and migrant workers who were excluded from the craft unions of the American Federation of Labor. It became famous for its revolutionary tactics of direct action, and for its songs and graphics.

1905

ROKEYA SAKAWAT HOSSEIN

"Sultana's Dream"

"We have no hand or voice in the management of our social affairs. In India man is lord and master, he has taken to himself all powers and privileges and shut up the women in the zenana."

"Why do you allow yourselves to be shut up?"

"Because it cannot be helped as they are stronger than women."

"A lion is stronger than a man, but it does not enable him to dominate the human race. You have neglected the duty you owe to yourselves and you have lost your natural rights by shutting your eyes to your own interests."

"But my dear Sister Sara, if we do everything by ourselves, what will the men do then?"

"They should not do anything, excuse me; they are fit for nothing. Only catch them and put them into the zenana."

Rokeya was a Bengali Muslim writer and feminist activist who founded the first Muslim girls' school in Calcutta in 1911. This story, which first appeared in a Madras English-language magazine, describes a feminist utopia: a tale of reverse purdah that imagines a world in which men are confined indoors and women rule public life. In Ladyland, women have also eliminated war and have harnessed science for progress—introducing air travel and solar power.

MAJI-MAJI REBELLION

1905

Password

Hongo or the European, which is the stronger? Hongo!

In 1905, several African tribes in Tanganyika rose up in violent protest against their German colonizers. After it was largely suppressed, the Germans proceeded to flush out the remaining rebels through a widespread and devastating famine. By the end, fifteen Europeans and between 200,000 and 300,000 insurgents had died.

TONKIN FREE SCHOOL

1905

"Indictment of Corrupt Customs"

Why is the roof of their [the Western] universe the broad lands and skies,
While we cower and confine ourselves to a cranny in our house?
Why can they jump straight, leap far,
While we shrink back and cling to each other?
Why do they rule the world,
While we bow our heads as slaves?
Take up a mirror, look at yourself.
Where on that face is there something to brag about?
Taking steps outward, we fear what others think,
We intend to try, but where's the ability?
Our spirit is as cold as ash,
Our body has the form of a shriveled tree.
We have eyes, but they seem to be blind.
Who will bring the lamp to light the path?
Our ears might as well not be there.
Who will bring the bell and ring it noisily?

The Tonkin Free School was founded by Vietnamese nationalists with the aim of reforming Vietnamese society through the dissemination of new ideas from the West and Japan, and replacing the Chinese character-based script with quoc ngu, *the Vietnamese system of writing used today. The school was closed down after just a few months by the French authorities, who also arrested the leading participants and suppressed the school's publications.*

1905

UPTON SINCLAIR

The Jungle

All day long the blazing midsummer sun beat down upon that square mile of abominations: upon tens of thousands of cattle crowded into pens whose wooden floors stank and steamed contagion; upon bare, blistering, cinder-strewn railroad tracks and huge blocks of dingy meat factories, whose labyrinthine passages defied a breath of fresh air to penetrate them; and there are not merely rivers of hot blood and carloads of moist flesh, and rendering-vats and soup cauldrons, glue-factories and fertilizer tanks, that smelt like the craters of hell—there are also tons of garbage festering in the sun, and the greasy laundry of the workers hung out to dry and dining rooms littered with food black with flies, and toilet rooms that are open sewers.

Sinclair spent seven weeks in the Chicago stockyards investigating the meat-packing industry. Socialist novelist Jack London called the novel that Sinclair subsequently wrote that was serialized in the Appeal to Reason, *"the Uncle Tom's Cabin of wage slavery," and it helped to inspire the creation of federal Meat Inspection and Pure Food and Drug Acts. Sinclair ran a radical campaign for governor of California in 1934, and only narrowly lost.*

1906

PHAN BOI CHAU

"Letter from Abroad Written in Blood"

Why was our country lost?
I submit the following:
First the monarch knew nothing of popular affairs;
Second the mandarins cared nothing for the people;
And third the people knew only of themselves.

State matters to the King, other affairs to the mandarins, the people said.
Hundreds of thousands, millions together worked
To build the foundations of our country.
The bodies, the resources are from the people;
The people are in fact the country, the country is the people's.
On the throne the King had complete license
And had a long time to drowse . . .
Blood is boiling in your heart,
Countrymen! Draw forth your swords,
There is Heaven, Earth, and Us,
That is what we call true unity!

One of the fathers of Vietnamese nationalism, Phan was living in Japan when this poem was written. He openly criticized French colonialism and called for Vietnamese liberation in a series of political tracts, later returning to Vietnam and forming the Vietnam Restoration League, modeled on Sun Yat-sen's Republican Party. He spent the last fifteen years of his life under house arrest.

OLIVE SCHREINER 1908

"The Native Question"

If, blinded by the gain of the moment, we see nothing in our dark man but a vast engine of labor; if to us he is not man, but only a tool; if dispossessed entirely of the land for which he now shows that large aptitude for peasant proprietorship for the lack of which among their masses many great nations are decaying; if we force him permanently in his millions into the locations and compounds and slums of our cities, obtaining his labor cheaper, but to lose what the wealth of five Rands could not return to us; if, uninstructed in the highest forms of labor, without the rights of citizenship, his own social organisation broken up, without our having aided him to participate in our own; if, unbound to us by gratitude and sympathy, and alien to us in blood and color, we reduce this vast mass to the condition of a great seething, ignorant proletariat—then I would rather draw a veil over the future of this land.

The themes of women's labor, racism, imperialism and pacifism populate the fiction and non-fiction works of South African writer and socialist Schreiner, who was also close with Eleanor Marx, Edward Carpenter and Gandhi. "The Native Question," written after twenty-some years lecturing on the need to transform South Africa into a multiracial and democratic federation of states, argued against public opinion for the resolution of racial tensions in South African society.

1908

WILLIAM SHEPPARD

Article from *Kassai Herald*

These great stalwart men and women, who have from time immemorial been free, cultivating large farms of Indian corn, peas, tobacco, potatoes, trapping elephants for their ivory tusks and leopards for their skins, who have always had their own king and a government not to be despised, officers of the law established in every town of the kingdom, these magnificent people, perhaps about 400,000 in number, have entered a new chapter in the history of their tribe . . .

How changed they are! Their farms are growing up in weeds and jungle, their king is practically a slave, their houses now are mostly only half-built single rooms and are much neglected. The streets of their towns are not clean and well-swept as they once were. Even their children cry for bread.

Why this change? You have it in a few words. There are armed sentries of chartered trading companies who force the men and women to spend most of their days and nights in the forests making rubber, and the price they receive is so meager that they cannot live upon it. In the majority of villages these people have not time to listen to the Gospel story, or give an answer concerning their soul's salvation.

Sheppard was an African American Presbyterian missionary who spent twenty years in Africa, primarily in the Congo Free State, and made great efforts to publicize the barbarities committed by King Leopold II's Force Publique. Sent to ensure a rubber quota and maintain the system of forced labor, they employed whips, raped women, burned villages and sometimes severed and collected the hands of rebels against Leopold's regime, as proof that they had subdued them.

CHARLES DOMINGO

1911

"Failure Among Europeans"

There is too much failure among all Europeans in Nyasaland. The three combined bodies—Missionaries, Government, and Companies or gainers of money—do form the same rule to look upon the native with mockery eyes . . . Instead of "Give," they say "Take away from." There is too much breakage of God's pure law as seen in James's Epistle, chapter five, verse four.

Domingo founded a Seventh-Day Adventist church in Nyasaland in 1911 and frequently criticized Christian missions and Europeans, noting the wide discrepancies between the theories they preached and their practice.

EMILIANO ZAPATA

1911

"Plan de Ayala"

The Revolutionary Junta of the State of Morelos will admit no transactions or compromises until it achieves the overthrow of the dictatorial elements of Porfirio Díaz and Francisco I. Madero, for the nation is tired of false men and traitors who make promises like liberators and who on arriving in power forget them and constitute themselves tyrants.

[Regarding] the fields, timber, and water which the landlords, *científicos*, or bosses have usurped, the pueblos or citizens who have the titles corresponding to those properties will immediately enter into possession of that real estate of which they have been despoiled by the bad faith of our oppressors . . .

Mexicans: consider that the cunning and bad faith of one man is shedding blood in a scandalous manner, because he is incapable of governing; consider that his system of government is choking the fatherland and trampling with the brute force of bayonets on our institutions; and thus, as we raised up our weapons to elevate him to power, we again raise them up against him for defaulting on his promises to the Mexican people and for having betrayed the revolution initiated by him; we are not personalists, we are partisans of principles and not of men!

Zapata allied with Madero in overthrowing the dictator Díaz, then denounced Madero's unwillingness to carry out land reform. The "Plan de Ayala" drew in part on the ideas of Ricardo Flores Magón, anarcho-syndicalist thinker and agitator whose slogan Tierra y Libertad *(Land and Freedom) became a watchword of the revolution. Zapata was ambushed in 1919; Magón died in Leavenworth Penitentiary in Kansas, having received a twenty-year sentence for "obstructing" the US war effort.*

1911

EMMA GOLDMAN

"Anarchism: What It Really Stands For"

Anarchism is the only philosophy which brings to man the consciousness of himself; which maintains that God, the State, and society are nonexistent, that their promises are null and void, since they can be fulfilled only through man's subordination. Anarchism is therefore the teacher of the unity of life; not merely in nature, but in man. There is no conflict between the individual and the social instincts, any more than there is between the heart and the lungs: the one the receptacle of a precious life essence, the other the repository of the element that keeps the essence pure and strong. The individual is the heart of society, conserving the essence of social life; society is the lungs which are distributing the element to keep the life essence— that is, the individual—pure and strong.

"Red Emma" to admirers and enemies alike, Goldman was a prolific writer who addressed a range of issues from homosexuality to atheism to the prison system. Arrested at various times for inciting to riot, distributing information on birth control and opposing the draft, she was eventually deported by the United States to Russia—where she opposed Soviet state oppression, especially after being told by Lenin that "there can be no free speech in a revolutionary period."

"Why I Became a Socialist"

The *Brooklyn Eagle* says, apropos of me, and socialism, that Helen Keller's "mistakes spring out of the manifest limitations of her development." . . . Oh, ridiculous *Brooklyn Eagle*! What an ungallant bird it is! Socially blind and deaf, it defends an intolerable system, a system that is the cause of much of the physical blindness and deafness which we are trying to prevent. The *Eagle* is willing to help us prevent misery provided, always provided, that we do not attack the industrial tyranny which supports it and stops its ears and clouds its vision. The *Eagle* and I are at war. I hate the system which it represents, apologizes for and upholds. When it fights back, let it fight fair. Let it attack my ideas and oppose the aims and arguments of Socialism. It is not fair fighting or good argument to remind me and others that I cannot see or hear. I can read. I can read all the socialist books I have time for in English, German and French. If the editor of the *Brooklyn Eagle* should read some of them, he might be a wiser man and make a better newspaper. If I ever contribute to the Socialist movement the book that I sometimes dream of, I know what I shall name it: Industrial Blindness and Social Deafness.

Keller was the first deaf-blind person to earn a college degree. She joined the Socialist Party in 1909, and sided with the IWW and with the radical wing of the party against Woodrow Wilson's war. She campaigned for women's suffrage, birth control, and workers' rights, wrote twelve books, helped to found the American Civil Liberties Union, and counted Charlie Chaplin and Mark Twain among her friends.

1911

WILLIAM "BIG BILL" HAYWOOD

"The General Strike"

The Socialists believe in the general strike. They also believe in the organization of industrial forces after the general strike is successful. So, on this great force of the working class I believe we can agree that we should unite into one great organization—big enough to take in the children that are now working; big enough to take in the black man; the white man; big enough to take in all nationalities—an organization that will be strong enough to obliterate state boundaries, to obliterate national boundaries, and one that will become the great industrial force of the working class of the world.

A hard-rock miner, Haywood was the keynote speaker at the Chicago founding convention of the IWW, which he called "the Continental Congress of the working class." He was the symbol of the Wobblies, which reached a peak of 100,000 members in the run-up to World War I, when Haywood and most of the union's leadership were convicted of sedition. He fled to the Soviet Union and is buried in the Kremlin wall.

1912

LAWRENCE STRIKERS

"Bread and Roses"

Our lives shall not be sweated from birth until
    life closes
Hearts starve as well as bodies, give us bread
    but give us roses
. . .
As we go marching, marching, we bring the
    greater days
The rising of the women means the rising of the
    race

> No more the drudge and idler, ten that toil
>   where one reposes,
> But a sharing of life's glories—bread and roses,
>   bread and roses!

Written by James Oppenheim, "Bread and Roses" has become associated with the Lawrence, Massachusetts textile strike, which was led by the IWW, lasted three months, and ended in a victory for the workers. Mary Heaton Vorse, the famed labor reporter, wrote: "There are 20,000 people there who, whatever else happens, can never again have the race hatreds and creed prejudices that they did before they had learned what working together may mean."

MOTHER JONES   1912

Speech to Striking Coal Miners

Be good, "Mother" is going to stay with you. I am going to Colorado. There was a sheriff in the county, and the mine owners asked for the troops, and the sheriff said, "You can send no troops, no militia into the county I have charge of. The men elected me." He was the sheriff, and he did not allow the Governor to send the troops in there. There was no tyranny in that county. Once in a while we licked a scab, we wanted to put brains in him, he had none. That sheriff is going to run for Secretary of State, and I am going out to sweep the state with him. I will put him into office, if it is the last thing I do. I want to put in all the officers, and we have got to put out the fellows who stand with the robbing class, and we have got to put them out of business, we have got to make an honest nation. You can't be honest today. A girl goes to school, to church, and prays to Jesus. On Monday she acts like the devil when she sells to you. The whole machinery of capitalism is rotten to the core. This meeting tonight indicates a milestone of progress of the miners and workers of the State of West Virginia. I will be with you, and the Baldwin guards will go. You will not be serfs, you will march, march, march on from milestone to milestone of human freedom, you will rise like men in the new day and slavery will get its death blow. It has got to die. Good night.

An organizer and tribune of the United Mine Workers of America, the some-time socialist Jones also campaigned against child labor in the textile mills, for Mexican revolutionaries jailed in the US—and against feminists and the Chinese in America, not uncommon among white labor agitators.

1913   BLACK WOMEN'S PROTEST

"Proclaim Their Womanhood"

Too long have they submitted
To white malignity;
No passes would they carry,
But to assert their dignity.
They vowed no more to fawn on or cringe,
Nor creep to the tyrant's power;
But to proclaim their womanhood,
Their inherent, God-given dower.

In May 1913, a procession of 600 black women marched through Bloemfontein in South Africa to protest the requirement that all African and Colored residents carry government-issued passes at all times. This poem was inspired by that event and appeared in the newspaper of the African Political Organization, which repre-sented the Colored voice in the Free State, signed by "Johnny the Office Boy."

1914   EMMELINE PANKHURST

My Own Story

The moving spirit of militancy is deep and abiding reverence for human life. In the latter course of our agitation I have been called upon to discuss our policies with many eminent men, politicians, liter-ary men, barristers, scientists, clergymen. One of the last-named, a high dignitary of the Church of England, told me that while he was a convinced suffragist, he found it impossible to justify our doing wrong that right might follow. I said to him: "We are not doing wrong—we are doing right in our use of revolutionary methods against private property. It is our work to restore thereby true values, to emphasize the value of human rights against property rights. You are well aware, sir, that property has assumed a value in the eyes of men, and the eyes of the law, that it ought never to claim. It is placed above all human values. The lives and health and happiness, and even the virtue of women and children—that is to say, the race itself—are being ruthlessly sacrificed to the god of property every day of the world."

To this my reverend friend agreed, and I said: "If we women are wrong in destroying private property in order that human values may be restored, then I say, in all reverence, that it was wrong for the Founder of Christianity to destroy private property, as He did when He lashed the money changers out of the Temple and when He drove the Gadarene swine into the sea."

It was absolutely in this spirit that our women went forth to war.

Pankhurst founded the Women's Social and Political Union, a militant all-women suffragist organization dedicated to "deeds, not words." The guerrilla campaign of burning letters and destroying mailboxes defended here divided the suffragist movement in England.

ITO NOE   1914

"Women's Problems"

"Women's Problems" are not just women's problems. They are major problems for human beings. They pose issues that both men and women must think about. But men use traditional customs as shields. Relying on a large number of adherents, they brandish overhead the real power they hold over society and suppress the assertions of serious people, jeering at them and relying on unjust, cowardly means to get rid of them. Ignorant women who for millions of years past have been taught to remain as slaves are unable to escape from the slavish disposition that has seeped into each one of their physical cells. Without any self-awareness, they go along with the arrogant men, and they look down on those who are seeking to fight on their behalf. No one among them thinks seriously about the issues. What a sad state of affairs . . .

Don't you recognize your wife and your children as human beings?

113

Don't you recognize them as "women?" Oh, what a painful affair. A pitiful affair. Take care. We are unable to just listen silently.

Ito was a feminist and anarchist activist and writer from a Japanese working-class family, who rebelled against her arranged marriage; wrote scathing critiques of misogynists, upper-class women and communists alike; and was brutally murdered by the military police. Here, she responds to an article by Shimoda Jiro, a prominent progressive male educator, on his views regarding women.

1914   MEKATILILI WA MENZA

Giriama Tale

And the Giriama said, who will give away his sons to go and be killed? You try taking the chicks. And Champion took the chick and the hen flapped and attacked him. And the Giriama said, you see what this hen has done? If you take our sons, we will do the same.

In 1913–14, an old woman, Mekatilili, led the Kenyan Giriama people in resistance against the British, personified in this story in the figure of Arthur Champion, the district commissioner. Mekatilili is the hen. The British demanded taxes and young men for labor from the Giriama; Mekatilili's charisma brought together Giriama women, powerless young men and elders to push back.

1914   JAMES CONNOLLY

"War—What It Means to You"

You are asked to stop and consider what this war will mean to the working class of this city and country.

It already means that increased prices will be demanded for all food and household necessities. In every bite of food you eat you will be compelled to pay for the war; and as you are already poor and have at the best of times a struggle to live the war will mean hunger and misery to thousands—less food on their tables, less clothes on their backs or beds, less coal for their fires, less boots and shoes on their children's feet and their own.

War will mean more unemployment and less wages. Already the

mills of Belfast are put on short time, which means starvation wages, ware-rooms are closing down, and all foundries and engineering works which make machinery for the Continent, if they have not closed down already, are getting ready to do so.

Thus before a shot has been fired by the British army on land, before a battle has been fought at sea, ruin and misery are entering the homes of the working people. What will be your case? Many thousands of you will die of slow starvation, or perish of cold and long-drawn-out misery before the end of the war if you suffer so much before it is begun.

Some people tell you it will be over in a fortnight. They said the same about the Boer War, but it lasted three years. And the Boer War was a mere picnic compared to what this war will be.

Born in Scotland to Irish immigrant parents, Connolly became a leader of the socialist movement in Scotland, Ireland and the United States, where he was a member of the Socialist Party and the IWW. He helped lead the Easter Rising of 1916, the precursor to the declaration of the Irish Republic in 1919. For his role in the Easter Rising, he was tied to a chair and shot by the British governemnt on May 12, 1916.

ANONYMOUS   1914

"Woe on Us Wingate"

Woe on us Wingate,
Who has carried off our corn,
Carried off our cotton,
Carried off our camels,
Carried off our children,
Leaving us only our lives,
For love of Allah, now leave us alone.

After Turkey sided with Germany in World War I, Britain declared Egypt a protectorate and made it the base for all British military operations in the Middle East, requisitioning its labor, properties and livestock for this purpose. Reginald Wingate was the high commissioner for the protectorate. Egyptians voiced their resentment in this popular song, and resentment turned into open revolt in 1919.

ROSA LUXEMBURG

"Junius Pamphlet"

Violated, dishonored, wading in blood, dripping filth—there stands bourgeois society. This is it. Not all spic and span and moral, with pretense to culture, philosophy, ethics, order, peace, and the rule of law—but the ravening beast, the witches' sabbath of anarchy, a plague to culture and humanity. Thus it reveals itself in its true, its naked form. In the midst of this witches' sabbath a catastrophe of world-historical proportions has happened: International Social Democracy has capitulated. To deceive ourselves about it, to cover it up, would be the most foolish, the most fatal thing the proletariat could do. . . .

Imperialism and all its political brutality, the chain of incessant social catastrophes that it has let loose, is undoubtedly a historical necessity for the ruling classes of the contemporary capitalist world. Nothing would be more fatal for the proletariat than to delude itself into believing that it were possible after this war to rescue the idyllic and peaceful continuation of capitalism. However, the conclusion to be drawn by proletarian policy from the historical necessity of imperialism is that surrender to imperialism will mean living forever in its victorious shadow and eating from its leftovers. . . .

It is our strength, our hope, that is mown down day after day like grass under the sickle. The best, most intelligent, most educated forces of international socialism, the bearers of the holiest traditions and the boldest heroes of the modern workers' movement, the vanguard of the entire world proletariat, the workers of England, France, Belgium, Germany, Russia—these are the ones now being hamstrung and led to the slaughter.

The blood-letting of the June days [1848] paralyzed the French workers' movement for a decade and a half. Then the blood-letting of the Commune massacres again retarded it for more than a decade. What is now occurring is an unprecedented mass slaughter that is reducing the adult working population of all the leading civilized countries to women, old people, and cripples. This blood-letting threatens to bleed the European workers' movement to death . . . This is an assault, not on the bourgeois culture of the past, but on the socialist culture of the future, a lethal blow against that force which carries the future of humanity within itself and which alone can bear the precious treasures of the past into a better society. Here capitalism lays bare its death's head; here it betrays the fact that its historical rationale is used up; its continued domination is no longer reconcilable to the progress of humanity.

The madness will cease and the bloody demons of hell will vanish only when workers in Germany and France, England and Russia finally awake from their stupor, extend to each other a brotherly hand, and drown out the bestial chorus of imperialist war-mongers and the shrill cry of capitalist hyenas with labor's old and mighty battle cry:

Proletarians of all lands, unite!

Written in prison to oppose the German Social-Democratic Party's (SDP) support for World War I, this pamphlet quickly became a rallying point for anti-war socialists, contributing to the split of the SPD in 1916, and the formation of the Spartacus League and later the Communist Party of Germany. Much of Luxemburg's argument about the development of capitalism and spread of imperialism builds on her most well-known treatise Accumulation of Capital. *She was murdered, along with her Spartacus league co-founder Karl Liebknecht, by right-wing paramilitaries during the Spartacist Uprising of 1919.*

ALFRED BRYAN   1915

"I Didn't Raise My Boy to Be a Soldier"

Ten million mothers' hearts must break
For the ones who died in vain
Head bowed down in sorrow
In her lowly years
I heard a mother murmur through her tears

I didn't raise my boy to be a soldier
I brought him up to be my pride and joy
Who dares to place a musket on his shoulder

117

To shoot some other mother's darling boy?
Let nations arbitrate their future troubles
It's time to lay the sword and gun away
There'd be no war today
If mothers all would say
I didn't raise my boy to be a soldier

An anthem of the American pacifist movement that preceded US entry into World War I, Bryan's song was condemned by Theodore Roosevelt, among other pro-war figures.

1915   CLYDE WORKERS' COMMITTEE

First Agitational Leaflet

We will support the officials just so long as they rightly represent the workers, but we will act independently immediately they misrepresent them. Being composed of delegates from every shop and untrammelled by obsolete rule or law, we claim to represent the true feeling of the workers. We can act immediately and according to the merits of the case and the desire of the rank and file.

The Clydeside shop stewards built a powerful rank-and-file movement during World War I, successfully challenging the class collaborationist policies of the union leaders by organizing a series of militant unofficial strikes. "Red Clydeside" became one of the British labor movement's strongest bastions.

1915   JOE HILL

Last Words

Don't waste any time in mourning—organize.

The most popular songwriter of the IWW, the Swedish-born American immigrant Hill was a hobo agitator, taking part in the Mexican Revolution and singing for Canadian railroad strikers. In 1914 he was charged with murder in Salt Lake City, and despite international protests against the frame-up that

*eventually enlisted both the Swedish government and Woodrow Wilson, Hill
was executed by firing squad. His famous last words were wired to fellow
Wobbly Big Bill Haywood.*

WILLIAM BLAKE $\qquad$ **1915**

"Jerusalem"

> I will not cease from mental fight,
> Nor shall my sword sleep in my hand,
> Till we have built Jerusalem
> In England's green and pleasant land.

*Set to music by Sir Hubert Parry in 1916, Blake's poem—actually an excerpt
of the preface to one of his prophetic books,* Milton—*became one of England's
most popular patriotic songs, preferred by King George V over "God Save the
King." Blake himself had been tried for sedition for having uttered such expressions as "Damn the King, damn all his subjects . . ." He was acquitted.*

EASTER RISING $\qquad$ **1916**

"The Dublin Brigade"

> There was much work to do in getting things right,
> But the old and the young were all anxious to fight.
> Every man worked hard at his own barricade,
> And rifles rang out from the Dublin Brigade.

*Though the Easter Rising of 1916 involved only a small military minority,
it transformed Irish politics. Anger over its defeat and the execution of its
leaders erupted into a decisive mass struggle during the War of Independence
of 1919–21.*

1917

RANDOLPH BOURNE

"Twilight of Idols"

In this difficult time the light that has been in liberals and radicals has become darkness. If radicals spend their time holding conventions to attest their loyalty and stamp out the "enemies within," they do not spend it in breaking intellectual paths, or giving us shining ideas to which we can attach our faith and conscience. The spiritual apathy from which the more naïve of us suffer, and which the others are so busy fighting, arises largely from sheer default of a clear vision that would melt it away . . . Our intellectuals consort with war boards in order to keep their minds off the question what the slow masses of the people are really desiring, or toward what the best hope of the country really drives . . .

A policy of "win the war first" must be, for the radical, a policy of intellectual suicide. Their support of the war throws upon them the responsibility of showing inch by inch the democratic gains, and of laying out a charter of specific hopes. Otherwise they confess that they are impotent and that the war is submerging their expectations, or that they are not genuinely imaginative and offer little promise for future leadership.

Bourne denounced Progressives like John Dewey for their support of the US's involvement in World War I. A democrat and cosmopolitan, he savaged at once smug high culture and the ideal of the American "melting pot," in the name of a "transnational" culture drawing on immigrant and native strains of expression. He died of influenza in 1918 at thirty-two.

1917

V. I. LENIN

The State and Revolution

In capitalist society, providing it develops under the most favorable conditions, we have a more or less complete democracy in the democratic republic. But this democracy is always hemmed in by the narrow limits set by capitalist exploitation, and consequently always remains, in effect, a democracy for the minority, only for the propertied classes, only for the rich. Freedom in capitalist society always remains about the same as it was in the ancient Greek republics: freedom for the slave-owners. Owing to the conditions of capitalist exploitation, the modern wage slaves are so crushed by want and poverty that "they cannot be bothered with democracy," "cannot be bothered with politics"; in the ordinary, peaceful course of events, the majority of the population is debarred from participation in public and political life . . . Democracy for an insignificant minority, democracy for the rich— that is the democracy of capitalist society.

. . .

In a higher phase of communist society, after the enslaving subordination of the individual division of labor, and with it also the antithesis between mental and physical labor, has vanished, after labor has become not only a livelihood but life's prime want, after the productive forces have increased with the all-around development of the individual, and all the springs of the cooperative wealth flow—only then can the narrow horizon of bourgeois law be crossed in its entirety and society inscribe on its banners: From each according to his ability, to each according to his needs!

Bolshevik revolutionary and Marxist theorist, Lenin governed the Soviet Union until he suffered a stroke in 1922, dying two years later. The State and Revolution *argues that the state is an instrument of ruling-class control, whether formally democratic or not.*

MOHAMMED ABDULLA HASSAN   1917

Letter to Colonel Swann

If the country were cultivated or if it contained houses or property, it would be worth your while to fight for it. But the country is all jungle, and that is no use to you. If you want bush and stones you can get these in plenty. There are also many ant-heaps, and the sun is very hot. All you can get from me is war and nothing else.

1918

SIDNEY WEBB

Clause IV of the Labour Party Constitution

To secure for the workers by hand or by brain the full fruits of their industry and the most equitable distribution thereof that may be possible upon the basis of the common ownership of the means of production, distribution and exchange, and the best obtainable system of popular administration and control of each industry or service.

Clause IV acquired iconic status in the British labor movement because of its explicit support of nationalization, and the implication that the Labour Party's ultimate aim was a fully socialized economy. Labour leader Hugh Gaitskell failed to amend it in 1959; Tony Blair removed it in 1995, two years before becoming Prime Minister.

1918

LU XUN

"Diary of a Madman"

. . . Suddenly someone came in. He was only about twenty years old and I did not see his features very clearly. His face was wreathed in smiles, but when he nodded to me his smile did not seem genuine. I asked him, "Is it right to eat human beings?"

Still smiling, he replied, "When there is no famine how can one eat human beings?"

I realized at once, he was one of them; but still I summoned up courage to repeat my question:

"Is it right?"

"What makes you ask such a thing? You really are . . . fond of a joke . . . It is very fine today."

"It is fine, and the moon is very bright. But I want to ask you: is it right?"

He looked disconcerted, and muttered: "No . . ."

"No? Then why do they still do it?"

"What are you talking about?"

"What am I talking about? They are eating men now in Wolf Cub Village, and you can see it written all over the books, in fresh red ink."

His expression changed, and he grew ghastly pale. "It may be so," he said, staring at me. "It has always been like that . . ."

"Is it right because it has always been like that?"

"I refuse to discuss these things with you. Anyway, you shouldn't talk about it. Whoever talks about it is in the wrong!"

I leaped up and opened my eyes wide, but the man had vanished. I was soaked with perspiration. He was much younger than my elder brother, but even so he was in it. He must have been taught by his parents. And I am afraid he has already taught his son: that is why even the children look at me so fiercely.

Wanting to eat men, at the same time afraid of being eaten themselves, they all look at each other with the deepest suspicion . . .

How comfortable life would be for them if they could rid themselves of such obsessions and go to work, walk, eat and sleep at ease. They have only this one step to take. Yet fathers and sons, husbands and wives, brothers, friends, teachers and students, sworn enemies and even strangers, have all joined in this conspiracy, discouraging and preventing each other from taking this step.

"You should change, change from the bottom of your hearts!" I said. "You must know that in future there will be no place for man-eaters in the world."

Widely considered to be the father of modern Chinese literature, Lu Xun was also the co-founder of the League of Left-Wing Writers, the editor of several left publications, including New Youth, and an early supporter of the Esperanto movement in China. The Gogol-inspired "Diary of a Madman," with its comparison of Chinese feudal society to cannibalism, became one of the representative works of the anti-Confucian New Culture Movement, which called for the creation of a new Chinese culture and society based on democracy and science. Although the communists claimed him as one of their own, he was never a member of the party.

TRISTAN TZARA

DADA Manifesto

I'm writing this manifesto to show that you can perform contrary actions at the same time, in one single, fresh breath; I am against action; as for continual contradiction, and affirmation too, I am neither for nor against them, and I won't explain myself because I hate common sense . . .

We are like a raging wind that rips up the clothes of clouds and prayers, we are preparing the great spectacle of disaster, conflagration and decomposition. Preparing to put an end to mourning, and to replace tears by sirens spreading from one continent to another. Clarions of intense joy, bereft of that poisonous sadness . . .

Every product of disgust that is capable of becoming a negation of the family is dada; DADA; acquaintance with all the means hitherto rejected by the sexual prudishness of easy compromise and good manners: DADA; abolition of logic, dance of those who are incapable of creation: DADA; every hierarchy and social equation established for values by our valets: DADA; every object, all objects, feelings and obscurities, every apparition and the precise shock of parallel lines, are means for the battle of: DADA; the abolition of memory: DADA; the abolition of archaeology: DADA; the abolition of prophets: DADA; the abolition of the future: DADA; the absolute and indisputable belief in every god that is an immediate product of spontaneity: DADA; the elegant and unprejudiced leap from one harmony to another sphere; the trajectory of a word, a cry, thrown into the air like an acoustic disc; to respect all individualities in their folly of the moment, whether serious, fearful, timid, ardent, vigorous, decided or enthusiastic; to strip one's church of every useless and unwieldy accessory; to spew out like a luminous cascade any offensive or loving thought, or to cherish it—with the lively satisfaction that it's all precisely the same thing—with the same intensity in the bush, which is free of insects for the blue-blooded, and gilded with the bodies of archangels, with one's soul. Liberty: DADA DADA DADA—the roar of contorted pains, the

interweaving of contraries and all contradictions, freaks and irrelevan-
cies: LIFE.

*Born in Romania and active in France, Tzara was an avant-garde artist and
self-proclaimed "president" of the Dada movement, whose oblique protests
against bourgeois culture and politics would later inform the Situationists and
the Beat Generation. Tzara's own political trajectory included fighting for the
Spanish Republicans, joining the Communist Party, and participating in the
French Resistance during World War II.*

EUGENE DEBS   1918
"Address to the Jury"

When great changes occur in history, when great principles are
involved, as a rule the majority are wrong. The minority are usually
right. In every age there have been a few heroic souls who have been
in advance of their time, who have been misunderstood, maligned,
persecuted, sometimes put to death. Long after their martyrdom
monuments were erected to them and garlands woven for their graves.
. . .

Chattel slavery has disappeared. But we are not yet free. We are
engaged today in another mighty agitation. It is as wide as the world.
It means the rise of the toiling masses who are gradually becoming
conscious of their interests, their power, and their mission as a class;
who are organizing industrially and politically and who are slowly but
surely developing the economic and political power that is to set them
free. These awakening workers are still in a minority, but they have
learned how to work together to achieve their freedom, and how to
be patient and abide their time.

*Debs—founder of the American Railway Union, leader of the Social Democratic
Party, and folk hero of the American Left—was tried for sedition for an anti-war
speech that discouraged enlistment in the military. Debs opposed "every war but
one; I am for that war with heart and soul, and that is the world wide war of the
social revolution." Convicted and sentenced to ten years in prison, Debs still gained
nearly a million votes for US president as a Socialist candidate while in jail.*

1918

Why Armenia Should Be Free

The day is not very far distant when, gathered around the great tribunal of justice, the representatives of all the nations of the globe—guilty or just—are to receive their punishment or reward . . . Behold! Into the Peace Congress Hall there enters an old woman, bathed in blood, clothed in rags, her face covered with wrinkles 3,000 years old, and completely exhausted. With her thoughtful eyes the venerable Mother Armenia will survey the countenances of all those present, and thus will she address the great figures of the world:

"Century after century my sons took part in all the strifes waged to safeguard justice and the freedom of suffering humanity. Three thousand years ago my sons struggled for 700 years against the despotism of Babylon and Nineveh, which eventually collapsed under the load of their own crimes. Fifteen centuries ago the Armenians resisted for 500 years the persecutions of the mighty Persian Empire to preserve their Christian faith. Since the 700s my sons have been the vanguard of Christian civilization in the East against Moslem invasions threatening for a while the very existence of all Europe . . .

"Here, before you, stand the representatives of those three nations which tried to destroy my sons . . . Look at this Turk; it was he who wished to wipe the very name of Armenia off the face of the map; but today, foiled in his attempt, he stands there like a criminal awaiting his sentence. And where is today the Tsar of Russia, who planned to occupy Armenia without the Armenians—the representative of that Empire before which the world trembled? And what has remained of the policies of the German Empire, in whose hands is the Baghdad railroad now, built at the cost of the blood of hundreds of thousands of Armenian women and children? Thus, those three modern malevolent empires, which tried to attain happiness through the blood of my sons, have received their just punishment.

"Such will be the fate in the future of all those who shall attempt similar crimes against Armenia. This is the message, gentlemen, handed down to us through 3,000 years of history.

"I have nothing more to add. I await your verdict with confidence."

Pasdermajian was a member of the Armenian Revolutionary Federation, which fought for Armenian independence from the Ottoman Empire and participated in the Armenian Resistance of 1914–18. It was during this time that the Armenian massacre took place, in which between 600,000 and 1.5 million Armenians were killed by Ottoman forces.

JOHN MACLEAN 1918

Speech from the Dock

I wish no harm to any human being, but I, as one man, am going to exercise my freedom of speech. No human being on the face of the earth, no government is going to take from me my right to speak, my right to protest against wrong, my right to do everything that is for the benefit of mankind. I am not here, then, as the accused: I am here as the accuser of capitalism dripping with blood from head to foot.

MacLean, a Scottish teacher, revolutionary and proponent of a Scottish Worker's Republic independent from Britain, was imprisoned for opposing the First World War. Tens of thousands of Glaswegian workers greeted him on his release from prison, and he was carried through the streets in triumph.

RABINDRANATH TAGORE 1919

"Walk Alone"

If they answer not to thy call, walk alone,
if they are afraid and cower mutely facing the wall,
O thou of evil luck,
open thy mind and speak out alone.

If they turn away, and desert you when crossing the wilderness,
O thou of evil luck,

trample the thorns under thy tread,
and along the blood–lined track travel alone.

If they do not hold up the light when the night is troubled with storm,
O thou of evil luck,
with the thunder flame of pain ignite thy own heart
and let it burn alone.

Tagore, a Bengali writer and the first Asian winner of the Nobel Prize for Literature, wrote more than 2,000 songs, including ones lionizing the Indian independence movement, though he was controversial in the movement for holding that British imperialism was "a political symptom of our social disease." "Walk Alone" was one of Gandhi's favorite songs.

1919

JOHN REED

Ten Days that Shook the World

In the relations of a weak Government and a rebellious people there comes a time when every act of the authorities exasperates the masses, and every refusal to act excites their contempt ... The proposal to abandon Petrograd raised a hurricane; Kerensky's public denial that the Government had any such intention was met with hoots of derision.

Pinned to the wall by the pressure of the Revolution (cried *Rabotchi Put*), the Government of "provisional" bourgeois tries to get free by giving out lying assurances that it never thought of fleeing from Petrograd, and that it didn't wish to surrender the capital ...

In Kharkov thirty thousand coal miners organized, adopting the preamble of the IWW constitution: "The working class and the employing class have nothing in common." Dispersed by Cossacks, some were locked out by the mine-owners, and the rest declared a general strike. Minister of Commerce and Industry Konovalov appointed his assistant, Orlov, with plenary powers, to settle the trouble. Orlov was hated by the miners. But the *Tsay-ee-kah* not only supported his appointment, but refused to demand that the Cossacks be recalled from the Don Basin ...

In Petrograd was ending a regional Congress of Soviets of the

North, presided over by the Bolshevik Krylenko. By an immense majority it resolved that all power should be assumed by the All-Russian Congress; and concluded by greeting the Bolsheviki in prison, bidding them rejoice, for the hour of their liberation was at hand. At the same time the first All-Russian Conference of Factory-Shop Committees declared emphatically for the Soviets, and continued significantly.

After liberating themselves politically from Tsardom, the working class wants to see the democratic regime triumphant in the sphere of its productive activity. This is best expressed by Workers' Control over industrial production, which naturally arose in the atmosphere of economic decomposition created by the criminal policy of the dominating classes . . .

Ten Days That Shook the World *was the first major account of the Russian Revolution to appear in America, published when its author was just twenty-two. A child of great privilege, Reed was a playboy who became a socialist, helped to organize the "Strike Pageant" in Madison Square Garden with Bill Haywood of the Wobblies, traveled with the insurgent forces of Pancho Villa, and was buried in the wall of the Kremlin after his death from typhus at the age of thirty-three.*

EUGEN LEVINÉ   1919

Last Speech

We Communists are all dead men on leave. Of this I am fully aware. I do not know if you will extend my leave or whether I will have to join Karl Liebknecht and Rosa Luxemburg. In any case I await your verdict with composure and serenity. Whatever your verdict, events cannot be stopped . . .

Pronounce your verdict if you deem it proper. I have only striven to foil your attempt to stain my political activity, the name of the Soviet Republic with which I feel myself so closely bound up, and the good name of the workers of Munich. Long live the Communist World Revolution.

Leviné, a revolutionary socialist and a leader of the German Spartacus League, thought the Munich Uprising—part of the German Revolution of 1918–9— was premature, but once overruled by social-democrats and independent socialists, he assumed leadership. The Munich Commune controlled the city for a month before it was toppled by the military and local groups, many of whom would later back Hitler. Leviné was found guilty of treason and executed on July 5, 1919.

1919

CHEN DUXIU

"Our Final Awakening"

We, having been living in one corner of the world for several decades, must ask ourselves what is the level of our national strength and our civilization. This is the final awakening of which I speak. To put it another way, if we open our eyes and take a hard look at the situation within our country and abroad, what place does our country and our people occupy, and what actions should we take? . . .

Our task today can be said to be the intense combat between the old and the modern currents of thought. Those with shallow views all expect this to be our final awakening, without understanding how difficult it is to put [constitutional government] into practice . . .

There is no difference between the shameful disgrace of submissiveness of men of ancient times hoping that sage rulers and wise ministers will practice benevolent government and present-day men hoping that dignitaries and influential elders will build a constitutional republic. Why should I reject the desires of dignitaries and influential elders, who are after all a part of the people, to build a constitutional republic? Only because a constitutional republic cannot be conferred by the government, cannot be maintained by one party or one group, and certainly cannot be carried on the backs of a few dignitaries and influential elders. A constitutional republic which does not derive from the conscious realization and voluntary action of the majority of the people is a bogus republic and bogus constitutionalism.

Chen was the editor of China's most influential journal of the day, New Youth, *a leader of the Xinhai Revolution of 1911 and the May Fourth Movement, and one of the co-founders, with Li Dazhao, of the Chinese Communist Party.*

"If We Must Die"

If we must die—let it not be like hogs
Hunted and penned in an inglorious spot,
While round us bark the mad and hungry dogs,
Making their mock at our accursed lot.
If we must die—O let us nobly die,
So that our precious blood may not be shed
In vain; then even the monsters we defy
Shall be constrained to honor us though dead!

McKay, the Jamaican-born Harlem Renaissance poet, was once a maverick member of the Harlem-based African Blood Brotherhood, the black affiliate of the Communist Party, although he would become disenchanted with communism by the end of his life. "If We Must Die" addresses the racial violence perpetrated against blacks during the "Red Summer of 1919," when whites attacked blacks in a series of bloody riots all over the US.

"Two Negro Radicalisms"

All over this land and in the West Indies Negroes are responding to the call of battle against the white man's Color Line. And, so long as this remains, the international dogma of the white race, so long will the new Negro war against it. This is the very Ethiopianism which England has been combatting from Cairo to the Cape.

Undoubtedly some of these newly-awakened Negroes will take to Socialism and Bolshevism. But here again the reason is racial. Since they suffer racially from the world as at present organized by the white race, some of their ablest hold that it is "good play" to encourage and give aid to every subversive movement within that white world which makes for its destruction "as it is." For by its subversion they have much to gain and nothing to lose. But they build on their own foundations. Parallel with the dogma of Class-Consciousness they run the dogma of Race-Consciousness. And they dig deeper. For the roots of Class-Consciousness inhere in a temporary economic order; whereas the roots of Race-Consciousness must of necessity survive any and all changes in the economic order. Accepting biology as a fact, their view is the more fundamental. At any rate, it is that view with which the white world will have to deal.

An immigrant to the US from the Virgin Islands, Harrison worked at different times for the Socialist Party and Marcus Garvey. Ultimately he promulgated his own radical nationalist thinking through two organizations he founded, the Liberty League and the International Colored Unity League.

1920   ALEXANDRA KOLLONTAI

"Communism and the Family"

The workers' state needs new relations between the sexes. Just as the narrow and exclusive affection of the mother for her own children must expand until it extends to all the children of the great proletarian family, the indissoluble marriage based on the servitude of women is replaced by a free union of two equal members of the workers' state who are united by love and mutual respect. In place of the individual and egoistic family, a great universal family of workers will develop, in which all the workers, men and women, will above all be comrades. This is what relations between men and women in the communist society will be like. These new relations will ensure for humanity all the joys of a love unknown in the commercial society of capitalism, a love that is free and based on the true social equality of happy young people, free in their feelings and affections.

Kollontai did not actually say that "the satisfaction of one's sexual desires should be as simple as getting a glass of water"—this was a misinterpretation of her statement that sexuality is "as natural as hunger or thirst"—but many were captivated by her argument that sex and the family needed to be shorn of bourgeois and patriarchal norms. She became the People's Commissar for Social

Welfare after the Bolshevik Revolution, founded the Women's Department of the Soviet Union, and was the world's first female ambassador as the Soviet representative to Norway.

HO CHI MINH   1920

"French Colonization on Trial"

Indochina is a darling daughter. She is worthy of mother France. She has all that the latter has: her government, her means, her justice, and also her little conspiracies. We will speak only of the two latter.

Justice is represented by a good lady holding scales in one hand and a sword in the other. As the distance between Indochina and France is so great, so great that, on arrival there, the scales lose their balance and the pans melt and turn into opium pipes and official bottles of spirits, the poor lady has only the sword left with which to strike. She even strikes innocent people, and innocent people especially . . .

Poor Indochina! You will die, unless your old-fashioned Youth comes to life.

After working as a baker in Harlem, where he was influenced by Marcus Garvey, Ho wound up in France via England, joined and then left the Socialist Party when it fractured on the issue of colonialism, and became the resident expert on colonialism in the French Communist Party. This diatribe was written while he was in Paris and smuggled into Indochina as a pamphlet, where it quickly became the "bible of nationalists." After Paris, Ho worked for the Comintern in Moscow and then proceeded to Shanghai, not returning to Vietnam until 1941 to lead the independence movement.

W. A. DOMINGO   1920

"The New Negro—What is He?"

Now, what are the aims of the New Negro? The answer to this question will fall under three general heads, namely, political, economic, and social.

In politics, the New Negro, unlike the Old Negro, cannot be lulled into a false sense of security with political spoils and patronage. A job is not the price of his vote ... The New Negro demands political equality ...

A word about the economic aims of the New Negro. Here, as a worker, he demands the full product of his toil. His immediate aim is more wages, shorter hours and better working conditions. As a consumer, he seeks to buy in the market, commodities at the lowest possible price.

The social aims of the New Negro are decidedly different from those of the Old Negro. Here he stands for absolute and unequivocal "social equality." He realizes that there cannot be any qualified equality. He insists that a society which is based upon justice can only be a society composed of social equals. He insists upon identity of social treatment. With respect to intermarriage, he maintains that it is the only logical, sound and correct aim for the Negro to entertain ...

The New Negro arrived upon the scene at the time of all other forward, progressive groups and movements—after the great world war. He is the product of the same world-wide forces that have brought into being the great liberal and radical movements that are now seizing the reins of political, economic and social power in all of the civilized countries of the world.

His presence is inevitable in these times of economic chaos, political upheaval and social distress. Yes, there is a New Negro. And it is he who will pilot the Negro through this terrible hour of storm and stress.

Jamaican journalist Domingo briefly edited Marcus Garvey's newspaper in Harlem before launching the Emancipator, *his own weekly publication of "scientific radicalism and fearless opinion." He later founded the pro-independence Jamaican Progressive League in New York City in 1936.*

"Develop the Peasantry"

Our China is a rural nation and most of the laboring class is made up of peasants. If they are not liberated, then our whole nation will not be liberated; their sufferings are the sufferings of our whole nation; their ignorance is the ignorance of our whole nation; the advantages and defects of their lives are the advantages and defects of all of our politics. Go out and develop them and cause them to know [that they should] demand liberation, speak out about their sufferings, throw off their ignorance and be people who will themselves plan their own lives.

In 1918, Li established an informal politics study group at Peking University, where he was head librarian. This group eventually became the "Marxist Research Society." Together with another of its members, Chen Duxiu, he later co-founded the Chinese Communist Party.

Response to al-Risafi

"Juda's" speech? Or acts of witchcraft? And Risafi's saying? Or lies
    of poetry . . .
Your poetry is of the choicest words, you are well-acquainted with
    the jewels of sea verse
But this sea is one of politics, if justice spreads high its low tide begins
Yes! He who has crossed the Jordan River is our cousin but he who
    comes from across the sea is suspicious . . .

Al-Bustani, a Lebanese poet who settled in Palestine, was an early opponent of the Balfour Declaration, which proclaimed Britain's intent to establish a "Jewish national home" in Palestine. This poem, written in response to Iraqi poet Ma'ruf Al-Risafi's praise of the first British High Commissioner, Herbert Samuel, pointed out the dangers to Palestine's Arab society posed by Jewish immigration and colonization.

1920

"Young Syria Will Never Submit to Old France"

Tell the pope, the clericalists, the capitalists and the politicians who aim at conquest that young Syria will never submit to old France.

Al-Kinana *was one among several Syrian newspapers that called for resistance against an imminent French invasion in 1920, meant to overthrow the first ever Arab republic under King Faisal. This slogan ran as a two-page headline in the paper. After crushing the resistance, the French ruled Syria until 1946.*

1920s

VERA FIGNER

Memoirs of a Revolutionist

My past experience had convinced me that the only way to change the existing order was by force. If any group in our society had shown me a path other than violence, perhaps I would have followed it; at the very least, I would have tried it out. But, as you know, we don't have a free press in our country, and so ideas cannot be spread by the written word. And so I concluded that violence was the only solution. I could not follow the peaceful path.

Growing up in Kazan, Russia, Figner was prevented—by state and father—from studying medicine. In 1872 she married, sold her dowry, and enrolled in the Department of Medicine at the University of Zurich. She joined Narod-naya Volya ("The Will of the People"), taking part in the formation of the paramilitary wing of the group and helping to assassinate Tsar Alexander II in 1881. She spent more than thirty years in prison and in internal and external exile, but lived until 1942.

"It Is Close at Hand"

Arise. Time is at hand.
   It is very close.
Stand up, brothers. Do you want to die lying there?
We now face our deepest winter.
Arise.
   Time is very short but we still have time.
If we miss this chance,
   The winter will freeze our lives.

Abdukhaliq, a Uyghur nationalist poet whose poems describe the lives of the Uyghur people under oppression, was killed by the Chinese government at the age of twenty-two in retaliation for the Hami Uprising of 1930–3. The Rebellion sought an end to Chinese rule in East Turkestan and the establishment of a Turkish Islamic Republic of East Turkestan in what is today Xinjiang Province. "Uyghur" was Abdukhaliq's pen name, and when he adopted it, the Chinese saw it as a nationalistic move.

REVOLUTIONARY WAR COUNCIL OF THE PERSIAN RED ARMY **1920**

Letter to Trotsky

With great difficulty and enduring all manner of privations we have succeeded in defeating the internal counterrevolution, which was nothing more nor less than the hireling of international capitalism. By the will of the working people, Soviet power has been organized in Persia, and this has set about creating a Persian Red Army on the lines on which Russia's Red Army was formed, in order to destroy the enslavers of the Persian people.

   "Long live the fraternal alliance of the Russian Red Army with the young Persian army!"

In 1920, the republican-socialist Jangal movement formed the Persian Soviet Socialist Republic in the Gilan province of Iran. Jangal volunteers had been trained by German, Austrian and Turkish officers. A year and a half later, the territory was captured by Reza Khan, and the Republic's leader, Mirza Kuchuk Khan, was caught and executed.

1921   KRONSTADT REBELS

Petropavlovsk Resolution and Demands

Our country is enduring a difficult moment. Hunger, cold and economic ruin have held us in an iron vice these three years already. The Communist Party, which rules the country, has become separated from the masses, and shown itself unable to lead her from her state of general ruin. It has not faced the reality of the disturbances which in recent times have occurred in Petrograd and Moscow. This unrest shows clearly enough that the party has lost the faith of the working masses. Neither has it recognized the demands presented by the workers. It considers them plots of the counter-revolution. It is deeply mistaken.

This unrest, these demands, are the voice of the people in its entirety, of all laborers. All workers, sailors and soldiers see clearly at the present moment that only through common effort, by the common will of the laborers, is it possible to give the country bread, wood, and coal, to dress the barefoot and naked, and to lead the Republic out of this dead end.

This will of all laborers, soldiers and sailors was definitively expressed at the Garrison Meeting of our town . . . in view of the fact that there were grounds to fear repression, and also due to threatening speeches by the representatives of authority, the Conference decided to form a Provisional Revolutionary Committee, to which to give all authority in governing the town and fortress.

Comrades and citizens! The Provisional Committee is deeply concerned that there should not be spilled a single drop of blood. It has taken emergency measures for the establishment of revolutionary order in the town and fortress, and at the forts. Comrades and citizens! Do not stop work. Workers, remain at your machines, sailors and soldiers in your units and at the forts. All Soviet workers and organizations must continue their work. The Provisional Revolutionary Committee calls all workers' organizations, all naval and trade unions, and all naval and military units and individual citizens to give it universal support and aid. The task of the Provisional Revolutionary Committee is a general, comradely effort to organize in the town and fortress means for proper and fair elections to a new Soviet. And so, comrades, to order, to calm, to restraint, and to a new Socialist construction for the good of all laborers.

The crews of the battleships Petropavlovsk and Sevastopol crafted these demands, and the next day, sailors, soldiers, and civilians in Kronstadt, a naval fortress in the Gulf of Finland, formed a provisional revolutionary committee—one in a wave of left-wing rebellions against Soviet Russia. The Bolshevik government attacked Kronstadt on March 7, and took the city on March 17 at a cost of more than ten thousand deaths. Thousands of rebels were executed.

KAZI NAZRUL ISLAM   1922

"The Rebel"

I am the magic flute of Orpheus—its music lulls
the heaving ocean into drowsy forgetfulness, and in sleep
it kisses the earth and soothes it to complete silence.
I am the flute in the hands of Krishna.
As I rage and rush, enveloping the boundless heavens,
The fires of all the hells down below flicker and die in panic!
I am the carrier of rebellion all over the earth.
. . .
And I shall rest, battle-weary rebel, only on the day
when the wails of the oppressed shall not rend the air and sky,
and the scimitar and the sword of the oppressor
shall not clang in the fierce arena of battle—
that day my rebel self, weary with fighting,
shall rest appeased.

Nazrul, known as the "rebel poet" of Bengali literature, was also a novelist, journalist, musician, songwriter, actor, and director. He was imprisoned often by the British, and this poem, his most famous, coincided with the non-cooperation movement—the first mass nationalist campaign of civil disobedience against British rule.

1922   SEN KATAYAMA

"To the Soldiers of the Japanese Army in Siberia"

Against the will and wishes of the workers and the peasants of Japan, the Japanese government has sent a large army to Siberia to fight against the Red Army and to devastate the workers' and peasants' country. We, the revolutionary proletarians in Japan, are yet too weak and powerless against the aggressive and oppressive militarist government to stop this most inhuman and bloody slaughter by the Japanese imperialist army in Siberia. The Japanese army has been losing the people's confidence ever since the fall of German militarism and the unjust Siberian invasion that has been undertaken by the militarist clique . . .

Proletarians of the world! This most outrageous invasion of the Japanese imperialists in Siberia can only be stopped by your concerted action at this critical moment. We, the Communist Party members and the revolutionary workers and peasants, are powerless before this powerful imperialist oppression although we are fighting against the imperialists at every possible step . . .

Katayama, an early member of the American Communist Party, became a Christian and a socialist during his education in America; edited the publication of the Iron Workers' Union and Trade Unions' Federation in Japan; was a rice farmer in Texas for many years; and returned to Japan as a journalist and intellectual, where he became the leader of the Japanese Communist movement and was jailed for his participation in the 1912 Tokyo streetcar strike. The Japanese Communist Party, which he co-founded in 1922, later became the sole political party to oppose Japanese involvement in World War II. Katayama died in the USSR and is buried in the Kremlin Wall.

HUDA SHAARAWI

1924

"Women Are Bright Stars"

. . . women are bright stars whose light penetrates dark clouds. They rise in times of trouble when the wills of men are tried. In moments of danger, when women emerge by their side, men utter no protest. Yet women's great acts and endless sacrifices do not change men's views of women. Through their arrogance, men refuse to see the capabilities of women. Faced with contradiction, they prefer to raise women above the ordinary human plane instead of placing them on a level equal to their own. Men have singled out women of outstanding merit and put them on a pedestal to avoid recognizing the capabilities of all women.

Shaarawi, an Egyptian feminist and nationalist activist, was a founder of several women's societies, including the Egyptian Feminist Union, and helped organize the first street demonstration by Egyptian women during the nationalist revolt in 1919. A social reformer, Shaarawi believed in education for women and came to oppose the veil.

VLADIMIR MAYAKOVSKY

1924

"Vladimir Ilyich Lenin"

Just guzzling,
>> snoozing
>>>> and pocketing pelf,
Capitalism
>> got lazy and feeble.
All blubber,
>> he sprawled
>>>> in History's way.
No
>> getting over
>>>> or past him.

141

So snug

in his world-wide
bed

he lay,

The one way out
was to blast him.

Mayakovsky's elegy to Lenin, written immediately following the leader's death, brought him fame throughout Russia. A self-described Communist Futurist, Mayakovsky was also one of Stalin's favorite poets and wrote plays satirizing Soviet philistinism and bureaucracy. He shot himself in 1930.

1925 NGUYEN AN NINH

"France in Indochina"

When a people has reached the point where they must choose between death and slavery, to taunt death is more virile. Violence ought to be condemned when it is unnecessary. But there are cases when violence must be accepted, for it represents the only recourse . . . If the masses taunt death rather than accept injustice and, on the other hand, if the colonialists refuse to give up their policy of oppression and exploitation without scruples, it is then the duty of the more courageous and the more devoted Vietnamese to think of methods of struggle that fit the time and to devise a form of resistance that is capable of fighting oppression. The prisoner who attempts to escape does not think about the death that may befall him during the evasion.

Nguyen, an unorthodox radical nationalist who was better known and more influential than Ho Chi Minh during the colonial era, became involved in the anarchist and socialist movements while studying to become a lawyer in France; was employed at a Parisian newspaper where Ho was also on staff; and made a living working as a fortune-teller before returning to Vietnam and founding the anti-colonial Nguyen An Ninh Secret Society, which disseminated anti-French propaganda and recruited hundreds of workers in Saigon. In 1926, he was arrested along with 115 members of his organization and deported to the island of Poulo Condore, where he died nearly twenty years later.

JOSÉ CARLOS MARIÁTEGUI — 1925
"Man and Myth"

What most clearly and obviously differentiates the bourgeoisie and the proletariat in this era is myth. The bourgeoisie finally has no myth. It has become incredulous, skeptical, nihilist. The reborn liberal myth has already aged. The proletariat has a myth: the social revolution. It moves toward this myth with a vehement and active faith. The bourgeoisie denies; the proletariat affirms. The bourgeois mind amuses itself with a rationalist critique of the methods, the theories, the technique of the revolutionaries. What incomprehension! The revolutionaries' power is not in their science; it is in their faith, their passion, their will. It is a religious, mystical, spiritual power. It is the power of myth.

Mariátegui was a Peruvian writer and thinker whose Seven Interpretive Essays on Peruvian Reality *helped make him one of the most influential Latin American Marxists of the 1900s.*

LAMINE SENGHOR — 1927
"The Negro's Fight for Freedom"

The Negroes have slept for too long. But beware! The man who has slept too well, and then awakes, will not fall asleep again . . .

We have assembled to defend ourselves against these injustices, these horrors I have mentioned. Young Negroes are beginning to see things clearly. We know and ascertain that we are French when they need us to let us be killed or make us labor. But when it comes to giving us rights, we are no longer Frenchmen but Negroes . . .

Senghor was an early Senegalese nationalist who joined the French Communist Party in 1924 and continued to fight for an independent Senegal. The speech was made before the League of Imperialism in Brussels.

1927

MAO ZEDONG

"Report on the Investigation of the Peasant Movement in Hunan"

Down with the local tyrants and evil gentry! All power to the peasants' associations! . . .

The most violent revolts and the most serious disorders have invariably occurred in places where the local tyrants, evil gentry and lawless landlords perpetrated the worst outrages. The peasants are clear-sighted. Who is bad and who is not, who is the worst and who is not quite so vicious, who deserves severe punishment and who deserves to be let off lightly—the peasants keep clear accounts, and very seldom has the punishment exceeded the crime . . .

A revolution is not a dinner party, or writing an essay, or painting a picture, or doing embroidery; it cannot be so refined, so leisurely and gentle, so temperate, kind, courteous, restrained and magnanimous. A revolution is an insurrection, an act of violence by which one class overthrows another. A rural revolution is a revolution by which the peasantry overthrows the power of the feudal landlord class. Without using the greatest force, the peasants cannot possibly overthrow the deep-rooted authority of the landlords which has lasted for thousands of years. The rural areas need a mighty revolutionary upsurge, for it alone can rouse the people in their millions to become a powerful force. All the actions mentioned here which have been labeled as "going too far" flow from the power of the peasants, which has been called forth by the mighty revolutionary upsurge in the countryside.

The Communist Party of China, initially focused on proletariat-led revolution, would take a sharp turn toward peasant- and mass-based revolution under the leadership of Mao. This report marks the beginning of that turn. Revolutionary mass mobilization would thus become the hallmark of his policies and thought on both domestic and international matters. As he later remarked, "US imperialism is a paper tiger"—weak in its lack of mass support.

"Last Will"

Prologue:
We, Sacco and Vanzetti, sound of body and mind,
Devise and bequeath to all we leave behind,
The worldly wealth we inherited at our birth,
Each one to share alike as we leave this earth.

To Wit:
To babies we will their mothers' love,
To youngsters we will the sun above.
To spooners who want to tryst the night,
We give the moon and stars that shine so bright.
To thrill them in their hours of joy,
When boy hugs maid and maid hugs boy.
To nature's creatures we allot the spring and summer,
To the doe, the bear, the gold-finch and the hummer.
To the fishes we ascribe the deep blue sea,
The honey we apportion to the bustling bee.
To the pessimist—good cheer—his mind to sooth,
To the chronic liar we donate the solemn truth.

And Lastly:
To those who judge solely seeking renown,
With blaring trumpets of the fakir and clown;
To the prosecutor, persecutor, and other human hounds,
Who'd barter another's honor, recognizing no bounds,
To the Governor, the Jury, who another's life they'd sell—
We endow them with the fiery depths of HELL!

The circumstances surrounding the wrongful arrest, trial and execution of Italian-American anarchists Nicola Sacco and Bartolemeo Vanzetti for armed robbery and murder remain contested to this day. The arrest came during a period of intense political repression—the "Red Scare" of 1919–20—and the testimonies of many witnesses who verified Vanzetti's alibi were virtually ignored for being given in Italian, making Sacco and Vanzetti into martyrs of the unjust and discriminatory legal system.

1927 KITAHARA TAISAKU

"Petition to the Emperor Over Discrimination Against the *Burakumin* in the Army"

I ran up to a point several meters from the Emperor, who was on horse-back, and took a kneeling position. I then took out the petition from my pocket and raised it high in my left hand shouting, "A petition, a peti-tion!" The Emperor appeared to be baffled by this untoward occurrence and looked down at me from atop his horse with a puzzled look. The general who was on horseback behind the Emperor . . . was shocked, and charged toward me with his saber uplifted shouting, "Arrest him, arrest him!" I was then grabbed from behind by a powerful pair of arms. When I looked around I saw Lieutenant Okuda's deathly pale face. His lips were trembling and he let out a groan and, grabbing me by my backpack, dragged me to a line to the left of the battalion. The cavalry troops under review marched in perfect formation, as if nothing at all had happened. My action was a "happening" that lasted only five minutes.

Kitahara was a member of the burakumin *caste in Japan—people engaged in "unclean work," similar to the Untouchables in India. At the beginning of the 1900s,* burakumin *were subject to the draft just like everyone else, but experienced brutal harassment and abuse within the military, often leading to suicides. Kitahara's act was extensively publicized, raising awareness about the* burakumin *nationwide, despite their relatively small numbers.*

1928 VICTOR SERGE

Year One of the Russian Revolution

The next years were to bring a number of fantastic spectacles: whole armies entering the field without munitions, fighting it out with sword and bayonet in mid-battle; treason at work in the General Staff and perhaps in the Court; sudden fortunes in the hands of manufacturers of war supplies; incompetent drunkards in responsible posts; a rakish *staretz* (or "holy old man"), Rasputin, as close adviser to the Tsar, appointing and dismissing ministers between one drunken orgy and the next; Russia sliding towards the abyss while the world watched. The war revealed the gangrene of the whole system . . .

The revolution did come into the streets: it came down from the factories with thousands of workers out on strike, to cries of "Bread! Bread!" The authorities saw it coming but could do nothing: it was not in their power to remedy the crisis. In the streets of Petrograd the troops fraternized with the workers' demonstrations, sealing the fate of the autocracy. The speed of events took the revolutionary organizations by surprise, even though they had been working towards this goal . . .

Three great problems cry out for urgent solution, expressed in the three words: peace, land, bread! Peace is wanted by millions of peasants and proletarians in the army, and the bourgeoisie cannot give it them because it is too busy waging its own war. Land is desired by millions of peasants: the bourgeoisie will not give it, because it is allied with the big landowners and because it rejects any attack on private property, the principle of its own domination. Bread is demanded by the proletariat of the cities: the bourgeoisie cannot give it, for the famine is the offshoot of its war and its policies . . . The overthrow of Tsardom has solved nothing. Another revolution has to be made.

This is what the masses feel and want. This is what the party of the proletariat knows and arms for.

The Belgian-born son of Russian immigrants, Serge published his first anarchist article at eighteen, was expelled from Belgium at nineteen, and was sentenced to solitary confinement in France at twenty-two. Thus began a lifetime of revolutionary activism that included episodes as a Bolshevik; as a journalist, editor, and translator for the Comintern; and as an exile and socialist critic of Stalin. He wrote this history of the Russian Revolution—as well as numerous essays, analyses, and novels—between stints in prison.

MOHANDAS K. GANDHI

Letter to Viceroy Lord Irwin

I know the dangers attendant upon the methods adopted by me. But the country is not likely to mistake my meaning. I say what I mean and think—and I have been saying for the last fifteen years in India, and outside for twenty years more, and repeat now that the only way to conquer violence is through non-violence pure and undefiled. I have said also that every violent act, word and even thought interferes with the progress of non-violent action. If in spite of such repeated warnings, people will resort to violence, I must disown responsibility save such as inevitably attaches to every human being for the acts of every other human being. But the question of responsibility apart, I dare not postpone action on any cause whatsoever if non-violence is the force the seers of the world have claimed it to be and if I am not to belie my own extensive experience of its working . . . If you say, as you have said, that the civil disobedience must end in violence, history will pronounce the verdict that the British Government, not bearing because not understanding non-violence, goaded human nature to violence, which it could understand and deal with. But in spite of the goading, I shall hope that God will give the people of India wisdom and strength to withstand every temptation and provocation to violence.

The Salt Satyagraha, which began with a march from Gandhi's ashram to the Dharasana Salt Works, sparked large-scale acts of civil disobedience against the British Raj by millions of Indians, and led to hundreds of marchers being beaten and more than 80,000 arrests. Gandhi was arrested the day before writing this letter. Earlier, he had written: "Truth (satya) implies love, and firmness (agraha) engenders and therefore serves as a synonym for force. I thus began to call the Indian movement Satyagraha, that is to say, the Force which is born of Truth and Love or non-violence, and gave up the use of the phrase 'passive resistance.'"

USA

USA is a slice of the continent. USA is a group of holding companies, some aggregations of trade unions, a set of laws bound in calf, a radio network, a chain of moving picture theaters, a column of stock-quotations rubbed out and written in by a Western Union boy on a blackboard, a public library full of old newspapers and dog-eared history books with protests scrawled on the margins in pencil. USA is the world's greatest river valley fringed with mountains and hills, USA is a set of bigmouthed officials with too many bank accounts. USA is a lot of men buried in their uniforms in Arlington Cemetery. USA is the letters at the end of an address when you are away from home. But mostly USA is the speech of the people.

The politics of Dos Passos' trilogy USA, which provided a sweeping look at American culture using a blend of fictional biography, newsreels and stream of consciousness, seemed to confirm his growing connection with the far left. But not long after, he began to drift toward the right, eventually coming to admire Joseph McCarthy.

The Empire Is a System

The empire is a system. It can wait. It can fatten its victims to render its digestion more enjoyable at a later time.

Known as "El Maestro," Albizu Campos was a leader of the Puerto Rican independence movement. He was leader of the Nationalist Party in Puerto Rico from 1930 until his death in 1965, and was imprisoned a number of times in the United States and Puerto Rico, including on charges of trying to overthrow the US government.

1930s

IBRAHIM TUQAN

"Lest We Lose"

You're the ones loyal to the cause
You're the ones who carry its burden
You're the ones who act without speech
God bless your strong arms!
A declaration from you equals an army
with all its military might
Your gatherings restore
the glory lost since Umayyad conquests
But we still have bits of country left in our hands
so rest awhile, lest we lose what remains.

Tuqan was Palestine's foremost revolutionary poet during the period of the British mandate (1917–48), and the author of what is informally considered the Palestinian national anthem.

1930s

ANONYMOUS

"Poem in Blood"

A rosy-cheeked woman here I am fighting side-by-side with you men!
On my shoulders weighs the hatred which is common to us.
The prison is my school, its inmates my friends.
The sword is my child, the gun my husband!

The Indochinese Communist Party included a women's organization; its members worked alongside men to resist the French and then the Americans, and many were killed. This poem was written by a female guerrilla on the walls of her prison cell, in her own blood, before she died. She had been tortured.

AUNT MOLLY JACKSON
1931

"I Am A Union Woman"

I was raised in Old Kentucky
Kentucky born and bred,
But when I joined the union,
They called me a Rooshian Red . . .
The bosses ride fine horses
While we walk in the mud,
Their banner is the dollar sign,
While ours is striped with blood.

After losing her husband and having her father and brother blinded in separate mining accidents, Jackson became an activist, joining the United Mine Workers and writing protest songs, including "I Am A Union Woman."

BHAGAT SINGH
1931

"Why I Am an Atheist"

Let me tell you, British rule is here not because God wills it but because they possess power and we do not dare to oppose them. Not that it is with the help of God that they are keeping us under their subjection but it is with the help of guns and rifles, bombs and bullets, police and militia and our apathy that they are successfully committing the most deplorable sin against society—the outrageous exploitation of one nation by another. Where is God? What is he doing? Is he enjoying all these woes of the human race? A Nero; A *Changez*: down with him.

In 1929, at the age of twenty and in response to the passage of the Defense of India Act, which gave British police more power, Singh threw a bomb into the central legislative assembly—as well as leaflets saying "it takes a loud voice to make the deaf hear." A revolutionary influenced by anarchism and Marxism, he wrote this pamphlet in prison, where he confessed to another murder in order

151

to turn his trial into a platform for the cause of independence and revolution. He was hanged in March, 1931.

1931   VICTOR RAÚL HAYA DE LA TORRE

Speech at Plaza de Acho

Even after 110 years of independence, forgotten are the true inheritors and masters of this land, the three million indigenous people who cannot read nor write . . .

. . . We must fight for the Peruvianization of the state and the economic incorporation of the majorities, the nation's vital force and the ones who have a right to take part in directing our destiny because of their great number and ability.

Consequently, we are a political force that means to rescue for the nation's majorities the mastery of the state.

Haya de La Torre was a Peruvian political theorist and the founder of the American Popular Revolutionary Alliance, which he hoped would become a continent-wide party.

1932   LALA HAR DAYAL

"Hints of Self-Culture"

The nation–state may be truly compared to the dinosaurs and the tyrannosaurus of the Mesozoic Age. Like those gigantic reptiles, the sovereign nation–state has a very small brain with which to think and plan, but tremendously powerful teeth and claws to tear and rend, to destroy and dismember.

The Oxford-educated Indian anarchist Dayal moved to America at the age of twenty-five, where he founded the pro-Indian-independence Ghadar Party and became involved with the IWW. In 1914, he was arrested for spreading anarchist literature.

"The Stalin Epigram"

Our lives no longer feel ground under them.
At ten paces you can't hear our words.

But whenever there's a snatch of talk
it turns to the Kremlin mountaineer,

the ten thick worms his fingers,
his words like measures of weight,

the huge laughing cockroaches on his top lip,
the glitter of his boot-rims.

Ringed with a scum of chicken-necked bosses
he toys with the tributes of half-men.

One whistles, another meows, a third snivels.
He pokes out his finger and he alone goes boom.

He forges decrees in a line like horseshoes,
One for the groin, one the forehead, temple, eye.

He rolls the executions on his tongue like berries.
He wishes he could hug them like big friends from home.

Six months after writing this poem, "acmeist" poet Mandelstam was arrested and sent into internal exile. The sentence was more lenient than what was received by many of Stalin's critics, usually explained by Stalin's interest in Mandelstam's fate. Upon release, Mandelstam wrote an "Ode to Stalin," but in 1938 he was arrested again and died in a concentration camp.

1933–4

ANTONIO GRAMSCI

"Voluntarism and Social Masses"

"Vanguards" without armies to back them up, "commandos" without infantry or artillery, these are transpositions from the language of rhetorical heroism—though vanguard and commandos as specialised functions within complex and regular organisms are quite another thing. The same distinction can be made between the notion of intellectual élites separated from the masses, and that of intellectuals who are conscious of being linked organically to a national-popular mass. In reality, one has to struggle against the above-mentioned degenerations, the false heroisms and pseudo-aristocracies, and stimulate the formation of homogeneous social blocs, which will give birth to their own intellectuals, their own commandos, their own vanguard—who in turn will react upon those blocs in order to develop them, and not merely so as to perpetuate their gypsy domination. Romanticism's Paris *bohème* too was intellectually at the root of many contemporary modes of thought which appear nonetheless to deride those *bohémiens*.

A founder and leader of the Communist Party of Italy, Gramsci was imprisoned by the Fascist government in 1926; at his trial, the prosecutor famously stated, "We must stop this brain from functioning for twenty years." Gramsci wrote more than thirty notebooks in prison that would revolutionize Marxist thought, most notably with his theory of hegemony and the role of the organic intellectual, and his critique of materialism; he died shortly after his release at the age of forty-six.

1935

ABD AL-RAHIM MAHMUD

"The Aqsa Mosque"

Honorable Prince! Before you stands a poet
whose heart harbors bitter complaint.
Have you come to visit the Aqsa Mosque

or to bid it farewell before its loss?
This land, this holy land, is being sold to all intruders
and stabbed by its own people!
And tomorrow looms over us, nearer and nearer!
Nothing shall remain for us but our streaming tears,
our deep regrets!

Mahmud was known as the "Cavalier Poet" or "Poet Martyr" of Palestine for fighting against his homeland's aggressors and dying on the battlefield in 1948. This poem was addressed to Prince Saud Ibn Abd al-Aziz of Saudi Arabia. The al-Aqsa Mosque is part of the Noble Sanctuary in Jerusalem, Islam's third holiest site; although Prince Saud was a reactionary figure, the poem reflects the efforts made by the Palestinian national movement to win support from other Arab states and princes against Zionist ambitions.

CARLOS BULOSAN   1935

"Factory Town"

These were the longest years of their lives;
These were the years when the whistle at four o'clock
Drove them to the yard, then they scurried
Home heavy with fatigue and hunger and love.
These were the years when the gigantic chimneys blocked
The skies with black smoke that reminded passersby
Of a serpent–like whip of life within, bleeding,
Scarred with disease and death. These were the years . . .

Immigrating to the US from the Philippines as a teenager with hopes of completing his education and becoming a writer, Bulosan was instead faced with racial discrimination and harsh conditions, and found work as a manual laborer. Radicalized by the Repatriation Act of 1935, which threatened Pinoys with deportation, Bulosan helped to organize Filipino resistance against these practices. Eventually achieving his dream of becoming a writer, he wrote of Filipinos in America and peasants in the Philippines, also becoming a voice of working-class Asian America.

1935

CLIFFORD ODETS

Waiting for Lefty

Agate: What's the answer, boys? The answer is, if we're reds because we wanna strike, then we take over their salute too! Know how they do it? *Makes Communist salute.* What is it? An uppercut! The good old uppercut to the chin! Hell, some of us boys ain't even got a shirt to our backs. What's the boss class tryin' to do—make a nudist colony out of us?

These slick slobs stand here telling us about bogeymen. That's a new one for the kids—the reds is bogeymen! But the man who got me food in 1932, he called me Comrade! The one who picked me up where I bled—he called me Comrade too! What are we waiting for . . . Don't wait for Lefty! He might never come.

The American playwright Odets was a member of the Communist Party and traveled to Cuba to study the political situation, where he was arrested for his communist views. Waiting for Lefty, *inspired by the New York taxi strike of 1934, brought him fame within the theater world and was performed as "Left theater" throughout the US. But during the McCarthy era he appeared as a friendly witness before the House Un-American Activities Committee, destroying his reputation as a radical.*

1935

W. E. B. DU BOIS

"Black Reconstruction"

This the American black man knows: his fight here is a fight to the finish. Either he dies or wins. If he wins it will be by no subterfuge or evasion of amalgamation. He will enter modern civilization here in America as a black man on terms of perfect and unlimited equality with any white man or he will not enter at all. Either extermination root and branch, or absolute equality. There can be no compromise. This the last great battle of the West.

Du Bois, herald of Pan-Africanism, co-founder of the NAACP, and critic of the Cold War, began the 1900s by positing the Color Line as the problem of the century, and ended by joining the Communist Party. In between, he attempted, as his biographer David Levering Lewis put it, "virtually every possible solution to the problem of 1900s racism—scholarship, propaganda, integration, national self-determination, human rights, cultural and economic separatism, politics, international communism, expatriation, third world solidarity."

MIKE GOLD   1935

"Ode to Walt Whitman"

O Walt Whitman, they buried you in the filth
The clatter speedup of a department store basement
But he rose from the grave to march with us
On the picket line of democracy . . .

The Lenin dreams of the kelleys and greenbaums
Deep in the gangrened basements
Where Walt Whitman's America
Aches, to be born—

Gold was a writer and literary critic who has been called the "Dean of US Proletarian Literature"—a tradition of writing characterized by the fervent class consciousness that emerged in the 1930s among some working-class writers. Gold's most famous work is his fictionalized autobiography, Jews Without Money, *a coming-of-age story ending with a leftist conversion; but his writings and poems—including this one—frequently appeared in the socialist journal* New Masses, *which he edited for many years.*

BUENAVENTURA DURRUTI   1936

Interview

We have always lived in slums and holes in the wall. We will know how to accommodate ourselves for a while. For you must not forget that we can also build. It is we who built these palaces and cities, here in Spain and America and everywhere. We, the workers. We can build others to take their place. And better ones. We are not in the least afraid of ruins. We are going to inherit the earth; there is not the slightest doubt about that. The bourgeoisie might blast and ruin its own world before it leaves the stage of history. We carry a new world here, in our hearts. That world is growing in this minute.

The Spanish anarchist started work at the age of fourteen in the León rail yards. He had to flee to France and then Argentina due to the activities of Los Solidarios, the anarchist group he founded, but in the 1930s returned to Spain to help coordinate armed resistance against Francisco Franco, and ultimately to lead the most famous anarchist militia, later known as the Durruti Column, in the Spanish Civil War. He was killed three months after giving this interview.

1936

NYO MYA

"A Hellhound at Large"

Escaped from Awizi a devil in the form of a black dog.

Had been during its brief span on earth a base object of universal odium and execration, sentenced to eternal damnation for churlishness, treachery, ruffianism, pettifogging, etc. A pimping knave with avuncular pretensions to some cheap wiggling wenches from a well-known hostel, he was also a hectic popularity hunter, shamming interest in sports, concerts and other extra-curricular student activities. His only distinguishing marks are buboes and ulcers due to errant whoring.

Will finder please kick him back to hell.

In the early 1930s, U Nu and Aung San, who would later become the leaders of the Burmese nationalist movement, were leader and secretary, respectively, of the Rangoon University Students' Union. In 1936, U Nu was expelled for criticizing the University president, and two days later, Aung San, the editor of the student union magazine Oway, *printed this piece (written by Nyo Mya but sometimes attributed to the pair). Aung San was also expelled, precipitating the 1936 student strike. Both went on to become leading figures of Burma's communist movement and are regarded as national heroes today.*

LA PASIONARIA

1936

Speech during the Siege of Madrid

No pasarán!

Dolores Ibarruri achieved international fame for her passionate speeches on behalf of the Republic during the Spanish Civil War, including the famous slogan "They shall not pass" she used in defense of Madrid when it came under siege by Franco in 1936. One of the first members of the Spanish Communist Party, she was jailed repeatedly, but also repeatedly escaped capture by fascists.

MAHMOUD ABOU DEEB

1936

"Rebellion in the Hills"

When the rebellion started, young men used to go to the hills and ambush the Jews and the English . . . Day and night, in the hills. The English and the Jews who came to the hills paid for it. The rebels beat the hell out of them . . . The rebellion continued despite their harshness. They stepped all over us until we couldn't take any more. This went on until the rebellion was smashed. How do you think it was smashed? Well, the English warned the villages that they would destroy every village and every town that shot at an English soldier . . .

Abou Deeb, a Palestinian refugee living in Lebanon, was only twelve when he witnessed the "Great Revolt," an anti-colonial uprising against British rule and Zionism that lasted for three years. Its suppression by the British, who used tactics based in collective punishment that Israel continues to employ, greatly weakened Palestinian society and paved the way for its collapse during the war in 1948, when Israel was created and the majority of Palestinian people were permanently expelled from their homes.

1936

GEORGE PADMORE

"The White Man's Burden"

The black man certainly has to pay dear for carrying the white man's burden.

Padmore, a leader of the international Pan-African movement, was born in Trinidad and was a student activist at Howard University in Washington, DC before becoming a member of the American Communist Party and moving to the USSR. Later, he broke with the Comintern and served as an advisor to Kwame Nkrumah in post-independence Ghana.

1937

B. R. AMBEDKAR

Annihilation of Caste

This anti-social spirit is not confined to caste alone. It has gone deeper and has poisoned the mutual relations of the sub-castes as well. In my province the Golak Brahmins, Deorukha Brahmins, Karada Brahmins, Palshe Brahmins, and Chitpavan Brahmins all claim to be sub-divisions of the Brahmin caste. But the anti-social spirit that prevails between them is quite as marked and quite as virulent as the anti-social spirit that prevails between them and other non-Brahmin castes. There is nothing strange in this. An anti-social spirit is found wherever one group has "interests of its own" which shut it out from full interaction with other groups, so that its prevailing purpose is protection of what it has got.

Ambedkar was born into the Dalit caste—the "Untouchables"—who were relegated to occupations considered impure, like butchering and waste removal. He was one of the first Dalits to obtain a college degree in India, eventually earning a law degree and multiple doctorates, and became the chief architect of the Indian constitution. This book is his most well-known, though he sparked the rise of many Dalit political parties and publications, as well as a revival of Buddhism in India.

ANGELO HERNDON

You Cannot Kill the Working Class

The trial was set for January 16, 1933. The state of Georgia displayed the literature that had been taken from my room, and read passages of it to the jury. They questioned me in great detail. Did I believe that the bosses and government ought to pay insurance to unemployed workers? That Negroes should have complete equality with white people? Did I believe in the demand for the self-determination of the Black Belt—that the Negro people should be allowed to rule the Black Belt territory, kicking out the white landlords and government officials? Did I feel that the working class could run the mills and mines and government? That it wasn't necessary to have bosses at all? I told them I believed all of that—and more . . .

The state held that my membership in the Communist Party, my possession of Communist literature, was enough to send me to the electric chair. They said to the jury: "Stamp this damnable thing out now with a conviction that will automatically carry with it a penalty of electrocution."

And the hand-picked lily-white jury responded: "We, the jury, find the defendant guilty as charged, but recommend that mercy be shown and fix his sentence at from eighteen to twenty years."

I had organized starving workers to demand bread, and I was sentenced to live out my years on the chain-gang for it. But I knew that the movement itself would not stop. I spoke to the court and said:

"They can hold this Angelo Herndon and hundreds of others, but it will never stop these demonstrations on the part of Negro and white workers who demand a decent place to live in and proper food for their kids to eat."

I said: "You may do what you will with Angelo Herndon. You may indict him. You may put him in jail. But there will come thousands of Angelo Herndons. If you really want to do anything about the case, you must go out and indict the social system. But this you will not do, for your role is to defend the system under which the toiling masses are robbed and oppressed.

"You may succeed in killing one, two, even a score of working-class organizers. But you cannot kill the working class . . ."

In 1932, the nineteen-year-old black communist Herndon organized a peaceful interracial hunger march and was arrested a week later for "attempting to incite insurrection," found guilty and sentenced to twenty years. However, the broad support he received from labor unions and civil rights groups eventually helped convince the Supreme Court to overturn the verdict, and the national publicity surrounding his trial helped to educate northerners about discrimination in the southern legal system.

1937 INTERNATIONAL AFRICAN SERVICE BUREAU

Editorial

No people, race or nationality has been oppressed, exploited and humiliated as the black people for centuries past up to the present day, and the Bureau was formed to assist by all means in our power the uncoordinated struggle of Africans and people of African descent against the oppression from which they suffer in every country . . . Our people are becoming alive to the nature of the struggle ahead. That struggle we shall pursue to the end, until economically, politically and socially, the Negro is everywhere as free as other men are.

The International African Service Bureau was a radical anti-colonial, Pan-African group founded in London and included West Indians, such as George Padmore, as well as African activists from Kenya to Sierra Leone, such as Jomo Kenyatta and Ras Makonnen.

1938 C. L. R. JAMES

A History of Negro Revolt

Today the Rhodesian copper miner, living the life of three shillings a week, is but another cog in the wheels of a creaking world economy, as uneconomic in the 1900s as a naked slave in the cotton fields of Alabama a hundred years ago. But Negro emancipation has expanded with the centuries; what was local and national in San Domingo and America is today an international urgency, entangled in the future of a hundred million Africans with all the hopes and fears of Western Europe. Though dimly, the political consciousness immanent in the historical process emerges in groping and neglected Africa . . . The African bruises and breaks himself against his bars in the interests of freedoms wider than his own.

James, a Trinidadian-born historian, novelist, critic, and peerless follower of cricket (it was he who wrote "What do they know of cricket who only cricket know?") helped organize the militant anti-colonial African Service Bureau in London and, at the urging of Trotsky, several American radical political and intellectual groups.

LEAD BELLY   **1938**

"Bourgeois Blues"

Well, them white folks in Washington they know how
To call a colored man a nigger just to see him bow
Lord, it's a bourgeois town
I got the bourgeois blues
Gonna spread the news all around

Lead Belly twice got himself released from jail using his musical talents, the first time by writing a song for Governor Pat Morris Nef, appealing for a pardon—which he got—and the second time by being "discovered" by musicologist Alan Lomax on a visit to Angelo Prison Farm. Described by newspapers as "the singing convict," Lead Belly became a musical celebrity and a close friend of Richard Wright.

"FB Eye Blues"

Woke up this morning
FB eye under my bed
Said I woke up this morning
FB eye under my bed
Told me all I dreamed last night, every word I said.

Wright became the most famous black writer in the world after the publication of his novel Native Son *in 1940. He had joined the Communist Party in 1932, and covered the Joe Louis–Max Schmeling fight for the sports pages of the CP paper, the* Daily Worker, *among other stories. He later wrote approvingly of the Third World movement Bandung conference, and died in exile in Paris.*

"Strange Fruit"

Southern trees bear strange fruit,
Blood on the leaves and blood at the root,
Black body swinging in the Southern breeze,
Strange fruit hanging from the poplar trees.

Pastoral scene of the gallant South,
The bulging eyes and the twisted mouth,
Scent of magnolia sweet and fresh,
Then the sudden smell of burning flesh!

Here is fruit for the crows to pluck,
For the rain to gather, for the wind to suck,
For the sun to rot, for the trees to drop,
Here is a strange and bitter crop.

Billie Holiday's record label wouldn't let her record this song, which originated in a poem that high-school teacher and Communist Meeropol—writing as

Lewis Allan—had published in the New York Teacher, *a union publication. So Holiday got a one-song exemption from her label and made the song a staple of her performances. Meeropol, whose two children—Lewis and Allan—died as infants, later adopted Robert and Michael Rosenberg when their parents Julius and Ethel were executed by the US government.*

DALTON TRUMBO   1939

Johnny Got His Gun

Remember this well you people who plan for war. Remember this you patriots, you fierce ones, you spawners of hate, you inventors of slogans. Remember this as you have never remembered anything else in your lives. We are men of peace, we are men who work and we want no quarrel. But if you destroy our peace, if you take away our work, if you try to range us one against the other, we will know what to do. If you tell us to make the world safe for democracy we will take you seriously and by god and by Christ we will make it so. We will use the guns you force upon us, we will use them to defend our very lives, and the menace to our lives does not lie on the other side of a no-man's-land that was set apart without our consent. It lies within our own boundaries here and now. We have seen it and we know it.

Trumbo, the screenwriter for Spartacus *and* Roman Holiday, *was also a member of the Communist Party USA and one of the Hollywood Ten—the first group of writers and directors to be blacklisted by the House Committee on Un-American Activities in 1947.* Johnny Got His Gun *is Trumbo's anti-war novel, which was serialized in the* Daily Worker *and piqued the interest of the FBI; long after the McCarthy era had passed, Trumbo would direct the film adaptation.*

1939

JOSEPHINE HERBST

Rope of Gold

Yes, they can shuffle the cards and stuff the deck and draw every ace but one. They can buy guns and bombs and bring in a crew from Germany, from Italy to rub us off. England will snuffle in the corner, France can hide her head . . . Satisfy the gluttons, spread the butter of peace. The smell of death. The sellout.

But they haven't got one little card.

We got the living, they got the dead. There's some guys won't sell out for a crust of bread.

Herbst was a prominent left journalist and one of America's foremost proletarian novelists. Rope of Gold, *her most accomplished work, drew on her experience touring the fronts of the Spanish Civil War in 1937—an experience that left her in personal despair.*

1940

BERTOLT BRECHT

"Short Description of a New Technique of Acting"

An old tradition leads people to treat a critical attitude as a predominantly negative one. Many see the difference between the scientific and artistic attitudes as lying precisely in their attitude to criticism. People cannot conceive of contradiction and detachment as being part of artistic appreciation. Of course such appreciation normally includes a higher level, which appreciates critically, but the criticism here only applies to matters of technique; it is quite a different matter from being required to observe not a representation of the world but the world itself in a critical, contradictory, detached manner.

To introduce this critical attitude into art, the negative element which it doubtless includes must be shown from its positive side: this criticism of the world is active, practical, positive. Criticizing the course of a river means improving it, correcting it. Criticism of society is ultimately revolution; there you have criticism taken to its logical conclusion and playing an active part. A critical attitude of this type is an operative factor of productivity; it is deeply enjoyable as such, and if we commonly use the term "arts" for enterprises that improve people's lives why should art proper remain aloof from arts of this sort?

Marxist poet and playwright Brecht's mordant pen was aimed at many targets, foremost among them the Nazis who forced him into exile in 1933, as well as the US Congress, which ordered his appearance before the House Un-American Activities Committee. As one of his poems from exile put it, "In the dark times / Will there also be singing? / Yes, there will also be singing / About the dark times."

LEON TROTSKY   1940

Testament

For forty-three years of my conscious life I have remained a revolutionist; for forty-two of them I have fought under the banner of Marxism. If I had to begin all over again I would of course try to avoid this or that mistake, but the main course of my life would remain unchanged. I shall die a proletarian revolutionist, a Marxist, a dialectical materialist, and, consequently, an irreconcilable atheist. My faith in the communist future of mankind is not less ardent, indeed it is firmer today, than it was in the days of my youth.

Natasha has just come up to the window from the courtyard and opened it wider so that the air may enter more freely into my room. I can see the bright green strip of grass beneath the wall, and the clear blue sky above the wall, and sunlight everywhere. Life is beautiful. Let the future generations cleanse it of all evil, oppression and violence, and enjoy it to the full.

Exiled from the Soviet Union in 1929 after losing his power struggle with Stalin, Trotsky spent the last three years of his life in Mexico. Long ill and fearing his impending death, he wrote the above testament. Mere months later, he was assassinated in his home by a Stalinist agent.

1940

"Out of the People"

It so happens that this war, whether those at present in authority like it or not, has to be fought as a citizen's war. There is no way out of that because in order to defend and protect this island, not only against possible invasion but also against all the disasters of aerial bombardment, it has been found necessary to bring into existence a new network of voluntary associations such as the Home Guard, the Observer Corps, all the ARP and fire-fighting services, and the like . . . They are a new type, what might be called the organized militant citizen. And the whole circumstances of their wartime life favor a sharply democratic outlook. Men and women with a gift for leadership now turn up in unexpected places. The new ordeals blast away the old shams. Britain, which in the years immediately before this war was rapidly losing such democratic virtues as it possessed, is now being bombed and burned into democracy.

During the summer of 1940, as many as one in three Britons tuned into the radio to listen to novelist and Yorkshire radical J. B. Priestley's "Postscript" radio broadcasts. Once the immediate crisis of the Blitz was past, these broadcasts were dropped, being considered altogether too anti-establishment.

1940

NÂZIM HIKMET

"Invitation"

Galloping from farthest Asia
and jutting out into the Mediterranean
like a mare's head
this country is ours.
Wrists in blood, teeth clenched, feet bare
on this soil that's like a silk carpet
this hell, this paradise is ours.

Shut the gates of servitude, keep them shut,
stop man worship another man
this invitation is ours.
To live, free and single like a tree
but in brotherhood like a forest
this longing is ours.

Turkish poet and writer Hikmet was frequently persecuted by the Turkish state and was imprisoned from 1940–50 for his revolutionary and pro-communist views. "Invitation" is one of his best-known poems.

GEORGE ORWELL   1940

Article in the *Evening Standard*

The totalitarian states can do great things, but there is one thing they cannot do: they cannot give the factory-worker a rifle and tell him to take it home and keep it in his bedroom. That rifle hanging on the wall of the working-class flat or laborer's cottage is the symbol of democracy. It is our job to see that it stays there.

Having fought with the Workers' Party of Marxist Unification (POUM) militia in Spain during the Civil War, Orwell envisioned the Home Guard— a defense organization in the British Army made up of volunteers—as a potential red guard. He was an enthusiastic member of his local unit in Hampstead.

WALTER BENJAMIN   1940

"Theses on the Philosophy of History"

To articulate the past historically does not mean to recognize it "the way it really was" (Ranke). It means to seize hold of a memory as it flashes up at a moment of danger. Historical materialism wishes to retain that image of the past which unexpectedly appears to man singled out by history at a moment of danger. The danger affects both the content of the tradition and its receivers. The same threat hangs over both: that of becoming a tool of the ruling classes. In every era the attempt must be made anew to wrest tradition away from a conformism that is about to overpower it. The Messiah comes not only as the redeemer, he comes as the subduer of Antichrist. Only that historian will have the gift of fanning the spark of hope in the past who is firmly convinced that *even the dead* will not be safe from the enemy if he wins. And this enemy has not ceased to be victorious.

Blending Marxist and Jewish thought, lyrically and across many disciplines, Benjamin was a friend and interlocutor of Bertolt Brecht, Theodor Adorno and Georg Lukács. Fleeing Vichy France across the French-Spanish border, his group was detained by Spanish troops. Benjamin took his own life that night. The "Theses on the Philosophy of History" is his last surviving work.

1941

YURI KOCHIYAMA

"Then Came the War"

Everything changed for me on the day Pearl Harbor was bombed. On that very day—December 7—the FBI came and they took my father. He had just come home from the hospital the day before. For several days we didn't know where they had taken him. Then we found out that he was taken to the federal prison at Terminal Island . . . By the time they brought him back, he couldn't talk. He made guttural sounds and we didn't know if he could hear . . . And I think the interrogation was very rough. My mother kept begging the authorities to let him go to the hospital until he was well, then put him back in the prison. They did finally put him there, a week or so later. But they put him in a hospital where they were bringing back all these American merchant marines who were hit on Wake Island. So he was the only Japanese in that hospital, so they hung a sheet around him that said, Prisoner of War . . .

You could see the hysteria of war.

Kochiyama, the radical Japanese American political activist who was interned for two years along with 110,000 other Japanese Americans during the Second World War, later became a member of Malcolm X's Organization for Afro-American Unity, and held him as he lay dying on the floor of Harlem's Audubon Ballroom in 1965.

A. PHILIP RANDOLPH

1942

"Why Should We March?"

A community is democratic only when the humblest and weakest person can enjoy the highest civil, economic, and social rights that the biggest and most powerful possess. To trample on these rights of both Negroes and poor whites is such a commonplace in the South that it takes readily to anti-social, anti-labor, anti-Semitic and anti-Catholic propaganda. It was because of laxness in enforcing the Weimar constitution in republican Germany that Nazism made headway. Oppression of the Negroes in the United States, like suppression of the Jews in Germany, may open the way for a fascist dictatorship. By fighting for their rights now, American Negroes are helping to make America a moral and spiritual arsenal of democracy. Their fight against the poll tax, against lynch law, segregation, and Jim Crow, their fight for economic, political, and social equality, thus becomes part of the global war for freedom.

Emerging from a poverty-stricken background in Florida, Randolph built the Brotherhood of Sleeping-Car Porters into one of the most powerful unions of black workers in America. Earlier he had been dubbed "the most dangerous black in America" by Attorney General Mitchell Palmer, and had organized support for strikers in Paterson, NJ, and Lawrence, MA, as well as opposition to World War I. He co-founded the black socialist magazine The Messenger, *and his threatened 1941 March on Washington pressured the US to desegregate the defense industries.*

MAREK EDELMAN

1943

"The Ghetto Fights"

The partisans' stand was so determined that the Germans were finally forced to abandon all ordinary fighting methods and to try new, apparently infallible tactics. Their new idea was to set fire to the entire brush-makers' block from the outside, on all sides simultaneously. In an instant fires were raging over the entire block, black smoke choked one's throat, burned one's eyes. The partisans, naturally, did not intend to be burnt alive in the flames. We decided to gamble for our lives and to attempt to reach the central ghetto area regardless of consequences. In the period preceding the last German extermination drive the Bund's activities were closely intertwined with the history of the ZOB [Jewish Combat Organization]. I think that never before had there existed a similar degree of unanimity and coordination of people of different political parties as during the various groups' collaboration in that period. We were all fighters for the same just cause, equal in the face of history and death. Every drop of blood was of precisely the same value.

On May 10th, 1943, the first period of our bloody history, the history of the Warsaw Jews, came to an end. The site where the buildings of the ghetto had once stood became a ragged heap of rubble reaching three stories high.

Those who were killed in action had done their duty to the end, to the last drop of blood that soaked into the pavements of the Warsaw ghetto.

We, who did not perish, leave it up to you to keep the memory of them alive—forever.

Edelman was one of a handful of young leaders of the Jewish Combat Organization, a force of some 220 poorly armed men and women who staged a desperate and doomed armed uprising in the Warsaw Ghetto in April 1943. He survived the war, remained in Poland and became an activist with the Polish union federation Solidarity.

1943   **THE WHITE ROSE**

Fourth Leaflet

We will not be silent. We are your bad conscience. The White Rose will not leave you in peace!

Beginning in June 1942, a group of students at the University of Munich formed a clandestine group and carried out a leafleting campaign calling for active opposition to the Nazi regime. The six core members of the group, including the sister and brother Sophie and Hans Scholl, were arrested in February 1943 and decapitated. In 2006, the anti-Iraq War blogger Raed Jarrar was prevented from boarding an airplane in New York until he changed his shirt, which bore the phrase "We will not be silent" in English and Arabic.

ERIC WILLIAMS   1944

Capitalism and Slavery

The history of our West Indian islands can be expressed in two simple words: Columbus and Sugar.

Williams was a historian and the founder of the People's National Movement in Trinidad and Tobago, which would usher in independence with Williams as its first President. His masterpiece, Capitalism and Slavery, *argued that the emancipation of slaves in Britain and elsewhere was motivated by economic and not humanitarian concerns. The work was so controversial in Britain that it would not be published there until 1964—twenty years after its US publication.*

THEODOR ADORNO   1944

"Imaginative Excesses"

Today, when the concept of the proletariat, unshaken in its economic essence, is so occluded by technology that in the greatest industrial country there can be no question of proletarian class-consciousness, the role of intellectuals would no longer be to alert the torpid to their most obvious interests, but to strip the veil from the eyes of the wise-guys, the illusion that capitalism, which makes them its temporary beneficiaries, is based on anything other than their exploitation and oppression. The deluded workers are directly dependent on those who can still just see and tell of their delusion. Their hatred of intellectuals has changed accordingly. It has aligned itself to the prevailing common-sense views. The masses no longer mistrust intellectuals because they betray the revolution, but because they might want it, and thereby reveal how great is their own need of intellectuals. Only if the extremes come together will humanity survive.

Adorno emigrated from Germany in 1934, where he had worked with Walter Benjamin and Ernst Bloch, to England and then the US, where he set up a research unit at UCLA with Max Horkheimer. Their co-authored Dialectic of Enlightenment *explores the self-destructive contradictions of the Enlightenment; in the preface to* Minima Moralia, *Adorno argues that "the social force of liberation may have temporarily withdrawn to the individual sphere."*

1945   FIFTH PAN-AFRICAN CONGRESS

Declaration to Colonial Powers

We are determined to be free. We want education. We want the right to earn a decent living, the right to express our thoughts and emotions, to adopt and create forms of beauty. We demand for Black Africa autonomy and independence. We will fight in every way we can for freedom, democracy, and social betterment.

The Pan-African Congress was a series of meetings, held during the interwar period, which sought the unification and liberation of African peoples. But it was not until the Fifth Congress, organized by Africans in Manchester, that members of the African Diaspora, including Afro-Caribbeans and African Americans, were included.

1945   LEOPOLD SENGHOR

"The Message"

I left my warm meal and the handling of many disputes.
Wearing nothing more than a *pagne* for the dewy mornings,
I had only words of peace as protection and to open every road.
And I too traversed rivers and forests full of dangers
Where vines hung more treacherous than snakes.
I went among people who would easily let fly a poisoned greeting.
But I held on the sign of recognition

And the spirits watched over my breath.
I saw the ashes of burned-out barracks and royal homes.
And under the mahogany trees we exchanged long speeches
And ceremonial gifts.
And I arrived at Elissa, the nest of falcons
Defying the pride of Conquerors.
I saw once again the old dwelling on the hill,
A village of long and lowering eyelashes.
I recited the message to the Guardian of our Blood:
The diseases the ruined trade, organized hunts,
And bourgeois decorum and the unlubricated scorn
Swilling the bellies of the slaves.

Senghor was the first Senegalese president, as well as a world-renowned cultural theorist, poet and originator of the concept of négritude, which embraces African culture in the face of Western colonialism. In "The Message," he laments the destruction of African tradition and returns to the age of the African empires.

MATSUSHIMA SHOTARO — 1946

"Food May Day" Protest Placard

Front:
Imperial Edict
The national polity has been maintained.
I am eating my fill.
You people, starve and die.
—Imperial sign and seal.

Back:
Why are we starving no matter how much we work?
Answer, Emperor Hirohito!

The Japanese government's broken food delivery system was the target of the Food May Day demonstrations, which attracted between 1.25 and 2 million participants nationwide. Matsushima, a Communist in Tokyo, was subsequently arrested for lese-majesty—insulting the emperor—and found guilty, though he was pardoned soon after.

1946   JUAN JOSÉ ARÉVALO

Speech on Labor

We are socialists because we live in the 1900s. Our revolution is not explained by the hunger of the masses but by their thirst for dignity . . . Our socialism does not, therefore, aim at ingenious distribution of material wealth to economically equalize men who are economically different. Our socialism aims at liberating men psychologically and spiritually. We aim to give each and every citizen not only the superficial right to vote, but the fundamental right to live in peace with his own conscience, with his family, with his property and with his destiny.

Arévalo was the reformist president of Guatemala who, with Jacobo Arbenz, presided over a period of free speech and political reform known as the "Ten Years of Spring." While in office, he sought to carry out agrarian reform, establish better labor protections, improve education and consolidate democracy. Those ten years were preceded by a military dictatorship and brought to a close by a CIA-backed coup.

1947   FAIZ AHMED FAIZ

"Freedom's Dawn: August 1947"

This pockmarked daybreak,
Dawn gripped by night,
This is not that much-awaited light
For which friends set out filled with hope
That somewhere in the desert of the sky
The stars would reach a final destination,
The ship of grief would weigh anchor . . .
Our leaders' style is changing,
Sexual pleasure permitted,
sadness for separation forbidden.
The cure does not help the fevered liver, heartburn or the settled eye.

That sweet morning breeze
Where did it come from?
Where did it disappear?
The roadside lamp has no news;
The heavy night weighs the same
The heart and eye await deliverance;
Forward, we have not yet reached our goal . . .

Pakistani journalist Faiz, one of the greatest Urdu language poets, spent four years in jail for complicity in the Rawalpindi Conspiracy of 1951, a failed attempt to overthrow the government, one of a succession that suppressed the Communist Party of Pakistan, with which Faiz was associated. He would be imprisoned several more times by various military dictators.

MIN SHENG PAO 1947

"Complete Exposure of the Cruel Countenance"

Imperialism wants to suppress our struggle for better living conditions with guns and knives and we must answer with more vigorous and larger-scale unified struggle. Imperialism declared Trade Unions to be illegal (or any other organization to be illegal) and not allowed to remain in public: then we are not afraid of being illegal and strongly determined to turn underground and to carry out secret activities. Imperialism wants to arrest the leaders of the workers and responsible members of the people's organizations: then they must use every method to protect the safety of our personnel. Imperialism orders its running dogs and their followers to oppress us: then we will use the same method against them. All in all, for the sake of our lives, we cannot procrastinate any more, nor can we give in any further but to fight our way out through struggle.

Widely known as the "voice of the Malayan Communist Party," the Min Sheng Pao *was the most widely distributed Chinese-language paper in the Federation of Malaya. Around this time, its editorials were becoming increasingly inflammatory, and a few days before this editorial was published, the paper's editor, Liew Yit Fan, was arrested for sedition.*

1947

"My Country on Partition Day"

. . . Rise, friend, see how many people
drag their chains of dented steel.
Behold the serpents slithering endlessly among them!
They've prohibited oppression among themselves
but for us they legalized all prohibitions!
They proclaim, "Trading with slaves is unlawful"
but isn't the trading of free people more of a crime?
In the West man's rights are preserved,
but the man in the East is stoned to death.
Justice screams loudly protecting Western lands
but grows silent when it visits us!
Maybe justice changes colors and shapes!
Live embers scorch our lips
so listen to our hearts speaking,
call on free men in every land
to raise the flag of justice where we stand.

*The United Nations approved the partition of Palestine in 1947, despite its
rejection by Palestinian Arabs and the fact that 90 percent of privately-held
land was Arab-owned. The partition initiated a civil war between the Arab and
Jewish communities, leading to the expulsion of Palestinians by Zionist militias
and culminating in the loss of Arab Palestine in 1948. Abu Salma, a Palestinian poet, was known as "The Olive Tree of Palestine."*

1947

JAWAHARLAL NEHRU

"Tryst with Destiny"

Long years ago we made a tryst with destiny, and now the time comes
when we shall redeem our pledge, not wholly or in full measure, but
very substantially. At the stroke of the midnight hour, when the world

sleeps, India will awake to life and freedom. A moment comes, which comes but rarely in history, when we step out from the old to the new, when an age ends, and when the soul of a nation, long suppressed, finds utterance. It is fitting that at this solemn moment we take the pledge of dedication to the service of India and her people and to the still larger cause of humanity ... The achievement we celebrate today is but a step, an opening of opportunity, to the greater triumphs and achievements that await us. Are we brave enough and wise enough to grasp this opportunity and accept the challenge of the future? ... A new star rises, the star of freedom in the East, a new hope comes into being, a vision long cherished materializes. May the star never set and that hope never be betrayed!

Given before the Indian National Congress close to midnight on the eve of India's independence, this speech represented a culminating moment in the hundred-year struggle against British rule. Nehru had been a leading figure in the movement and was independent India's first prime minister.

KURIHARA SADAKO　　ca. 1947

"Let Us Shake Hands"

"Hello American soldiers,"
Call out little militarists,
Throwing away their toy guns.
They were busy with their game of war
Until only yesterday.

"Hello American soldiers," they call.
In their little hearts spring out longings
Toward people of unfamiliar race.

"Hello American soldiers!
Was it you who fought our fathers until only yesterday?
But you smile at us brightly:
You are not the beast
That grown-ups had made us believe."

We want to touch your big hands
We want to shake hands with you.

Although Kurihara lived in Hiroshima during World War II, only four miles from where the bomb was dropped, she survived and achieved fame for her poems about her city. "Let Us Shake Hands" was censored by the Supreme Commander of the Allied Powers.

1948   JORGE ELIÉCER GAITÁN

"Oration for Peace"

Señor Presidente, our flag is in mourning; this silent multitude, the mute cry from our hearts, asks only that you treat us . . . as you would have us treat you. We say to you finally, your Excellency: Fortunate are those who understand that words of peace and harmony should not conceal sentiments of rancor or enmity. Badly advised are those in the government who conceal behind kind words their lack of respect for all people. They will be marked in the pages of history by the finger of infamy!

Gaitán, the leader of the Colombian Liberal Party, delivered this speech at the conclusion of his "March of Silence," a memorial for victims of state violence that Gabriel García Márquez called "the most moving of all the marches ever held in Colombia." He was assassinated on the street just a few months later, touching off the Bogotazo, a popular uprising that left thousands dead and much of the city in ruins, and marking the beginning of the period known as La Violencia.

1948   MUHAMMAD MAHDI AL-JAWAHIRI

"The Martyr's Day"

Woe to a State run by incompetents who fancy
that the Government can be maintained by the whip!

Al-Jawahiri, a leading Iraqi poet associated with Iraq's Communist Party, served in the Iraqi government after the 1958 revolution and later went into exile. "The Martyr's Day" was written after the wathba *(leap) in 1948, a nationalist upsurge that helped galvanize opposition to the country's alliance with Britain. Al-Jawahiri lived for nearly a century, from the late Ottoman era through the British mandate to independence.*

TO HUU   **1948**

"Guerrilla Woman"

The night is shorter than the road
its path more intricate than the tiny lanes
that curve the surface of my baby daughter's palm.
Yet I will wound this land, our own, with trenches,
With pits for the French when they march this path,
beds for the French to sleep in,
groves in the land for the enemy of the land.
The ditches must go deeper than my hatred.
The work must fly faster than my tears . . .

You can drown the calls of my children,
but you can never hush the rhythm of my naked hands
clawing the frozen mud that will continue.

To Huu was Vietnam's most celebrated revolutionary poet—although by 1948, he had become a cultural czar, ruthlessly enforcing cultural orthodoxy in Viet Minh liberated zones and persecuting dovish intellectuals, whom he labeled "revisionists" and "Trotskyists."

AMERICAN JEWISH INTELLECTUALS   **1948**

Letter Protesting Menachem Begin

Among the most disturbing political phenomena of our times is the emergence in the newly created state of Israel of the "Freedom Party" (*Tnuat Haherut*), a political party closely akin in its organization, methods, political philosophy and social appeal to the Nazi and Fascist parties . . .

A shocking example was their behavior in the Arab village of Deir Yassin . . . On April 9 the *New York Times* reported that terrorist bands had attacked this peaceful village, which was not a military objective in the fighting, killed most of its inhabitants—240 men, women, and children—and kept a few of them alive to parade as captives through the streets of Jerusalem. Most of the Jewish community was horrified at the deed, and the Jewish Agency sent a telegram of apology to King Abdullah of Trans-Jordan. But the terrorists, far from being ashamed of their act, were proud of this massacre, publicized it widely, and invited all the foreign correspondents present in the country to view the heaped corpses and the general havoc at Deir Yassin . . .

In the light of the foregoing considerations, it is imperative that the truth about [the leader of the party] Mr Begin and his movement be made known in this country . . .

This letter to the New York Times, *written to protest Begin's planned visit to America, was signed by Albert Einstein and Hannah Arendt, among many other Jewish intellectuals in the United States. Haherut was infamous for its militant actions and eventually merged into Likud in 1988; Begin would serve as Israel's prime minister from 1977 to 1983.*

1948

TAN MALAKA

"Introduction" to *Gerpolek*

We are now pushed to the margin. As we know in the economic, financial and military fields our room for action is extremely limited. This is the result of two years of negotiations. The unity of the people in the struggle against capitalism and imperialism no longer exists . . .

How vast is the change from the first six months of the Revolution! At that time, seventy million Indonesians were determined to fight against capitalism and imperialism. All the instruments and resources of power were then in the hands of the Indonesian people. The entire people took the initiative in creating an army and paramilitary forces, which guarded our coasts while all the towns and all the villages were firmly united, for defense and attack!

Is it possible to reignite the spirit of August 17, 1945? But even if history ultimately determines the course of events, we, as human beings and members of our society, must not sit with our hands in our laps while watching the waves that constantly strike the deck of the ship of state, and menace it with shipwreck. I feel that the only endeavor that can possibly rescue the ship of state from the rocks is to form guerrilla forces everywhere, on land and on the sea.

Tan Malaka, today a National Hero in Indonesia, was the leader of the Indonesian Communist Party until his exile by the regime; the Comintern point-man for Southeast Asia; and, returning to Indonesia post-independence after over twenty years in exile, leader of the opposition to the Republic, for which he was jailed and then later murdered by the military. A radical leftist who pushed for an alliance between Marxists and progressives, and who criticized Lenin's policy of snuggling up to the colonial bourgeoisie, Tan Malaka also clashed on occasion with the Communist Party leadership. "Gerpolek" is an acronym for "The Political and Economic Movement" in Indonesian. This book was intended for peasant fighters in the struggle against the Dutch, and written while he was in prison.

WOODY GUTHRIE   **1948**

"Deportee"

The skyplane caught fire over Los Gatos Canyon
The great ball of fire it shook all our hills
Who are these dear friends who are falling like dry leaves?
Radio said, "They are just deportees" . . .
To fall like dry leaves and rot on our topsoil
And be known by no names except "deportees."

The iconic American folksinger Guthrie was also a committed leftist, writing briefly for the Communist newspaper the Daily Worker. *"Deportee" describes a plane crash in 1948, in which twenty-eight migrant workers, who were being deported back to Mexico from California, were killed.*

ca. 1948 SAEKI JINZABURO

"Raping Mothers"

Seizing married women,
Raping mothers in front of their children—
This is the Imperial Army.

Despite the suppression of information in Japan about Japanese brutality in Manila and the Rape of Nanking after World War II, these atrocities became well publicized during the Tokyo War Crimes Trial. Some of Saeki's poems were censored by the Supreme Commander of the Allied Powers.

1949 ALBERT EINSTEIN

"Why Socialism?"

I have now reached the point where I may indicate briefly what to me constitutes the essence of the crisis of our time. It concerns the relationship of the individual to society. The individual has become more conscious than ever of his dependence upon society. But he does not experience this dependence as a positive asset, as an organic tie, as a protective force, but rather as a threat to his natural rights, or even to his economic existence. Moreover, his position in society is such that the egotistical drives of his make-up are constantly being accentuated, while his social drives, which are by nature weaker, progressively deteriorate. All human beings, whatever their position in society, are suffering from this process of deterioration. Unknowingly prisoners of their own egotism, they feel insecure, lonely, and deprived of the naïve, simple, and unsophisticated enjoyment of life. Man can find meaning in life, short and perilous as it is, only through devoting himself to society.

The economic anarchy of capitalist society as it exists today is, in my opinion, the real source of the evil. We see before us a huge community of producers the members of which are unceasingly striving to deprive each other of the fruits of their collective labor—not by force, but on the whole in faithful compliance with legally established rules. In this respect, it is important to realize that the means of production—that is to say, the entire productive capacity that is needed for producing consumer goods as well as additional capital goods—may legally be, and for the most part are, the private property of individuals.

This crippling of individuals I consider the worst evil of capitalism. Our whole educational system suffers from this evil. An exaggerated competitive attitude is inculcated into the student, who is trained to worship acquisitive success as a preparation for his future career.

I am convinced there is only one way to eliminate these grave evils, namely through the establishment of a socialist economy, accompanied by an educational system which would be oriented toward social goals. In such an economy, the means of production are owned by society itself and are utilized in a planned fashion. A planned economy, which adjusts production to the needs of the community, would distribute the work to be done among all those able to work and would guarantee a livelihood to every man, woman, and child. The education of the individual, in addition to promoting his own innate abilities, would attempt to develop in him a sense of responsibility for his fellow-men in place of the glorification of power and success in our present society.

Renouncing his German citizenship and leaving the country, never to return again after the Nazi rose to power, Einstein remained a committed public intellectual for the rest of his life. His democratic socialist beliefs were reaffirmed in his various political activities, including his membership in the NAACP, opposition to nuclear proliferation, and criticism of the prevailing McCarthyist attitudes in the United States.

ALDO LEOPOLD   1949

A Sand County Almanac

Our bigger-and-better society is now like a hypochondriac, so obsessed with its own economic health as to have lost the capacity to remain healthy. The whole world is so greedy for more bathtubs that it has lost the stability necessary to build them, or even to turn off the tap.

Nothing could be more salutary at this stage than a little healthy contempt for a plethora of material blessings.

The American conservationist Leopold was a founder of the Wilderness Society, one of the most radical environmental organizations from the 1930s to the 1970s.

1949   **SIMONE DE BEAUVOIR**

The Second Sex

If her functioning as a female is not enough to define woman, if we decline also to explain her through "the eternal feminine," and if nevertheless we admit, provisionally, that women do exist, then we must face the question "what is a woman?"

To state the question is, to me, to suggest, at once, a preliminary answer. The fact that I ask it is in itself significant. A man would never set out to write a book on the peculiar situation of the human male. But if I wish to define myself, I must first of all say: "I am a woman"; on this truth must be based all further discussion. A man never begins by presenting himself as an individual of a certain sex; it goes without saying that he is a man. The terms masculine and feminine are used symmetrically only as a matter of form, as on legal papers. In actuality the relation of the two sexes is not quite like that of two electrical poles, for man represents both the positive and the neutral, as is indicated by the common use of man to designate human beings in general; whereas woman represents only the negative, defined by limiting criteria, without reciprocity. In the midst of an abstract discussion it is vexing to hear a man say: "You think thus and so because you are a woman"; but I know that my only defense is to reply: "I think thus and so because it is true," thereby removing my subjective self from the argument. It would be out of the question to reply: "And you think the contrary because you are a man," for it is understood that the fact of being a man is no peculiarity. A man is in the right in being a man; it is the woman who is in the wrong . . . She is simply what man decrees; thus she is called "the sex," by which is meant that she appears essentially to the male as a sexual being. For him she is sex—absolute sex, no less. She is defined and differentiated with reference to man and not he with reference to her; she is the incidental, the inessential as opposed to the essential. He is the Subject, he is the Absolute—she is the Other.

First published in Les Temps Modernes—*the journal Beauvoir co-founded with Jean-Paul Sartre and Maurice Merleau-Ponty*—The Second Sex *linked existentialist philosophy to feminism. In 1971, she signed the Manifesto of the 343—343 women admitting to having had an abortion (which was then illegal).*

YAMASHIRO TOMOE   ca. 1950

Bog Rhubarb Shoots

Uichi's wife wondered if she had not lost her mind, and went near the well. There, some women from the neighborhood were saying, "He won his gold stripes by doing brutal things to the Koreans. He did shady things to get wealthy. The mighty gods made it possible for him to keep a mistress who herself has done shady, dishonest things. Nothing good ever comes of people who bring into their home someone who has earned the hatred of others. After all, there is a God. People who are hated will bring trouble by fire or by water. Just wait and see. Nothing good will come of this."

But when they saw Uichi's wife, they made no effort to include her in their circle and did not even speak to her.

Toward evening, the woman and her maid arrived from the town in a rickshaw. The [mistress] stepped onto the new tatami in the annex with her pure white silk socks and quietly closed the sliding doors. Uichi's wife could not remember anything about the house after that. The only thing she remembers is the laughter that came from the room in the annex.

She set the house on fire and grabbed the rope by the well that she had used for thirty years and slid down into the bottom, hoping to vanish from the world. She doesn't know how or by whom she was restored to this world. When she regained consciousness she was being questioned by the police.

She set the fire, but she did not see what happened. The flames shot upwards through the night already darkened by the blackouts to guard against air raids. The main house, the shed, the storehouse, and the annex turned into pillars of fire. They did not have time to save the town woman's chests or dressers. They all turned into ashes. When Uichi's wife, now an arsonist, was told all this, she was bewildered. Because she had set fire to the house during the blackouts, she was sentenced to ten years in prison. Because of extenuating circumstances, however, the sentence was reduced to eight years, and she was sent to the Miyoshi penitentiary to serve her sentence. Here, she was dressed in red like the other prisoners.

Yamashiro, a novelist, communist labor organizer and activist in Japan's postwar agrarian reform and anti-war movements, spent much of World War II imprisoned for harboring "dangerous thoughts." There, she met a woman serving time for arson, whose life story became the basis for this "non-fiction novelette." Most of her novels are about poor rural women.

1950s

DEDAN KIMATHI

"I Do Not Lead Rebels"

I do not lead rebels, but I lead Africans who want their self-government and land. My people want to live in a better world than they met when they were born. I lead them because God never created any nation to be ruled by another nation forever.

Dedan Kimathi was a leader in the Mau Mau Uprising in Kenya against the British colonizers, for which he was executed in 1957. He allegedly spoke these words to fellow fighters while in the forest. During the eight-year Mau Mau Uprising in Kenya, thirty-two European settlers and 200 British soldiers were killed, compared with 20,000 Mau Mau rebles and 1,000 of their supporters. An additional 70,000 Kikuyu civilians were interned under brutal conditions for many years.

"United Fruit Company"

When the trumpet blared everything
on earth was prepared
and Jehovah distributed the world
to Coca-Cola Inc., Anaconda,
Ford Motors and other entities:
the United Fruit Inc.
reserved for itself the juiciest,
the central seaboard of my land,
America's sweet waist.
It rebaptized these lands
as "Banana Republics,"
and over the slumbering corpses,
upon the restless heroes,
who conquered renown,
freedom and flags,
it established the comic opera:
it alienated self-destiny,
regaled Caesar's crowns,
unsheathed envy, drew
the dictatorship of flies:
Trujillo flies, Tacho flies,
Carías flies, Martínez flies,
Ubico flies, flies soaked
in humble blood and jam,
drunk flies that drone
over the common graves,
circus flies, clever flies
versed in tyranny.

Among the bloodthirsty flies
the Fruit Co. disembarks,

ravaging coffee and fruits
for its ships that spirit away
our submerged lands' treasures
like serving trays.

Meanwhile, in the seaports'
sugary abysses,
Indians collapsed, buried
in the morning mist:
a body rolls down, a nameless
thing, a fallen number,
a bunch of lifeless fruit
dumped in the rubbish heap.

Neruda, the Nobel Prize-winning poet, was also a one-time Chilean Communist Party senator. The United Fruit Company came to control vast tracts of land in Central and South America. The violent suppression of a workers' strike in 1928 came to be known as the "Banana Massacre"; estimates of the number of dead range from 47 to 2,000.

1951

EDUARDO CHIBAS

Last Words

People of Cuba, keep awake. This is my last knock at your door.

Chibas was a Cuban politician and radio personality who inveighed against government corruption, and although avowedly anti-communist, he made a strong impression on the young Fidel Castro. For his radio broadcast on August 5, 1951, Chibas had promised to provide evidence that the education minister was embezzling money, but come that day, he was unable to deliver. Believing that the only way for him to make good on his promise was to kill himself, he spoke these final words on the air and shot himself as he left the studio.

"Montage of a Dream Deferred"

What happens to a dream deferred?
Does it dry up
like a raisin in the sun?
Or fester like a sore—
And then run?
Does it stink like rotten meat?
Or crust and sugar over—
like a syrupy sweet?
Maybe it just sags
like a heavy load.
Or does it *explode*?

In the thick of the Harlem Renaissance, Hughes wrote, "We young Negro artists who create now intend to express our individual dark-skinned selves without fear or shame. If white people are pleased we are glad. If they are not, it doesn't matter. We know we are beautiful. And ugly too." In the 1930s Hughes spent a year in the Soviet Union and campaigned with leftists, but in later years he had an ambivalent relationship to the left.

LILLIAN HELLMAN

1952

Letter to HUAC

I cannot and will not cut my conscience to fit this year's fashions.

Hellman, author of the plays The Children's Hour *and* The Little Foxes, *and of celebrated memoirs, refused to testify about other people when called by the House Un-American Activities Committee. Her longtime love, leftist detective novelist Dashiell Hammett, author of* Red Harvest *and* The Maltese Falcon, *was imprisoned for his refusal to testify, blacklisted, and sued for back taxes.*

LUIS TARUC

Born of the People

All the hundreds of peasants, soldiers, and civilians, who have died in the fields and barrios. None will be forgotten; all will be remembered, all honored.

Our friends in Manila refer to us as being "outside." That is incorrect terminology. For seven of the past eight years I've lived as I am living now, in the forests, in the swamps, wanted and hunted (with a price of 100,000 pesos on my head today, dead or alive), but never have I felt truly "outside." Rather, we are on the inside, close to the heart of the people. We are on the inside of the struggle. Whoever joins in the struggle today, whoever joins the people's movement, has an inside place in the most decisive events of our time. That is a proud and enviable role.

We do not live normally, of course. The life of a guerrilla has many strange features. The soldiers in the nearby huts, for instance, are sleeping in the daytime—they do so because at night is the time they move. They are more content with a moonless night than with the midday sun, for then they are unseen. The plain below changes hands at night: in the daytime it is an oppressed area, ruled by MPs [military police] and civilian guards, but when night falls it becomes a liberated region, where the people receiver soldiers with open arms.

Soon, when the sun of our victory comes, the day, too, will be ours . . .

I could show . . . the exact places where I worked in the fields, the places where the constabulary shot down striking peasants, and the locations of the largest landed estates. I could point out the barrio and tell them how its people live, the possessions they have, the extent of their education, and how much of a chance they have to be happy. I could indicate the barrios where landlords ejected tenants before, and where the PC's shoot them now. I could show them Clark Field, where the American Army owns a whole corner of Pampanga for ninety-nine years. I would prove that any ideology that would better the lives of the people is foreign to those who rule and exploit the people . . .

Here in this small hut on the side of a mountain, looking out upon the soil that bred me, upon the land of the people of whom I was born, I complete this book, which is more their record than mine. The struggle of which I have written, and to which I have tried to contribute, is still not completed, but it will be, and the people will triumph . . .

The sun is going down. The squadron awakes. I must go. In the barrios the people are waiting for us.

It is necessary now to get on with the work that needs to be done.

Taruc was a peasant leader of the Huk (Hukbalahap) Rebellion, a peasant-based communist insurgency against the Philippine government that lasted for eight years. In 1944 it had 10,000 to 12,000 active male and female members. Born of the People *is Taruc's memoir of his guerrilla fighting years; Nelson Mandela used it as a reference in guerrilla warfare during his time as commander-in-chief of Spear of the Nation, the military arm of the African National Congress.*

MOHAMMAD MOSSADEGH   1953

"My Greatest Sin"

Yes, my sin—my greater sin . . . and even my greatest sin is that I nationalized Iran's oil industry and discarded the system of political and economic exploitation by the world's greatest empire . . . This at the cost to myself, my family; and at the risk of losing my life, my honor and my property . . . With God's blessing and the will of the people, I fought this savage and dreadful system of international espionage and colonialism.

A popular and respected leader, Mossadegh was Iran's democratically elected prime minister until he was deposed in a CIA-backed coup d'état, tried and placed under house arrest for much of the remainder of his life. These words are from a speech he gave during his trial. The incident remains a source of anger in Iran toward the United States, and served as one of the ideological motivations for the overthrow of the Shah in 1979.

1954

ADELAIDE CASELY HAYFORD

"Opposition"

Truly a prophet is without honor in his own country. I can never quite fathom why I met with such universal opposition. Had I been starting a brothel, the antagonism could not have been worse.

Hayford was a Sierra Leonean crusader for women's rights and one of the first black West African women to enter into public life, establishing a girls school that promoted the cause of cultural nationalism and fighting against the inequities of British colonial rule—the first African-owned and -run schools in Freetown. Here, she reflects upon the community reaction to her efforts, including the widespread skepticism among whites about the need to educate women or Africans in general.

1954

EDWARD MURROW

"See It Now"

We must not confuse dissent with disloyalty. We must remember always that accusation is not proof and that conviction depends upon evidence and due process of law. We will not walk in fear, one of another. We will not be driven by fear into an age of unreason, if we dig deep in our history and our doctrine, and remember that we are not descended from fearful men—not from men who feared to write, to speak, to associate and to defend causes that were, for the moment, unpopular.

Murrow, the CBS journalist whose signature sign-off—"good night, and good luck"—was a testament to the uncertainty of his times is best known for his critical analysis of McCarthyism and the Red Scare on his show, "See It Now." Senator McCarthy appeared on the show to offer his rebuttal just one month after this segment; Murrow's commentary contributed to McCarthy's downfall.

LOLITA LEBRÓN

Words Upon Arrest

I did not come here to kill. I came here to die.

Dolores "Lolita" Lebrón Sotomayor was a Puerto Rican nationalist who was imprisoned for twenty-five years for an attack on the United States House of Representatives in 1954. After her release, she returned to Puerto Rico and continued to fight for Puerto Rican independence, including the struggle to remove the US Navy from Vieques Island.

LYN PEDERSON

"The Importance of Being Different"

Homosexuals have some problems heterosexuals don't have. Agreed? That's as far as we go. Once we try to list or analyze the problems, or suggest remedies . . . agreement vanishes. The Mattachine Society, née Foundation, and ONE magazine hope to tackle said problems, but the means remain in dispute. And there is no little disagreement on the ends. Are homosexuals in any important way different from other people? If so, ought that difference be cultivated, or hidden under a bushel, or extirpated altogether? For myself, I must say with the French legislator, who had something quite different on his mind, "Vive la différence!"

Jim Kepner, pioneering leader and documenter of the gay rights movement from the 1940s through to his death in 1997, claimed that "homosexuals are natural rebels" for their non-conformity to the hetero-normative world. But his defense of the right to be different was also directed at the gay community itself, within which he sought to be an individual. Here he writes under a pseudonym, Lyn Pederson.

1955

ALEX COMFORT

Speech at Inaugural Meeting of the CND

For many years now, and most evidently since last year, the salient new factor in the politics of Europe has been the growing discontent of ordinary men and women with the policies of inhumanity; of anger and disillusion with compromises, double talk and cruelty, and with the complete lack of principle which has become the rule in government since Hitler. . . .

That is the function of the campaign which we are launching here tonight: to make every individual reassume the moral responsibility for opposing public insanity. The issue is one for direct action by every one of us. We are not at the mercy of the Government, nor of events, nor of the policy of other nations, nor of the world situation, if we are prepared as a public to be sufficiently combative . . .

Within the coming weeks we intend to raise throughout the country a solid body of opposition to the whole strategy of moral bankruptcy and ceremonial suicide which the hydrogen bomb epitomizes, to all the mentally under-privileged double-talk by which it has been justified. I would urge every one of us at this meeting to go home determined to become a living focus of that opposition . . .

Sanity is always hardest to restore at the summit—the air there is rarefied. It seems to affect the brain. We can reassert it at the base. The people must take over—you must take over. The leaders of all the parties are waiting, as they always wait on any issue of principle, to follow public opinion. We can coerce them . . .

We can make Britain offer the world something which is virtually forgotten—moral leadership. Let us make this country stand on the side of human decency and human sanity—alone if necessary. It has done so before. If it does so again I do not think we need fear the consequences.

Comfort was speaking at the founding meeting of the Campaign for Nuclear Disarmament, held at the Central Hall, Westminster, on February 17, 1955. CND was to become the most important protest movement in Britain during the late 1950s and early 1960s, with major revivals in both the 1980s and the 2000s.

Speech at the Opening of the Bandung Conference

No task is more urgent than that of preserving peace. Without peace our independence means little. The rehabilitation and upbuilding of our countries will have little meaning. Our revolutions will not be allowed to run their course ... We, the peoples of Asia and Africa, 1,400,000,000 strong, far more than half the human population of the world, we can mobilize what I have called the Moral Violence of Nations in favor of peace. We can demonstrate to the minority of the world which lives on the other continents that we, the majority, are for peace, not for war, and that whatever strength we have will always be thrown on to the side of peace ...

Ahmed Sukarno was a leader of the Indonesian independence movement against Dutch colonial rule and the first president of Indonesia, whose political philosophy was a blend of nationalism, Marxism and Islam. Under his leadership, Indonesia joined the Non-Aligned Movement, which Sukarno saw as a counterweight to the colonialist and neo-colonialist Cold War superpowers, and hosted the Bandung Conference to strengthen Afro-Asian solidarity.

BERTRAND RUSSELL ET AL. **1955**

The Russell–Einstein Manifesto

Most of us are not neutral in feeling, but, as human beings, we have to remember that, if the issues between East and West are to be decided in any manner that can give any possible satisfaction to anybody, whether Communist or anti-Communist, whether Asian or European or American, whether White or Black, then these issues must not be decided by war. We should wish this to be understood, both in the East and in the West.

There lies before us, if we choose, continual progress in happiness, knowledge, and wisdom. Shall we, instead, choose death, because we cannot forget our quarrels? We appeal as human beings to human beings: Remember your humanity, and forget the rest. If you can do so, the way lies open to a new Paradise; if you cannot, there lies before you the risk of universal death.

Seven years before the Cuban Missile Crisis, several of the world's most brilliant scientists and mathematicians released this statement condemning the stockpiling and use of nuclear weapons by the Cold War powers. Alongside the philosopher and mathematician Russell, the signatories included physicists Albert Einstein, Max Born and Joseph Rotblat. Rotblat's research on nuclear fallout would become one of the major factors behind the signing of the Partial Test Ban Treaty in 1963.

1955   WOMEN'S POLITICAL COUNCIL

The Montgomery Bus Boycott

Another Negro woman has been arrested and thrown in jail because she refused to get up out of her seat on the bus for a white person to sit down. It is the second time since the Claudette Colvin case that a Negro woman has been arrested for the same thing. This has to be stopped. Negroes have rights, too, for if Negroes did not ride the buses, they could not operate. Three-fourths of the riders are Negroes, yet we are arrested, or have to stand over empty seats. If we do not do something to stop these arrests, they will continue. The next time it may be you, or your daughter, or mother. This woman's case will come up on Monday. We are, therefore, asking every Negro to stay off the buses Monday in protest of the arrest and trial. Don't ride the buses to work, to town, to school, or anywhere on Monday. You can afford to stay out of school for one day if you have no other way to go except by bus. You can also afford to stay out of town for one day. If you work, take a cab, or walk. But please, children and grown-ups, don't ride the bus at all on Monday . . .

Rosa Parks's arrest for refusing to give up her bus seat to a white man has, as they say, made history—together with the men and women behind the subsequent Montgomery bus boycott, which lasted for 381 days, crippling the bus system and bringing an end to racially segregated seating on Montgomery public buses. This pamphlet was widely distributed by the Women's Political Council, with Jo Ann Robinson at its head, just days after Parks's arrest.

FORUGH FARROKHZAD   **1955**

"Call to Arms"

Only you, O Iranian woman, have remained
in bonds of wretchedness, misfortune, and cruelty;
if you want these bonds broken,
grasp the skirt of obstinacy.

Do not relent because of pleasing promises,
never submit to tyranny;
become a flood of anger, hate and pain,
excise the heavy stone of cruelty.

It is your warm embracing bosom
that nurtures proud and pompous man;
it is your joyous smile that bestows
on his heart warmth and vigor.

Farrokhzad's poetry inspired much debate in Iran, and she became an iconic figure in radical circles following her death at thirty-two. "A Call to Arms" was widely circulated and critical of the patriarchal bent of modernization in Iran; it has since sparked many discussions within Iran about modernity in the Third World.

FEDERATION OF SOUTH AFRICAN WOMEN   **1956**

Letter of Protest

Raids, arrests, loss of pay, long hours at the pass office, weeks in the cells awaiting trial, forced farm labor—this is what the pass laws have brought to African men . . . punishment and misery, not for a crime, but for the lack of a pass. We African women know too well the effect of this law upon our homes, upon our children. We who are not African women know how our sisters suffer . . .

On August 9, 20,000 South African women converged on Pretoria to present their letters of protest to the Prime Minister. Their target was a pass system that allowed police and government agents to arrest any men without an official pass. At the time of the rally, the government was considering extending the policy to include women. Today, August 9 is celebrated as National Women's Day in South Africa.

1956

UMM KULTHUM

"Egypt Speaks of Herself"

He taught us how to build glory
So that we conquered the world.
Not through hope will the price be obtained.
The world must be taken through struggle.

When Britain, France and Israel invaded Egypt for nationalizing the French-owned Suez Canal, the Egyptians mounted a heroic resistance, and this song, sung by the "Diva of the East," could be heard throughout Cairo's streets.

1956

GAMAL ABDEL NASSER

Speech in Alexandria

If rumor in Washington tries to represent that Egypt is not strong enough to warrant American aid, then I say: "Choke on your fury, but you will never succeed in ordering us about or in wielding your tyranny over us, because we know our path—that of freedom, honor and dignity . . . We shall yield neither to force nor to the dollar."

Nasser, president of Egypt for over fifteen years, was the main proponent of pan-Arab nationalism in the Middle East during the Cold War. He brutally suppressed communism and the Muslim Brotherhood, ordering mass arrests. In 1956, he nationalized the French- and British-owned Suez Canal in retaliation for the withdrawal of funding by the US and the UK for the Aswan Dam. This is from the speech he gave in Alexandria, announcing the act. The UK, France and Israel responded by invading Egypt, and the subsequent war, known as the Tripartite Aggression, solidified Arab nationalist sentiment throughout the region.

ALLEN GINSBERG   1956

"Howl"

I'm with you in Rockland
where we wake up electrified out of the coma
by our own souls' airplanes roaring over the
roof they've come to drop angelic bombs the
hospital illuminates itself imaginary walls collapse O skinny legions run outside O starry-
spangled shock of mercy the eternal war is
here O victory forget your underwear we're
free

Ginsberg, for whom the "best minds" of his generation were outcasts and mad, imagines the insane breaking free of their cells and tearing down their walls. "Rockland" refers to a psychiatric facility where Ginsberg met Carl Solomon, to whom "Howl" is dedicated. Ginsberg and his fellow Beat Generation poets combined rampant drug use with political activism against militarism, sexual repression and the consumer-driven world.

RIGOBERTO LÓPEZ PÉREZ   1956

Letter to Mother Before Assassinating Somoza

Seeing that all efforts to return Nicaragua to being (or becoming for the first time) a free country without shame or stain have been futile, I have decided that I should be the one to try to initiate the beginning of the end of this tyranny . . .

I hope you will take this calmly. You must understand that my act is a duty that any Nicaraguan who truly loves his homeland should have carried out a long time ago. This has not been a sacrifice, but a duty I hope I've fulfilled.

López Pérez, a Nicaraguan poet and musician, assassinated the dictator Anastasio Somoza García. Somoza was succeeded by his son Luis who, together with his brother Anastasio, would rule the country either directly or indirectly for the next twenty-three years. Despite their widespread corruption and the brutality of their regimes, they were supported by successive US administrations for their anti-Communist views.

1957   JIT POUMISAK

The Real Face of Thai Saktina

Surely this broad movement of the Thai People which opposes and denounces imperialism and *saktina* [feudalism] is an auspicious sign revealing that the Thai People of today are now fully awake. They have been able to identify clearly the enemies who plunder them and skin them alive and suck the very marrow from their bones . . .

Whether in the economic sphere where rents and interest are sky-high and the ragged peasant, drowned in a sea of debt, has become economically ruined and landless, a hired farm laborer, someone who in the end sells his labor; or in the political sphere where we find corruption, fraud, and utter ruin in government circles, the wielding of legitimate power by important people and the grabbing for power among themselves, oppression of the People through unjust use of the law, and exploitation through heavy taxation; or in the cultural sphere where we find inequities between the classes in society, widening moral deterioration because of Western influence, and the monopolization of literature and the arts in the hands of a small group—all these experiences taken together teach the Thai People to see that the root cause lies in imperialism (including its underlings, the compradore-capitalists and aristo-capitalists) and *saktina*.

Jit was a Marxist intellectual, poet, archaeologist, composer and historian who was jailed for dissent from 1958 to 1965, then retreated to the jungle with the illegal Communist Party and was shot in 1966. The Real Face of Thai *Saktina was his most influential work.*

DJAMILA BOUHIRED   1957
"The Most Beautiful Day"

It was the most beautiful day of my life because I was confident that I would be dying for the sake of the most wonderful story in the world ... I still remember that on returning from the courtroom to the prison, when our brother prisoners shouted to us to ask what our sentence was, we replied with the hymn that those condemned to death would sing and that begins "God is Most Great . . . Our sacrifice is for the motherland."

Bouhired, a member of the National Liberation Front (FLN) from her student days, would come to be known as the "Arab Joan of Arc." She placed one of the three café bombs that marked the beginning of the Battle of Algiers, and was later captured, tortured and sentenced to death. Her execution was commuted just before it was to be carried out; these are her reflections about that day. The FLN waged guerrilla warfare against the French until Algerian independence was achieved, lasting eight years and resulting in between 960,000 and 1.5 million Algerian deaths, and 28,600 French casualties.

GUY DEBORD   1958
"Theses on Cultural Revolution"

2
Art can cease being a report about sensations and become a direct organization of more advanced sensations. The point is to produce ourselves rather than things that enslave us.

4
An international association of Situationists can be seen as a coalition of workers in an advanced sector of culture, or more precisely as a coalition of all those who demand the right to work on a project that

is obstructed by present social conditions; hence as an attempt at organizing professional revolutionaries in culture.

6

Those who want to supersede the old established order in all its aspects cannot cling to the disorder of the present, even in the sphere of culture. In culture as in other areas, it is necessary to struggle without waiting any longer for some concrete appearance of the moving order of the future. The possibility of this ever-changing new order, which is already present among us, devalues all expressions within existing cultural forms. If we are ever to arrive at authentic direct communication (in our working hypothesis of higher cultural means: the construction of situations), we must bring about the destruction of all the forms of pseudocommunication. The victory will go to those who are capable of creating disorder without loving it.

7

In the world of cultural decomposition we can test our strength but never use it. The practical task of overcoming our discordance with this world, that is, of surmounting its decomposition by some more advanced constructions, is not romantic. We will be "revolutionary romantics," in Lefebvre's sense, precisely to the degree that we fail.

Debord was best known as a founding member of the Situationist International, an avant-garde movement focused on creating experiences of life— "situations"— alternative to the existing capitalist order. The Situationists rose to prominence during the May 1968 uprisings in France, with Debord's work Society of the Spectacle *serving as an influence on the burgeoning student movement of the time.*

1958   **FIDEL CASTRO**

"History Will Absolve Me"

Remember that today you are judging an accused man, but also that you yourselves will be judged not once, but many times, as often as these days are submitted to scrutiny in the future. What I say here will be repeated many times, not because it comes from my lips, but because the problem of justice is eternal and the people have a deep sense of justice, above and beyond the hairsplitting of jurisprudence. The people wield simple but implacable logic, in conflict with all that is absurd and contradictory.

Furthermore, if there is in the world a people that utterly abhors favoritism and inequality, it is the Cuban people. To them, justice is symbolized by a maiden with a scale and a sword in her hands. Should she cower before one group and furiously wield that sword against another group, then, to the people of Cuba, the maiden of justice would seem nothing more than a prostitute brandishing a dagger. My logic is the simple logic of the people . . .

The guilty remain at liberty with weapons in hand—weapons which continually threaten the citizens. If all the weight of the law does not fall upon the guilty, because of cowardice, or because of domination of the courts, and if then all the magistrates and judges do not resign, I pity you. And I regret the unprecedented shame that will fall upon the judicial power.

I know that imprisonment will be as hard for me as it has ever been for anyone, filled with cowardly threats and wicked torture. But I do not fear prison, as I do not fear the fury of the miserable tyrant who took the lives of seventy of my comrades.

Condemn me. It does not matter. History will absolve me.

Castro made this speech just before being sentenced to fifteen years in prison for his role in the attack on the Moncada Barracks, an opening blow in the Cuban Revolution that ultimately overthrew dictator Fulgencio Batista. Castro, a lawyer, led the defense of his fellow defendants, and spoke extemporaneously for four hours. He wrote up the speech in prison and smuggled it out in matchboxes.

ROBERT F. WILLIAMS   1959
"We Must Fight Back"

Some Negro leaders have cautioned me that if Negroes fight back, the racist will have cause to exterminate the race. This government is in no position to allow mass violence to erupt, let alone allow twenty million Negroes to be exterminated. It is instilled at an early age that men who violently and swiftly rise to oppose tyranny are virtuous examples to emulate. I have been taught by my government to fight. Nowhere in the annals of history does the record show a people delivered from bondage by patience alone.

Williams formed the Black Armed Guard against racist violence in Monroe, North Carolina, where KKK membership numbered over 10,000, and was a proponent of armed self-defense against the pacifist and nonviolent stance of Martin Luther King, Jr. Facing persecution from both the FBI and opponents of desegregation, he fled to Cuba and then China, returning to the US several years later.

1959   C. WRIGHT MILLS

The Power Elite

The power elite is not an aristocracy, which is to say that it is not a political ruling group based upon a nobility of hereditary origin. It has no compact basis in a small circle of great families whose members can and do consistently occupy the top positions in the several higher circles which overlap as the power elite. But such nobility is only one possible basis of common origin. That it does not exist for the American elite does not mean that members of this elite derive socially from the full range of strata composing American society. They derive in substantial proportions from the upper classes, both new and old, of local society and the metropolitan 400.

Mills, the leading American radical sociologist of the 1960s, offered an incisive new analysis of postwar American society in The Power Elite, *which argued that the country was ruled by political, business, and military figures who constituted an elite stratum wielding disproportionate power and influence. He would become an intellectual beacon for the New Left after his death.*

"The Roots of Bureaucracy"

The worker and the bureaucrat are equally necessary for the transition towards socialism. As long as the working masses are still in that stage of intellectual pauperism left over from the centuries of oppression and illiteracy, the management of the processes of production must fall to the civil servant.

Officialdom still dominates society and lords over it, yet it lacks the cohesion and unity which would make of it a separate class in the Marxist sense of the word. The bureaucrats enjoy power and some measure of prosperity, yet they cannot bequeath their prosperity and wealth to their children. They cannot accumulate capital, invest it for the benefit of their descendants: they cannot perpetuate themselves or their kith and kin.

Of course, even small privileges contribute to the tension between the worker and the bureaucrat, but we should not mistake that tension for a class antagonism, in spite of some similarities which on closer examination would prove only very superficial. What we observe here is rather the hostility between members of the same class, between, say, a skilled miner and an unskilled one, between the engine driver and a less expert railwayman . . . When the organized is no longer the dumb and dull and helpless muzhik, when the cook is no longer the old scullion, then indeed the gulf between the bureaucrat and the worker can disappear. What will remain will be the division of functions, not of social status.

The old Marxist prospect of "withering away" of the state may seem to us odd. But let us not play with old formulas which were part of an idiom to which we are not accustomed. What Marx really meant was that the state should divest itself of its oppressive political functions. And I think this will become possible only in a society . . . free from cults, dogmatism and orthodoxies—in such a society the antagonism between brainwork and manual labour will really wither away, as will the division between the organizers and the organized. Then, and only then, it will be seen that if bureaucracy was a faint prelude to class society, bureaucracy will mark the fierce ferocious epilogue to class society—no more than an epilogue.

Born in Poland, Deutscher joined the Polish Communist Party as a young man, moved to the UK just months before the German invasion that would spark the Second World War, and became a popular left intellectual in the 1960s through his work as a Marxist academic and journalist. Today he is best remembered for his authoritative, three-volume biography of Leon Trotsky. "The Roots of Bureaucracy" was a lecture delivered when he was teaching at the London School of Economics.

1960   ANONYMOUS

Poem by Korean Elementary-School Student

> On the way home from school,
> Bullets flew through the air
> And blood covered the streets.
> The lonely discarded book bag
> Was as heavy as it could be.
> I know, yes, we all know
> Even if Mom and Dad say nothing
> Why our brothers and sisters were bleeding.

On March 15, 1960, a student demonstration against the fraudulent election victory of South Korean strongman Syngman Rhee was attacked by police. One month later, the body of student protester Kim Ju-yul washed ashore, his skull split open by a tear-gas grenade. The public outrage would eventually result in the April Revolution, which would end Rhee's rule.

MAURICE BLANCHOT, CLAUDE LANZMANN, JEAN-PAUL SARTRE, ET AL.

1960

"Manifesto of the 121"

Neither a war of conquest nor a war of "national defense" nor a civil war, the war in Algeria has little by little become an autonomous action on the part of the army and a caste which refuse to submit in the face of an uprising which even the civil power, aware of the general collapse of colonial empires, seems ready to accept.

Today, it is principally through the will of the army that this criminal and absurd combat is maintained; and this army, by the important political role that many of its higher representatives have it play—at times acting openly and violently outside any form of legality, betraying the ends confided in it by the nation—compromises and risks perverting the nation itself by forcing the citizens under its orders to become the accomplices of a seditious and degrading action. Must we be reminded that fifteen years after the destruction of the Hitlerite order, French militarism has managed to bring back torture and restore it as an institution in Europe?

The undersigned . . . declare:

• We respect and judge justified the refusal to take up arms against the Algerian people.

• We respect and judge justified the conduct of those French men and women who consider it their obligation to give aid and protection to the Algerians, oppressed in the name of the French people.

• The cause of the Algerian people, which contributes decisively to the ruin of the colonial system, is the cause of all free men and women.

When the "Manifesto of the 121" was published, the Algerian War had already been underway for six years. Criticizing the government's war against the native Algerian population, including the French forces' resort to torture, the 121 intellectuals who signed the manifesto included some of the most recognized names in French public life. With mounting domestic opposition, France and Algeria negotiated independence, bringing an end to the war two years later.

1960s DOM HÉLDER CÂMARA

"When I Give Food to the Poor"

When I give food to the poor, they call me a saint. When I ask why the poor have no food, they call me a communist.

Câmara was Archbishop of Olinda and Recife in Brazil. He was active in the Catholic Action movement, preached nonviolence, and was famous for creating the "church of the poor," a group of Third World bishops concerned with issues of social justice.

1960s SMASH THE SECURITY TREATY

"The Constitution of Japan—A Correct Interpretation"

We, the Armed Forces of the United States occupying Japan, acting on behalf of the United States and in place of the parliament chosen in Japan by menaces and bribery, determined that we shall secure for ourselves the fruits of peaceful cooperation with all nations under the control of the United States and the blessings accruing from money-making ventures throughout the Japanese archipelago, and resolved to stir up the calamities of war willingly and whenever it is in the interests of the United States, do proclaim that sovereign power does not reside in the Japanese people and do firmly establish this constitution. The governance of Japan shall be in accordance with the strict dictates of the government of the United States, its authority stemming from the military might of the occupying army, its power exercised as proxy for the occupation forces, and its benefits enjoyed by monopoly enterprises. This is the principle established by the government of the United States upon which this Constitution is founded. We reject and revoke all constitutions, laws, ordinances and rescripts in conflict herewith.

Japan's "Peace Constitution," drawn up under the postwar Allied Occupation and famous for its renunciation of the right to wage war, cleared the way for the establishment of local US bases to "protect" Japan, in the absence of a standing military. This satirical rewrite of the Japanese constitution was penned by the Smash the Security Treaty group, which emerged from protests in the 1960s and continues to oppose the US military presence in Japan.

TEWOLDE REDDA   1960s
"Shigey Habuni"

Give me my torch
How long can you deceive me?
What have I done
That you deny me my torch?

Resistance to Ethiopian hegemony was growing in Eritrea in the 1960s, and the Mahber Yeatra Asmara, a radical nationalistic cultural association, put on many public performances. While they were largely censored by the authorities, the artists camouflaged their political messages in their songs. "Shigey Habuni" was one of the more popular ones.

OUSMANE SEMBÈNE   1960
God's Bits of Wood

Ever since they left Thiès, the women had not stopped singing. As soon as one group allowed the refrain to die, another picked it up, and new verses were born at the hazard of chance or inspiration, one word leading to another and each finding, in its turn, its rhythm and its place. No one was very sure any longer where the song began, or if it had an ending. It rolled out over its own length, like the movement of a serpent. It was as long as a life.

Sembène, a renowned Senegalese filmmaker and writer, was also a communist and trade union activist, having participated in 1947 in a months-long work-ers' strike along the Dakar-Niger railway in colonial Senegal, upon which he based his seminal novel God's Bits of Wood. *In this extract, he describes a women's rally in Dakar demanding equal wages, old age pensions, family allowances and proper housing.*

1960

PATRICE LUMUMBA

"Lumumba Is an African"

Africa will tell the West that today it desires the rehabilitation of Africa, a return to the roots, a revalorization of moral values. The African personality must be expressed: that is the meaning of our policy of positive neutrality. Africa will have no blocs such as you have in Europe. Instead there will be active African solidarity. The common-wealth regime, which is just a disguise for continuing the colonial regime, is going to fall soon. You see, gentlemen, they are trying to distort your focus when they call our government a communist government, in the pay of the Soviet Union, or say that Lumumba is a communist, an anti-white: Lumumba is an African.

Lumumba, the celebrated Congolese independence leader, became the first prime minister of the Republic of Congo in 1960. Two months later, he was deposed, and just a few days after that, a CIA-backed coup d'état organized by Colonel Joseph Mobutu would strip him of his power entirely. Six months later, Lumumba was assassinated by the Belgian government; Mobutu would rule using authoritarian means for over thirty years.

1960

PHYLLIS NTANTALA

"The Widows of the Reserves"

Call it what you may. But if they be prostitutes it is not of their own choosing. It is the system that has kept them on starvation wages so that they and their children can perish slowly but surely; a system that has made them barren and their men impotent; a system that has demoralized and dehumanized a whole people—making the ratio of women to men in the Reserves as high as eight to one and so enabling the man who has the energy and the means to have as many women as he chooses; a system that has kept the men in the towns in a perpetual state of war, in battle-camps where masturbation, homosexuality, and rape are the order of the day, and turning otherwise decent human beings into beasts which see a woman not as a human being but as a source of sexual satisfaction alone.

Ntantala is a South African activist, educator and writer. "The Widows of the Reserves" describes the degradation of African families; the hardships experienced by women who remain in rural lands and by women who join their husbands in the cities; and the strength and ingenuity with which these women fight back.

FRANTZ FANON   **1961**

The Wretched of the Earth

History teaches us that the battle against colonialism does not run straight along the lines of nationalism. For a long time the native devotes his energies to ending definite abuses: forced labor, corporal punishment, inequality of salaries, limitations of political rights, etc. This fight for democracy against the oppression of mankind will slowly leave the confusion of neo-liberal universalism to emerge, sometimes laboriously, as a claim to nationhood. It so happens that the unpreparedness of the educated classes, the lack of practical links between them and the mass of the people, their laziness and, let it be said, their cowardice at the decisive moment of the struggle will give rise to tragic mishaps.

National consciousness, instead of being the all-embracing crystallization of the innermost hopes of the whole people, instead of being the immediate and most obvious result of the mobilization of the people, will be in any case an empty shell, a cruel and fragile travesty of what it might have been. The faults that we find in it are quite sufficient explanation of the facility with which, when dealing with young and independent nations, the nation is passed over, for the race and the tribe is preferred to the state. These are the cracks in the edifice which show the process of retrogression that is so harmful to national effort and national unity. We shall see that such retrograde steps, with the weaknesses and serious dangers they entail, are the historic result of the incapacity of the national middle class to nationalize popular action, that is to say their incapacity to see into the reasons for that action . . .

The works of Fanon—psychiatrist, writer and revolutionary—have inspired anticolonial movements throughout the world, and The Wretched of the Earth *is his most well known. Born in Martinique, Fanon studied with Aimé Césaire, fought in the French Army, became a psychiatrist, joined Algeria's National Liberation Front and dictated* Wretched *on his deathbed.*

1961

WU HAN

Hai Rui's Dismissal

Hai Rui:
You say the common people are tyrannized,
but do you know the gentry injures them?
Much is made at court of the gentry's oppression,
but do you know of the poverty
endured by the common people?
You pay lip service to the principle
that the people are the roots of the state.
But officials still oppress the masses
while pretending to be virtuous men.
They act wildly as tigers
and deceive the emperor.
If your conscience bothers you
you know no peace by day or night.

Wu was a member of the Three-Family Village, a group of Chinese intellectuals critical of many Communist government policies in the late 1960s; Hai Rui was a Ming official who fought intransigently for the people's economic rights. In this play, Wu highlighted the corruption of the monarch and system that Hai Rui opposed, implicitly drawing a parallel between Hai Rui and Peng Dehuai, a prominent military leader who had been dismissed for criticizing Mao's policies in the Great Leap Forward.

"A Guerrilla's Words"

Because my country is beautiful
like a sword in the air
and bigger now and even
still more beautiful,
I speak out and defend it
with my life.
I don't care what traitors
say
we've blocked the way
with thick tears
of steel.
The sky is ours.
Ours our daily bread.
We've sown and harvested
the wheat and the land,
ours too
and always ours
the sea,
the jungles
and the birds.

Heraud was a Peruvian poet and guerrilla fighter with the Revolutionary Left Movement, a group inspired by the Cuban Revolution. Unable to win significant popular support, Heraud was killed in 1963.

1962

JALAL AL-E-AHMAD

Occidentosis

To remain only consumers of the machine, to submit utterly to this 1900s juggernaut, is the road we have followed thus far. This road has led us to our present circumstances—occidentosis. We live on hand-outs from the West, which comes around every few years to give credit and aid so we can go on buying its industrial goods and replacing the junked machines. This is an easy road and one that solves the problem of our indolence, aimlessness, and idleness. And if this road led us to a point where we were free of disorder in our affairs and the threat of bankruptcy, there would be no need to say much about it. And as for retreating into our own cocoon, this is something no cricket has ever done. We are a nation engaged in transformation and if we suffer from such a confusion of values in both life and thought, it is because we are shedding our old skin. You might say we are studying the conditions of our permit to enter a new realm.

The writer and public intellectual Al-e-Ahmad's Occidentosis *became an influential work among radical students and was suppressed by the Shah. It was a diagnosis of Iran's condition, and was responsible for some of the ideological ferment that led to the Iranian Revolution of 1979.*

1962

OBAFEMI AWOLOWO

Adventures in Power, Book One: My March through Prison

I have been an unyielding advocate of a Federal Constitution for Nigeria. I have all along, with other leaders of this country, been a very active and constructive participant in all the constitutional conferences which have taken place since 1953, and which have culminated not only in the attainment of independence but in the production of a Constitution of which Nigerians are very proud.

This Constitution is now being gradually violated.

I have also fought against anything which savours of injustice. It is thus an irony of history that, as one of the architects of Nigeria's independence, I have spent almost half of Nigeria's three years of independence under one form of confinement or another . . .

Awolowo was a Nigerian socialist politician, union organizer and journalist who introduced free primary education and universal health-care until the age of eighteen in western Nigeria. In 1962, he was convicted on charges of conspiring with the government of Kwame Nkrumah in Ghana to overthrow the federal government. He made this statement after the verdict was passed.

SAM COOKE   **1963**

"A Change Is Gonna Come"

I was born by the river in a little tent
Oh and just like the river I been a runnin' ever since
It's been a long, a long time coming but I know
A change gon' come oh yes it will
It's been too hard living but I'm afraid to die
Cuz I don't know what's up there beyond the sky
It's been a long, a long time coming but I know
A change gon' come oh yes it will.

A soul and R&B pioneer, Cooke paved the way for the successes of artists like Aretha Franklin and Marvin Gaye. Written in the year of Cooke's death, "A Change Is Gonna Come" was a consciously political statement about the realities of the segregated South, and would later become an anthem for the civil rights movement.

NGUYEN TUONG TAM   **1963**

Suicide Note

Let history be my judge, I refuse to accept any other judgment. The arrest and detention of nationalist opposition elements is a serious crime, and it will cause the country to be lost into the hands of the

Communists. I oppose these acts, and sentence myself to death . . . as a warning to those who would trample upon freedom of every kind.

A writer, critic, and politician, Nguyen was part of the Vietnamese anticolonial movement during much of the 1940s, then broke with the Communist movement in the 1950s. Accused by the government of Ngo Dinh Diem of complicity in an abortive coup attempt in 1960 and facing trial, he poisoned himself with veronal-laced whiskey.

1963   **BETTY FRIEDAN**

The Feminine Mystique

The problem lay buried, unspoken, for many years in the minds of American women. It was a sense of dissatisfaction, a yearning. Each suburban housewife struggled with it alone as she made beds, shopped for groceries, matched slipcover material, ate peanut butter sandwiches with her children, chauffeured Cub Scouts and Brownies, lay beside her husband at night—she was afraid to ask the silent question—"Is this all?" . . . It is no longer possible to ignore that voice, to dismiss the desperation of so many women. This is not what being a woman means, no matter what the experts say.

It is no longer possible to blame the problem on loss of femininity: to say that education and independence and equality with men have made American women unfeminine.

The problem that has no name is not a matter of loss of femininity, or too much education. It is far more important than anyone recognizes. It may be the key to our future as a nation and a culture. We can no longer ignore that voice within women that says: "I want something more than my husband and my children, and my home."

Friedan's The Feminine Mystique *was the launching point for second-wave feminism, focusing on the social processes that pressured middle-class women to forfeit their individual identity to the structure of family. A co-founder of the National Organization for Women, Friedan also fought for abortion rights.*

1963

Cat's Cradle

There is no reason goodness cannot triumph over evil, so long as the angels are as organized as the mafia.

In the course of his literary career, the American novelist Vonnegut often addressed the themes of anti-authoritarianism, free will and technology from a humanistic perspective, and has named characters after Eugene Debs and Leon Trotsky.

NELSON MANDELA

1964

"An Ideal for Which I Am Prepared to Die"

I do not . . . deny that I planned sabotage. I did not plan it in a spirit of recklessness, nor because I have any love of violence. I planned it as a result of a calm and sober assessment of the political situation that had arisen after many years of tyranny, exploitation, and oppression of my people by the whites . . . The hard facts were that fifty years of non-violence had brought the African people nothing but more and more repressive legislation, and fewer and fewer rights . . .

We want equal political rights, because without them our disabilities will be permanent . . . It is not true that the enfranchisement of all will result in racial domination. Political division, based on color, is entirely artificial and, when it disappears, so will the domination of one color group by another. The ANC has spent half a century fighting against racialism. When it triumphs it will not change that policy.

This then is what the ANC is fighting. Their struggle is a truly national one. It is a struggle of the African people, inspired by their own suffering and their own experience. It is a struggle for the right to live. During my lifetime I have dedicated myself to this struggle of the African people. I have fought against white domination, and I have fought against black domination. I have cherished the ideal of a democratic and free society in which all persons live together in harmony and with equal opportunities. It is an ideal which I hope to live for and to achieve. But if needs be, it is an ideal for which I am prepared to die.

Mandela, who spent nearly thirty years in prison, opened his trial for sabotage with this statement. The African National Congress sought to resist apartheid through peaceful means until the Sharpeville Massacre of 1960, in which sixty-nine black protesters were killed. Mandela was the leader of its military wing, Umkhonto we Sizwe ("Sphere of the Nation"), which was established after this incident.

1964   **MARIO SAVIO**

Speech before Free Speech Movement Sit-In

There's a time when the operation of the machine becomes so odious, makes you so sick at heart, that you can't take part; you can't even passively take part. And you've got to put your bodies upon the gears and upon the wheels, upon the levers, upon all the apparatus, and you've got to make it stop. And you've got to indicate to the people who run it, to the people who own it, that unless you're free, the machine will be prevented from working at all!

One of the most prominent American student leaders of the 1960s, Savio was a key figure in the Free Speech Movement at the University of California, Berkeley. After giving this speech on the steps of Sproul Hall before a crowd of 4,000, he was arrested along with 800 others and sentenced to 120 days in jail.

1964   **HERBERT MARCUSE**

One-Dimensional Man

The critical theory of society possesses no concepts which could bridge the gap between the present and its future; holding no promise and showing no success, it remains negative. Thus it wants to remain loyal to those who, without hope, have given and give their life to the Great Refusal.

Marcuse was a former student of Martin Heidegger and one of the Frankfurt School intellectuals who fled Nazi Germany. Propelled to intellectual fame by the success of One-Dimensional Man, *which became a mainstay of the 1960s student movement, Marcuse became known in some circles as the father of the New Left. The work was a critique of the social repression occurring in both the Soviet Union and the capitalist West.*

MALCOLM X   1964
"The Ballot or the Bullet"

Uncle Sam's hands are dripping with blood, dripping with the blood of the black man in this country. He's the earth's number-one hypocrite. He has the audacity—yes, he has—imagine him posing as the leader of the free world . . . Let the world know how bloody his hands are. Let the world know the hypocrisy that's practiced over here. Let it be the ballot or the bullet. Let him know that it must be the ballot or the bullet.

Given less than a month after Malcolm's much-publicized break with the Nation of Islam, his "Ballot or Bullet" speech marked his willingness to form an alliance with the civil rights movement. He said he saw "America through the eyes of the victim," and that "it is only after slavery and prison that the sweetest appreciation of freedom can come."

AMILCAR CABRAL   1964
"The Role of the Petty Bourgeoisie"

If I may put it this way, I think one thing that can be said is this: the revolutionary petty bourgeoisie is honest: i.e., in spite of all the hostile conditions, it remains identified with the fundamental interests of the popular masses. To do this it may have to commit suicide but it will not lose: by sacrificing itself it can reincarnate itself, but in the condition of workers or peasants. In speaking of honesty I am not trying to establish moral criteria for judging the role of the petty bourgeoisie when it is in power; what I mean by honesty, in a political context, is total commitment and total identification with the toiling masses.

Cabral, a communist intellectual, guerrilla and leader in the anticolonial movements in the Portuguese colonies of Guinea-Bissau and Angola, was assassinated just months before Guinea-Bissau achieved independence. Some 6,000 of Cabral's guerrilla fighters were killed in the course of the eleven-year war.

1964

JEAN-PAUL SARTRE

"Why I Decline the Nobel"

A writer must refuse to allow himself to be transformed into an institution.

Sartre was the first winner to voluntarily decline the Nobel Prize. In 1945, he had declined France's highest honor, the Legion d'honneur. In a public letter, Sartre added that if he accepted the award, he would effectively be taking sides in the Cold War, which he refused to do.

1964

NINA SIMONE

"Mississippi Goddam"

You don't have to live next to me
Just give me my equality
Everybody knows about Mississippi
Everybody knows about Alabama
Everybody knows about Mississippi Goddam.

Written in response to the murder of civil-rights activist Medgar Evers in Mississippi and the burning of a church in Birmingham, in which four African American children died, Nina Simone's "Mississippi Goddam" was boycotted in several Southern states. The song was performed before a crowd of 40,000 at one of the Selma-to-Montgomery marches that marked a high point of the civil rights movement.

FANNIE LOU HAMER 1965

"Sick and Tired"

I am sick and tired of being sick and tired.

Born in Jim Crow Mississippi and sterilized without her knowledge by a white doctor, Hamer shot to fame in 1964 when she helped challenge the all-white Mississippi delegation to the Democratic Party convention, prompting Democratic president Lyndon Johnson to deride her as "that illiterate woman." She later ran for Congress and became a critic of the Vietnam War.

CASEY HAYDEN AND MARY KING 1965

"Sex and Caste"

The caste system perspective dictates the roles assigned to women in the movement, and certainly even more to women outside the movement. Within the movement, questions arise in situations ranging from relationships of women organizers to men in the community, to who cleans the freedom house, to who holds leadership positions, to who does secretarial work, and who acts as a spokesman for groups.

Regarded as one of the first documents of the women's liberation movement, "Sex and Caste" addressed the authors' experiences as volunteers in the Student Nonviolent Coordinating Committee, which, though committed to achieving racial equality, was run by men who expected the women in the organization simply to cook meals and take notes.

1965

PAUL POTTER

"We Must Name that System"

We must name that system. We must name it, describe it, analyse it, understand it and change it. For it is only when that system is changed and brought under control that there can be any hope for stopping the forces that create a war in Vietnam today or a murder in the South tomorrow or all the incalculable, innumerable more subtle atrocities that are worked on people all over—all the time.

Potter was president of Students for a Democratic Society—which grew from a tiny offshoot of a longstanding socialist group to a national organization with some 350 chapters, the flagship group of the American student New Left. Potter delivered this speech to a crowd of 25,000, at an SDS-organized anti–Vietnam War march on Washington.

1965

JORGE REBELO

Poem

Come, brother, and tell me your life
come, show me the marks of revolt
which the enemy left on your body

Come, say to me "Here
my hands have been crushed
because they defended
The land which they own"

"Here my body was tortured
because it refused to bend
to invaders"

"Here my mouth was wounded
Because it dared to sing
My people's freedom"

Come brother and tell me your life,
come relate to me the dreams of revolt
which you and your fathers and forefathers
dreamed
in silence
through shadowless nights made for love

Come tell me these dreams become
war,
the birth of heroes,
land reconquered,
mothers who, fearless,
send their sons to fight.

Come, tell me all this, my brother.
And later I will forge simple words
which even the children can understand
words which will enter every house
like the wind
and fall like red hot embers
on our people's souls.

In our land
Bullets are beginning to flower.

Rebelo, a lawyer and poet, was responsible for the Liberation Front of Mozambique's (FRELIMO) propaganda campaign and acted as the editor of Mozambique Revolution. *FRELIMO is a Marxist-Leninist political party in Mozambique and was an anticolonial liberation movement whose guerrilla force of 7,000 fought against a Portuguese force of 60,000 soldiers in the early 1970s.*

1965   ERNESTO "CHE" GUEVARA

"From Algiers, for Marcha: The Cuban Revolution Today"

At the risk of seeming ridiculous, let me say that the true revolutionary is guided by a great feeling of love. It is impossible to think of a genuine revolutionary lacking this quality . . .

The leaders of the revolution have children just beginning to talk, who are not learning to call their fathers by name; wives, from whom they have to be separated as part of the general sacrifice of their lives to bring the revolution to its fulfillment; the circle of their friends is limited strictly to the number of fellow revolutionists. There is no life outside of the revolution.

In these circumstances one must have a great deal of humanity and a strong sense of justice and truth in order not to fall into extreme dogmatism and cold scholasticism, into isolation from the masses. We must strive every day so that this love of living humanity will be transformed into actual deeds, into acts that serve as examples, as a moving force.

This article was written in the form of a letter to Carlos Quijano, editor of Marcha, *a weekly published in Montevideo. Guevara wrote it while on the three-month trip during which he addressed the United Nations General Assembly and visited Algeria and other African countries. He also later said that "a people without hatred cannot vanquish a brutal enemy."*

1966   GILLO PONTECORVO

Battle of Algiers

Journalist: M. Ben M'Hidi, don't you think it's a bit cowardly to use women's baskets and handbags to carry explosive devices that kill so many innocent people?

Ben M'Hidi: And doesn't it seem to you even more cowardly to drop napalm bombs on defenseless villages, so that there are a thousand times more innocent victims? Of course, if we had your airplanes it would be a lot easier for us. Give us your bombers, and you can have our baskets.

Directed by the Italian filmmaker Gillo Pontecorvo and based in part on a memoir of the Algerian War by National Liberation Front commander Saadi Yacef, Battle of Algiers *has become one of the most influential, as well as celebrated, depictions of guerrilla war, counterinsurgency tactics, and national liberation struggles. The film was debated avidly by radicals the world over— reportedly it was the favorite film of the German Red Army Faction's Andreas Baader—and screened at the Pentagon for Defense Department officials waging war in Iraq. Yacef himself appears in the film, which was banned in France for five years and had some of its torture scenes censored when it was first released in the US and UK.*

HUGO BLANCO   1966
"To My People"

To be a revolutionary is to love the world, to love life, to be happy. So, he doesn't flee from life, he understands that it is his duty to live for the fight, and he enjoys life.

But neither must he flee from death!

Because you can fight as well by dying; you can transform the world as well by dying. Because you can love life as well by dying! Because you live even through death! So, you must also accept death.

And for the Peruvian revolutionary, death is no disgrace. It can be no disgrace that my blood will flow to that red and militant river, wherever the blood of Lucho Zapata, of De la Puente, of Lobaton, of Heraud, of Vallejos, of Velando flows and fights on.

In the 1960s, Blanco led a Quechua peasant uprising in Peru. He was captured by the military and sentenced to twenty-five years, then exiled in 1976. He wrote "For My People" in El Frontón Penal Colony. After returning to Peru, he founded the Workers Revolutionary Party and served in the Peruvian senate until he had to flee the country again following President Alberto Fujimori's suspension of democratic rule in 1992. Today he is back in Peru.

1966

STOKELY CARMICHAEL

"Black Power!"

I do not want to be a part of the American pie. The American pie means raping South Africa, beating Vietnam, beating South America, raping the Philippines, raping every country you've been in. I don't want any of your blood money. I don't want to be part of that system. We must question whether or not we want this country to continue being the wealthiest country in the world at the price of raping everybody else.

Carmichael, leader of the Student Nonviolent Coordinating Committee and one-time Honorary Prime Minister of the Black Panther Party, popularized the slogan "Black Power" and coined the phrase "institutional racism." An icon of the Black Power movement, he nonetheless responded to Casey Hayden and Mary King's memo "Sex and Caste" that the "only position for women in SNCC is prone."

1967

WOLE SOYINKA

"Death in the Dawn"

Traveler you must set forth
At dawn.
I promise marvels of the holy hour
Presages as the white cock's flapped
Perverse impalement—as who would dare
The wrathful wings of man's Progression . . .
But such another Wraith! Brother,
Silenced in the startled hug of
Your invention—is this mocked grimace
This closed contortion—I?

Soyinka, the Nigerian poet, playwright and winner of the Nobel Prize for Literature, was sent to solitary confinement by one Nigerian dictator and sentenced to death in absentia by another. Much of his writing has been concerned with "the oppressive boot and the irrelevance of the color of the foot that wears it."

OGINGA ODINGA 1967

Not Yet Uhuru

We fought for *uhuru* so that people may rule themselves. Direct action, not underhand diplomacy and silent intrigue by professional politicians, won *uhuru*, and only popular support and popular mobilization can make it meaningful.

Oginga Odinga was a chief of the Luo tribe in Kenya, a leader in the independence movement, and the country's first vice president. Not Yet Uhuru *is his autobiography; the title expresses his sentiment that independence had not yet been achieved, the government having become mired in red tape and power struggles.*

RÉGIS DEBRAY 1967

Testimony at Court Martial

It is not the job of a Frenchman to teach a Bolivian military prosecuting attorney the history of his country. But since so much reference has been made to that history, gentleman, here are the facts of history. Thus, Bolivia was liberated from the Spanish by men who came from every corner of Latin America to help found Bolivia and all of Latin America. And similarly the same fraternal union of Latin Americans, tested in combat and the life of the battle campaign itself, will liberate Bolivia from Yankee imperialism.

For Che the true difference, the true frontier, is not the one which separates a Bolivian from a Peruvian, a Peruvian from an Argentinian, an Argentinian from a Cuban. It is the one which separates Latin Americans from Yankees.

Debray, the distinguished French philosopher and historian, was invited by Che Guevara to join his ill-fated guerrilla expedition to Bolivia in 1966 as a chronicler. Debray accepted, and was eventually arrested by the Bolivian military, tortured, brought to trial, found guilty and sentenced to thirty years in prison. A worldwide campaign in his favor won the support of French President Charles de Gaulle, and after a few years he was released.

1967

KWAME NKRUMAH

"African Socialism Revisited"

Islamic civilization and European colonialism are both historical experiences of the traditional African society, profound experiences that have permanently changed the complexion of the traditional African society. They have introduced new values and a social, cultural, and economic organization into African life. Modern African societies are not traditional, even if backward, and they are clearly in a state of socio-economic disequilibrium. They are in this state because they are not anchored to a steadying ideology.

The way out is certainly not to regurgitate all Islamic or Euro-colonial influences in a futile attempt to recreate a past that cannot be resurrected. The way out is only forward, forward to a higher and reconciled form of society, in which the quintessence of the human purposes of traditional African society reasserts itself in a modern context—forward, in short, to socialism, through policies that are scientifically devised and correctly applied . . .

It is the elimination of fancifulness from socialist action that makes socialism scientific. To suppose that there are tribal, national, or racial socialisms is to abandon objectivity in favor of chauvinism.

Nkrumah led the Gold Coast's fight for independence against the British in the 1940s and 1950s, then became the leader of Ghana once independence was achieved. Here, he argues against Leopold Senghor's "African Socialism" for its romanticizing of traditional African society. Despite his avowed socialist stance and his work as a labor organizer prior to becoming prime minister, once in power he introduced the 1955 Trade Union Act, which made strikes illegal.

"Footnotes to the Book of Setback"

3

My grieved country,
In a flash
You changed me from a poet who wrote love poems
To a poet who writes with a knife.

20

Arab children,
Corn ears of the future,
You will break out chains.
Kill the opium in our heads,
Kill the illusions.
Arab children,
Don't read about our windowless generation,
We are a hopeless case.
We are as worthless as watermelon rind.
Don't read about us,
Don't ape us,
Don't accept us,
Don't accept our ideas,
We are a nation of crooks and jugglers.
Arab children,
Spring rain,
Corn ears of the future,
You are a generation
That will overcome defeat.

A Syrian poet, publisher, and diplomat, Qabbani was one of the most revered contemporary poets in the Arab world. "Footnotes" was composed immediately after the Arab defeat in the Six Day War, and is highly critical of the Arab leadership. As a result, Qabbani's books were banned in Egypt, and he was barred from entering the country.

1967   MIGUEL ÁNGEL ASTURIAS

"The Latin American Novel: Testimony of an Epoch"

If you write novels merely to entertain—then burn them! This might be the message delivered with evangelical fervor since if you do not burn them they will anyway be erased from the memory of the people where a poet or novelist should aspire to remain. Just consider how many writers there have been who—down the ages—have written novels to entertain! And who remembers them now? On the other hand, how easy it is to repeat the names of those amongst us who have written to bear witness.

To bear witness. The novelist bears witness like the apostle. Like Paul trying to escape, the writer is confronted with the pathetic reality of the world that surrounds him—the stark reality of our countries that overwhelms and blinds us and, throwing us to our knees, forces us to shout out: WHY DO YOU PERSECUTE ME?

Our books do not search for a sensationalist or horrifying effect in order to secure a place for us in the republic of letters. We are human beings linked by blood, geography and life to those hundreds, thousands, millions of Latin Americans that suffer misery in our opulent and rich American continent. Our novels attempt to mobilize across the world the moral forces that have to help us defend those people.

Asturias, a Guatemalan writer, won both the Lenin Peace Prize and the Nobel Prize for Literature. These words are taken from his Nobel Prize acceptance speech. He devoted much of his work to the struggles of the indigenous people of his native country, and was a diplomat under socialist Jacobo Arbenz, whose government was toppled by a US-backed military coup d'etat in 1954, after which Asturias was stripped of his citizenship and exiled.

HUEY P. NEWTON

1967

"The Correct Handling of a Revolution"

The people make revolution; the oppressors, by their brutal actions, cause resistance by the people. The vanguard party only teaches the correct methods of resistance.

Newton was a student of Marxist political theory, co-founded the Black Panther Party, and was sentenced to fifteen years in prison for the alleged murder of a police officer, although the conviction was eventually overturned. Newton was also shot in the incident, and although he was admitted to hospital, he was chained to the bed and recalls being interrogated while he was in the operating room.

H. RAP BROWN

1967

"Violence"

Violence is as American as cherry pie.

A Justice Minister of the Black Panther Party and a chairman of the Student Nonviolent Coordinating Committee, Brown spent the greater part of his youth ducking weapons and rioting charges. In 2000, he was sentenced to life in prison for the murder of a police officer.

MARTIN LUTHER KING, JR.

1967

"Beyond Vietnam: A Time to Break Silence"

A true revolution of values will soon look uneasily on the glaring contrast of poverty and wealth. With righteous indignation, it will look across the seas and see individual capitalists of the West investing huge sums of money in Asia, Africa, and South America, only to take the profits out with no concern for the social betterment of the countries, and say, "This is not just."

Four years after he famously proclaimed "I Have a Dream" in one of the defining moments of the civil rights movement, Martin Luther King, Jr. spoke out against US involvement in the Vietnam War and became the subject of much criticism among civil rights leaders, the public and the press. Lyndon Johnson withdrew an invitation for him to the White House.

1968

TARIQ ALI

Street Fighting Years

As the Vietnamese successes inspired the students, so now the triumph of the students inspired the workers. France slipped into a prerevolutionary solution without an awareness on the part of the workers who made it possible that their actions had begun to pose the question as to who ruled France. The upsurge swept the whole country. Then a million workers went on strike. It was the biggest general strike in the history of capitalism and the scale of the events was much greater than the 1905 upheavals in tsarist Russia. It was no longer just the students and the workers who were involved. Farmers and peasants brought their tractors and compost onto the streets; lawyers and magistrates, architects and astronomers came out for change. They were backed by the newsreaders of ORTF, who declared that they were fed up with feeding "shit" to the population. And, as if to stress the truly national character of the discontent, the striptease artistes of the Folies Bergère joined the big marches, chanting "*De Gaulle assassin!*"

Lahore-born British writer, filmmaker, and activist Ali was the president of the Oxford Union in 1965, visited Régis Debray in prison in Bolivia just before Che was assassinated in 1967—where he told Bolivian officials, "If you torture me the whole night and I can speak Spanish in the morning, I'll be grateful to you for the rest of my life"—led an anti–Vietnam War march on the American embassy in London in 1968, and became a leading figure of the British New Left. An editor of New Left Review, *he has written the* Islam Quintet *and two dozen books on world history and politics.*

Pedagogy of the Oppressed

This, then, is the great humanistic and historical task of the oppressed: to liberate themselves and their oppressors as well. The oppressors, who oppress, exploit, and rape by virtue of their power, cannot find in this power the strength to liberate either the oppressed or themselves. Only power that springs from the weakness of the oppressed will be sufficiently strong to free both. Any attempt to "soften" the power of the oppressor in deference to the weakness of the oppressed almost always manifests itself in the form of false generosity; indeed, the attempt never goes beyond this. In order to have the continued opportunity to express their "generosity," the oppressors must perpetrate injustice as well. An unjust social order is the permanent fount of this "generosity," which is nourished by death, despair, and poverty. That is why the dispensers of false generosity become desperate at the slightest threat to its source.

True generosity consists precisely in fighting to destroy the causes which nourish false charity. False charity constrains the fearful and subdued, the "rejects of life," to extend their trembling hands. True generosity lies in striving so that these hands—whether of individuals or entire peoples—need be extended less and less in supplication, so that more and more they become human hands which work and, working, transform the world.

One of the world's most influential educators, Freire won international recognition for his breakthroughs in teaching literacy in northeastern Brazil. The 1964 military coup put an end to that, leading to a brief imprisonment and fifteen years of exile, during which he wrote Pedagogy of the Oppressed *and other books that influenced teachers and activists from the US to South Africa (where Steve Biko drew on Freire's ideas). After moving back to Brazil in 1980, Freire joined the Workers Party, and when the party prevailed in 1988 municipal elections, he was appointed secretary of education for São Paulo.*

1968

Paris Graffiti

Be realistic, demand the impossible.

Graffiti was an ever-present backdrop to the events of May 1968 in France, which started with student strikes and occupations but eventually involved the largest general strike that had ever stopped the economy of an industrialized country, and prompted President Charles de Gaulle to flee the country.

1968

DENNIS BRUTUS

"The Guerrillas: For the Fighting Men in Southern Africa"

3

. . . a sense of lost opportunity like a squall of rain
marching away leaving an aching hollowness
while the big ants crawl over the torn flesh and the
black streaks of crusted blood.
Who will break through the barriers of indifferent
bone and stubborn flesh and the great waves of
newsprint gruel?
O my friends where are the voices to plead your cause
to roar your challenge to trumpet your heroism?
to speak the words of brave resolve that you live
and die?

4

There is such a pleasure at last in handling a cool
efficient weapon most modern, highly automatic and
moving off at the ready—
wishing they could see at home—the friends, and
especially the children, and imaging the deeds of

flame and terror—terror from this weapon, terrible
and cold.

5

Chiefly it is a job to be done, with drills to be followed
and observed, the enemy an analysable factor
or a brute so deadly that he must die first: but sometimes there comes the thought of home the angry
longing of the exile and the fierce will to smash an
evil cruel thing.

*Brutus was a South African journalist and activist who was imprisoned with
Nelson Mandela. In 1961, just a few years before this poem was published,
18,000 people were arrested for demonstrating against the Sharpeville
massacre, in which 168 blacks were killed. The anti-apartheid movement was
henceforth forced underground.*

DANIEL COHN-BENDIT AND
GABRIEL COHN-BENDIT

1968

Obsolete Communism: The Left-Wing Alternative

Reader, you have come to the end of this book, a book that wants to
say only one thing: between us we can change this rotten society.
Now, put on your coat and make for the nearest cinema. Look at their
deadly lovemaking on the screen. Isn't it better in real life? Make up
your mind to learn to love. Then, during the interval, when the first
advertisements come on, pick up your tomatoes or, if you prefer, your
eggs, and chuck them. Then get out into the street, and peel off all the
latest government proclamations until underneath you discover the
message of the last days of May and June.

Stay awhile in the street. Look at the passers-by and remind yourself: the last word has not yet been said. Then act. Act with others, not
for them. Make the revolution here and now. It is your own. *C'est
pour toi que tu fais la révolution.*

*Nicknamed "Danny the Red" both because of his political leanings and the
color of his hair, Daniel Cohn-Bendit became a well-known student activist*

and a public face of the French student movement in 1968. With Obsolete
Communism, *written with his brother Gabriel, he stirred the anger of the
French Communist Party, prompting its leader, Georges Marchais, to denounce
him as a "son of the upper bourgeoisie." Cohn-Bendit became a supporter of
the Green movement and a proponent of the European constitution and enjoyed
success in the European Parliamentary elections of 2009.*

1968 COLUMBIA STUDENT DEMONSTRATIONS

Graffiti

Up against the wall Motherfuckers!

*Discovering that their university was working with the Institute for Defense
Analyses (a think tank linked to the US Department of Defense), Columbia
University students occupied several of its buildings in the spring of 1968 in
protest. This slogan—taken from an Amiri Baraka poem, "Black People!"—
was scrawled on the wall in the mathematics building. The police ended the
demonstrations violently, resulting in 700 arrests.*

1968 VALERIE SOLANAS

"SCUM Manifesto"

The sick, irrational men, those who attempt to defend themselves
against their disgustingness, when they see SCUM barrelling down on
them, will cling in terror to Big Mama with her Big Bouncy Boobies,
but Boobies won't protect them against SCUM; Big Mama will be
clinging to Big Daddy, who will be in the corner shitting in his force-
ful, dynamic pants. Men who are rational, however, won't kick or
struggle or raise a distressing fuss, but will just sit back, relax, enjoy the
show and ride the waves to their demise.

*The "SCUM Manifesto"—SCUM being an acronym for Society for Cutting
Up Men—was a radical feminist text calling for the gendercide of men. Its
author, Solanas, later became infamous for her assassination attempt on Andy
Warhol.*

"Intellectual Freedom"

Intellectual freedom is essential to human society—freedom to obtain and distribute information, freedom for open-minded and unfearing debate, and freedom from pressure by officialdom and prejudices. Such a trinity of freedom of thought is the only guarantee against an infection of people by mass myths, which, in the hands of treacherous hypocrites and demagogues, can be transformed into bloody dictatorship. Freedom of thought is the only guarantee of the feasibility of a scientific democratic approach to politics, economics and culture.

Sakharov became a world-famous dissident with his essay "Reflections on Progress, Peaceful Coexistence, and Intellectual Freedom," which was circulated in samizdat form and published outside the Soviet Union. He became one of the founders of the Moscow Human Rights Committee and was awarded the Nobel Peace Prize in 1975. After being arrested for protesting the Soviet invasion of Afghanistan, Sakharov was sent into internal exile where he spent six years under tight surveillance. Sakharov died in 1989—just after the beginning of the USSR's dissolution.

ED SANDERS **1968**

"Predictions for Yippie Activities"

1. Poetry readings, mass meditation, flycasting exhibitions, demagogic yippie political arousal speeches, rock music, and song concerts will be held on a precise timetable throughout the week August 25–30.

. . .

8. The Yippie Ecological Conference will spew out an angry report denouncing scheiss-poison in the lakes and streams, industrial honky-fumes from white killer industrialists, and exhaust murder from a sick hamburger society of automobile freaks; with precise total assault solutions to these problems.

9. There will be public fornication whenever and wherever there is an aroused appendage and willing aperture.

10. Poets will re-write the bill of rights in precise language, detailing ten thousand areas of freedom in OUR OWN LANGUAGE, to replace the confusing and vague rhetoric of 200 years ago.

11. Reporters and media representatives will be provided free use of dope and consciousness altering thrill-chemicals for their education and refreshment.

12. Pissed off hordes of surly draft eligible poets will somehow confront conventioneers with 16 tons of donated fish eyes.

Created by Abbie Hoffman, Jerry Rubin, Sanders and others to exemplify Hoffman's dictum that "a modern revolutionary heads for the television station, not the factory," the Yippies—later, the Youth International Party—brought counterculture theatricality to the American antiwar movement and New Left. In 1968, the Yippies launched their Festival of Life at the Democratic Convention in Chicago, and nominated a pig for president—which was arrested along with human protesters. Chicago police also staged a massive police riot, and Hoffman, Tom Hayden, Dave Dellinger and others—the Chicago Eight— were tried for incitement.

1969   **WALTER RODNEY**

"The Groundings with My Brothers"

The little black girl plays with a white doll, identifying with it as she combs its flaxen hair. Asked to sketch the figure of a man or a woman, the black schoolboy instinctively produces a white man or a white woman. This is not surprising, since until recently the illustrations in our textbooks were all figures of Europeans. The few changes which have taken place have barely scratched the surface of the problem. West Indians of every color still aspire to European standards of dress and beauty. The language which is used by black people in describing ourselves shows how we despise our African appearance. "Good hair" means European hair, "good nose" means a straight nose, "good complexion" means a light complexion. Everybody recognizes how incongruous and ridiculous such terms are, but we continue to use them and to express our support of the assumption that white Europeans have the monopoly of beauty, and that black is the incarnation of ugliness. That is why Black Power advocates find it necessary to assert that BLACK IS BEAUTIFUL.

Guyanese scholar and political activist Rodney was a prominent Pan-Africanist and was important to Black Power movements in the Caribbean and North America, while writing defining works of African history, such as How Europe Underdeveloped Africa. *Rodney's activism brought him from Guyana to London and Tanzania; his agitation in Jamaica on behalf of the working poor instigated what came to be known as the Rodney Riots, leading to his being banned from the country in 1968. He was assassinated in 1980 while running for office in Guyana.*

ERICH FRIED   1969

"Revised Version"

Imagine socialism
freed of everything
That upsets you

Ask yourself
who then would be
really upset

He and no other is
and remains
your real enemy

Fried, who was regarded in the 1960s and 1970s as the greatest German poet after Brecht, briefly joined the left-wing Young Austria movement in his youth, fled his native Austria after Hitler's invasion and settled in London, where he lived for the rest of his life. This poem was dedicated to his close friend, the writer Ernst Fischer, and was written after the Soviet occupation of Czechoslovakia in August 1968.

1969

"Power Anywhere Where There's People"

We in the Black Panther Party, because of our dedication and understanding, went into the valley knowing that the people are in the valley, knowing that our plight is the same plight as the people in the valley [sic], knowing that our enemies are on the mountain, to our friends are in the valley, and even though it's nice to be on the mountaintop, we're going back to the valley. Because we understand that there's work to be done in the valley, and when we get through with this work in the valley, then we got to go to the mountaintop. We're going to the mountaintop because there's a motherfucker on the mountaintop that's playing King, and he's been bullshitting us. And we've got to go up on the mountaintop not for the purpose of living his lifestyle and living like he lives. We've got to go up on the mountaintop to make this motherfucker understand, goddamnit, that we are coming from the valley!

As a key organizer with the Chicago branch of the Black Panthers, Hampton brokered a truce among gang members in the city and organized the multiracial Rainbow Coalition of activists. He was murdered in 1969 by the Chicago Police Department, with the help of the FBI. This speech was delivered at Olivet Church earlier that year.

1969

FRANK BARDACKE

"Who Owns People's Park?"

A long time ago the Costanoan Indians lived in the area now called Berkeley . . . They believed that the land was under the care and guardianship of the people who used it and lived on it. Catholic missionaries took the land away from the Indians . . . They ripped it off in the name of God. The Mexican Government . . . drew up some papers which said they legally owned it. No Indians signed those papers. The Americans were not fooled by the papers. They had a stronger army than the Mexicans. They beat them in a war and took the land. The American Government sold the land to some white settlers. The Government gave the settlers a piece of paper called a land title in exchange for some money. All this time there were still some Indians around who claimed the land. The American Army killed most of them. The piece of paper saying who owned the land was passed around among rich white men . . . Finally some very rich men, who run the University of California, bought the land. Immediately these men destroyed the houses that had been built on the land. The land went the way of so much other land in America—it became a parking lot. We are building a park on the land. We will take care of it and guard it, in the spirit of the Costanoan Indians. When the University comes with its land title we will tell them: "Your land title is covered with blood. We won't touch it. Your people ripped off the land from the Indians a long time ago. If you want it back now, you will have to fight for it again."

Built as a community project near the University of California, Berkeley, People's Park drew the ire of Governor Ronald Reagan, and became the scene of a confrontation between students and police in May 1969, leading to numerous injuries before the park was allowed to remain open.

GAY CHEERLEADERS   1969

"Stonewall Girls"

We are the Stonewall girls
We wear our hair in curls
We have no underwear
We show our pubic hairs!

During the Stonewall Riots—a series of spontaneous demonstrations against a police raid on the Stonewall Inn, a gay bar in Greenwich Village—a group of gay cheerleaders chanted "Gay Power" along with this cheer. The riots would spark the gay rights movement, spawning the Gay Liberation Front that would lead the movement for years.

1969

CÉSAR CHÁVEZ

Letter from Delano

Our strikers here in Delano and those who represent us throughout the world are well trained for this struggle. They have been under the gun, they have been kicked and beaten and herded by dogs, they have been cursed and ridiculed, they have been stripped and chained and jailed, they have been sprayed with the poisons used in the vineyards; but they have been taught not to lie down and die nor to flee in shame, but to resist with every ounce of human endurance and spirit. To resist not with retaliation in kind but to overcome with love and compassion, with ingenuity and creativity, with hard work and longer hours, with stamina and patient tenacity, with truth and public appeal, with friends and allies, with mobility and discipline, with politics and law, and with prayer and fasting. They were not trained in a month or even a year; after all, this new harvest season will mark our fourth full year of strike and even now we continue to plan and prepare for the years to come. Time accomplishes for the poor what money does for the rich.

A migrant farmworker in California who wasn't able to attend high school, Chávez, with Dolores Huerta, formed the United Farm Workers, which brought a modicum of justice to the fields through strikes and boycotts of grapes and lettuce. The UFW's slogan "Si Se Puede" became a watchword of renewed Latino and immigrant militancy in the US.

1969

INDIANS OF ALL TRIBES

Alcatraz Proclamation

We, the Native Americans, reclaim the land known as Alcatraz Island in the name of all American Indians by right of discovery.

We wish to be fair and honorable in our dealings with the Caucasian inhabitants of this land, and hereby offer the following treaty:

We will purchase said Alcatraz Island for twenty-four dollars (24) in glass beads and red cloth, a precedent set by the white man's purchase of a similar island about 300 years ago. We will give to the inhabitants of this island a portion of the land for their own to be held in trust by the American Indian Government and by the Bureau of Caucasian Affairs to hold in perpetuity—for as long as the sun shall rise and the rivers go down to the sea. We will further guide the inhabitants in the proper way of living. We will offer them our religion, our education, our life-ways, in order to help them achieve our level of civilization and thus raise them and all their white brothers up from their savage and unhappy state.

We feel that this so-called Alcatraz Island is more than suitable for an Indian reservation, as determined by the white man's own standards. By this we mean that this place resembles most Indian reservations in that:

It is isolated from modern facilities, and without adequate means of transportation.

It has no fresh running water.

It has inadequate sanitation facilities.

There are no oil or mineral rights.

There is no industry and so unemployment is very great . . .

The population has always been held as prisoners and kept dependent upon others.

Further, it would be fitting and symbolic that ships from all over the world, entering the Golden Gate, would first see Indian land, and thus be reminded of the true history of this nation. This tiny island would be a symbol of the great lands once ruled by free and noble Indians.

From 1969–71, the Indians of All Tribes occupied Alcatraz Island, announcing their intent to establish education, ecology and cultural centers. Although none of this was achieved, the occupation was successful in bringing negative publicity to the government's Indian termination policy, which had been adopted in the 1940s and sought to assimilate American Indians into mainstream society; the policy was subsequently rescinded by Richard Nixon.

MUTIMATI BARNABÉ JOÃO

"I, the People"

I, the people
Know the strength of the earth which bursts like a bomb
of grain.
I make this strength a faithful friend.

The wind blows with strength
The water runs with strength
The fire burns with strength.

In my growing arms I'll spread out cloths of sail
To seize the wind and take its strength into production.
My hands will grow until they make a circle of oars
To seize the strength of water and put it into production.
My growing lungs will blow the forge of my heart
To seize the strength of fire in production.

I, the people
I'm going to learn to fight at Nature's side
I'm going to be comrade-in-arms to the four elements.

The colonial tactic is to abandon the People in Nature
Making the People Nature's enemy.

I, the Mozambican people,
I'm going to know all my great strengths.

Mutimati Barnabé João is one of the pseudonyms of Portuguese-born poet and painter Grabato Dias, who was also a Marxist guerrilla fighter in Mozambique against the Portuguese.

"Communiqué #1"

Freaks are revolutionaries and revolutionaries are freaks. If you want to find us, this is where we are. In every tribe, commune, dormitory, farmhouse, barracks and townhouse where kids are making love, smoking dope and loading guns—fugitives from Amerikan justice are free to go.

For Diana Oughton, Ted Gold and Terry Robbins, and for all the revolutionaries who are still on the move here, there has been no question for a long time now—we will never go back.

Within the next fourteen days we will attack a symbol or institution of Amerikan injustice. This is the way we celebrate the example of Eldridge Cleaver and H. Rap Brown and all black revolutionaries who first inspired us by their fight behind enemy lines for the liberation of their people.

Never again will they fight alone.

Taking their name from a Bob Dylan lyric—"You don't need a weatherman to know which way the wind blows"—a faction of Students for a Democratic Society staged a series of confrontations with the Chicago police in 1969 under the rubric Days of Rage. After a number of Weather people were killed working on bombs in a New York City townhouse, the remaining members, including Mark Rudd, Bernhardine Dohrn, and Bill Ayers, declared a state of war against the US government and carried out a score of bombings.

"No Vietcong Ever Called Me Nigger"

I ain't got no quarrel with them Vietcong. No Vietcong ever called me Nigger.

Ali joined the Nation of Islam at twenty-two, opposed the Vietnam War, was convicted for draft evasion and stripped of his title as heavyweight champion of the world as a result. Draft evasion reached a historic peak in the US during the Vietnam War, with over 200,000 people reported delinquent over the span of the war; with no way of prosecuting such numbers, President Carter was forced to grant amnesty to all draft offenders in 1977.

1970   RADICALESBIANS

"The Woman-identified Woman"

Lesbian is the word, the label, the condition that holds women in line. When a woman hears this word tossed her way, she knows she is stepping out of line. She knows that she has crossed the terrible boundary of her sex role. She recoils, she protests, she reshapes her actions to gain approval. Lesbian is a label invented by the man to throw at any woman who dares to be his equal, who dares to challenge his prerogatives (including that of all women as part of the exchange medium among men), who dares to assert the primacy of her own needs . . . For a lesbian is not considered a "real woman." And yet, in popular thinking, there is really only one essential difference between a lesbian and other women: that of sexual orientation—which is to say, when you strip off all the packaging, you must finally realize that the essence of being a "woman" is to get fucked by men.

Lesbian activists staged a "zap" at the Second Congress to Unite Women in New York City to protest the exclusion of lesbian speakers from the Congress and distributed copies of this ten-paragraph manifesto, written by a group that included Rita Mae Brown and Artemis March.

1970   PAT MAINARDI

"The Politics of Housework"

Liberated women—very different from women's liberation! The first signals all kinds of goodies, to warm the hearts (not to mention other parts) of the most radical men. The other signals—housework.

Pat Mainardi was a member of Redstockings, a New York–based Marxist feminist group that coined the phrase "the personal is political" and engaged in street theatre and speakouts on abortion and other subjects that were taboo at the time.

THREE MARIAS   **1971**

"Second Letter IV"

If a woman refuses to love the man who loves her (having been conditioned since the day she was born to lead her life hoping and waiting and most assuredly not fighting for the right to be strong-willed and express her wrath freely, since once these rights were secured, they would be considered as weapons being used against the man), such a woman will be accused of being ungrateful. Hence we three will be accused of being ungrateful, we will be regarded as peculiar creatures, and the courageous battles we wage will be dismissed as mere literary skirmishes, though their roots lie much deeper, the fruit of vines that have intertwined, grown, and been toughened as we have trained ourselves to be more conscious of ourselves as women, as something more than vineyards for men.

We are deflowering myths, and we have allowed ourselves to be deflowered. But let men not take us to be willing victims. Let them take possession of me if they can. Or you, if you can. Let Mariana take possession of herself by writing of herself within her cloister, thus acquiring her measure of freedom and self-realization by way of her writing; a woman who writes and boasts of being a woman even though she is a nun, flouting the law, order, uses and customs, the habit that she wears.

In 1972, the Portugese feminists known as the Three Marias—Maria Velho da Costa, Maria Isabel Barreno and Maria Teresa Horta—were arrested for their indictment of Portugal's machismo society in their book New Portugese Letters. *The nun referred to in the last sentence was Mariana Alcoforado, a Portuguese girl who in the 1600s was sent to a convent and struck up an affair with a French officer; the Three Marias used her letters to her lover,* Letters of a Portuguese Nun, *as a literary model.*

RODOLFO "CORKY" GONZALES

"I Am Joaquin"

I have come a long way to nowhere,
unwillingly dragged by that
monstrous, technical,
industrial giant called
Progress
and Anglo success . . .
in a country that has wiped out
all my history,
stifled all my pride,
in a country that has placed a
different weight of indignity upon
my
age-
old
burdened back.
Inferiority
is the new load . . .
I sometimes
sell my brother out
and reclaim him
for my own when society gives me
token leadership
in society's own name.

Gonzalez, a former boxer, founded the first Mexican-American civil rights organization, Crusade for Justice. His epic poem brought to life key figures and events in Mexican and Mexican-American history, and was reprinted in barrio newspapers throughout the southwestern US, posted on telephone poles, and eventually adapted into a play.

JOHN LENNON

1971

"Power to the People"

A million workers working for nothing
You better give 'em what they really own
We got to put you down
When we come into town
Power to the people, right on.

Lennon wrote "Power to the People" after an interview he gave to Tariq Ali and Robin Blackburn—"I just felt inspired by what they said"—but later felt embarrassed about the song's simplicity, agreeing with Hunter S. Thompson's statement that the song had been written ten years too late. Nonetheless, Lennon was one of the most successful leftist rockers, penning songs about Angela Davis, women's liberation and working-class revolution.

ANTONIO AGOSTINHO NETO

1971

"Farewell at the Hour of Parting"

My mother
(all black mothers
whose sons have gone)
you taught me to wait and hope
as you hoped in difficult hours
But life
killed in me the mystic hope
I do not wait now
I am he who is awaited
It is I my mother
hope is us
your children
gone for a faith that sustains life . . .

Tomorrow we shall sing anthems of freedom
when we commemorate
the day of the abolition of this slavery
We are going in search of light
your children mother
(all black mothers
whose sons have gone)
Go in search of life.

Neto, first president of Angola and leader of the Movement for the Liberation of Angola, wrote this poem to commemorate the tenth anniversary of the Angolan armed struggle for independence. Forced labor was abolished in 1961, the year the war began, after revolts on coffee plantations resulted in 50,000 deaths.

1971

DANIEL ELLSBERG

"Mass Murder"

For me as an American to read, in our own official secret documents, about the origins of the conflict and of our participation in it was to see our involvement—and the killing we had done and were still doing—naked of any shred of legitimacy from the beginning. That strengthened and extended backward in time the conclusion I had drawn in May, in Ohio: the immorality of our deliberately prolonging the killing by a single additional day, or bomb, or death.

. . .

If the war was unjust, as I now regarded it, that meant that every Vietnamese killed by Americans or by the proxies we had financed since 1950 had been killed by us without justification. I could think of no other word for that but murder. Mass murder.

In 1971, US military analyst Daniel Ellsberg leaked the Pentagon Papers, a top-secret document detailing US government decision-making processes during the Vietnam War. Though he was tried for espionage, it came to light during the trial that Nixon's "White House plumbers"—who would go on to orchestrate the Watergate break-in—had broken into Ellsberg's psychiatrist's office and bugged his phones; the charges against him were dismissed.

MARVIN GAYE

1971

"What's Going On"

Father, father
We don't need to escalate
You see, war is not the answer
For only love can conquer hate
You know we've got to find a way
To bring some lovin' here today.

Gaye's "What's Going On"—one of the biggest hits of his career—indirectly addressed police brutality and popular protest in America. The album on which the track is found is a song cycle chronicling a Vietnam War veteran's disillusionment upon returning home.

ALI SHARIATI

1972

"Red Shi'ism vs Black Shi'ism"

The history of Islam follows a strange path; a path in which gangsters and ruffians from the Arab, Persian, Turk, Tartar and Mongol dynasties all enjoyed the right to the leadership of the Muslim community and to the caliphate of the Prophet of Islam, to the exclusion of the family of the Prophet and the rightful Imams of Islam. And Shi'ism begins with a "No"; a "No" which opposes the path chosen by history, and rebels against history. It rebels against a history which, in the name of the Qur'an, kings and caesars, follows the path of ignorance, and in the name of tradition, sacrifices those brought up in the house of the Qur'an and the Traditions!

Shi'ites do not accept the path chosen by history. They deny the leaders who ruled the Muslims throughout history and deceived the majority of the people through their succession to the Prophet, and then by their supposed support of Islam and fight against paganism. Shi'ites turn their backs on the opulent mosques and magnificent palaces of the caliphs of Islam and turn to the lonely mud house of Fatima. Shi'ites, who represent the oppressed, justice-seeking class in the caliphate system, find in this house whatever and whoever they have been seeking . . .

The minds of the people are prepared. The hearts of the enslaved masses are throbbing for revolt under the curtain of secrecy. One spark will be sufficient . . .

Shariati, the "ideologue of the Iranian Revolution," was a sociologist, revolutionary and public intellectual who devised an Islamic political ideology to compete with Marxism in its commitment to social justice and political liberation. In this essay, Shariati contrasts Red Shi'ism, which is concerned with salvation for the masses, with the Black Shi'ism of the clerics. He was arrested numerous times for subversive political activity.

1973   VICTOR JARA

"Estadio Chile"

There are five thousand of us here
in this small part of the city.
We are five thousand.
I wonder how many we are in all
in the cities and in the whole country?
Here alone
are ten thousand hands which plant seeds
and make the factories run.
How much humanity
exposed to hunger, cold, panic, pain,
moral pressure, terror and insanity?
Six of us were lost
as if into starry space.
One dead, another beaten as I could never have believed
a human being could be beaten.
The other four wanted to end their terror—
one jumping into nothingness,
another beating his head against a wall,

but all with the fixed stare of death.
What horror the face of fascism creates!

They carry out their plans with knifelike precision.
Nothing matters to them.
To them, blood equals medals,
slaughter is an act of heroism.
Oh God, is this the world that you created,
for this your seven days of wonder and work?
. . .
The blood of our President, our compañero,
will strike with more strength than bombs and machine guns!
So will our fist strike again!
How hard it is to sing
when I must sing of horror.
Horror which I am living,
horror which I am dying.
To see myself among so much
and so many moments of infinity
in which silence and screams
are the end of my song.
What I see, I have never seen
What I have felt and what I feel
Will give birth to the moment.

The words of Jara, a poet and songwriter whose work was infused with political imagery, helped propel Salvador Allende to power. Following Pinochet's coup against Allende, Jara was tortured and killed in Chile Stadium. Before being shot, his hands were broken while soldiers asked him to play for them; he is said to have died singing "Venceremos" ("We Will Win"). This was his last poem, written in the stadium and smuggled out in a comrade's shoe.

1973

SALVADOR ALLENDE

Farewell Speech

Surely, this will be the last opportunity for me to address you. The Air Force has bombed the antennas of Radio Magallanes. My words do not have bitterness but disappointment. May they be a moral punishment for those who have betrayed their oath . . . Given these facts, the only thing left for me is to say to workers: I am not going to resign!

Placed in a historic transition, I will pay for loyalty to the people with my life. And I say to them that I am certain that the seeds which we have planted in the good conscience of thousands and thousands of Chileans will not be shriveled forever. They have force and will be able to dominate us, but social processes can be arrested by neither crime nor force. History is ours, and people make history.

Workers of my country: I want to thank you for the loyalty that you always had . . .

The people must defend themselves, but they must not sacrifice themselves. The people must not let themselves be destroyed or riddled with bullets, but they cannot be humiliated either.

Workers of my country, I have faith in Chile and its destiny. Other men will overcome this dark and bitter moment when treason seeks to prevail. Keep in mind that, much sooner than later, great avenues will again be opened, through which will pass the free man, to construct a better society.

Long live Chile! Long live the people! Long live the workers!

Allende, the socialist president of Chile, gave this speech on live radio, with gunfire and explosions audible in the background, following the US-backed coup d'état against him led by General Augusto Pinochet. He died moments later.

CARLOS FONSECA # 1973

Havana Speech

Those of us who propose to wage a struggle to liberate our country and make freedom a reality must rescue our own traditions and put together the facts and figures we need in order to wage an ideological war against our enemy. This ideological war has to go step by step with the war we carry out arms in hand. I would even say that, to the same extent that we are able to use our rifles effectively, we will also be able to revive our people's historical traditions, and to the same extent that we master our popular traditions, we will also be able to find ourselves able to use our rifles successfully.

Fonseca was a student of Augusto César Sandino and the founder of the Sandinista National Liberation Front (FSLN). He was killed by the Nicaraguan National Guard in 1976. Upon hearing of Fonseca's death, Nicaragua's dictator, Anastasio Somoza Debayle, is said to have cried, "Say it again! Say it again!" Three years later, the FSLN overthrew Somoza.

SAMORA MACHEL # 1973

"The Emancipation of Women"

The emancipation of women is not an act of charity, the result of a humanitarian or compassionate attitude. The liberation of women is a fundamental necessity for the Revolution, the guarantee of its continuity and the precondition for its victory. The main objective of the Revolution is to destroy the system of exploitation and build a new society which releases the potentialities of human beings, reconciling them with labor and with nature. This is the context within which the question of women's emancipation arises.

After joining the Front for the Liberation of Mozambique (FRELIMO) and commanding its troops in the war against Portuguese colonial rule, Machel, a committed Marxist with the support of the peasantry, became the first President

1973   BESSIE HEAD

A Question of Power

As she fell asleep, she placed one soft hand over her land. It was a gesture of belonging.

Head, one of Africa's most celebrated female writers, was born to a black father and white mother in apartheid South Africa, dabbled in Pan-Africanism in her youth, and created characters who struggle with their racial identity and sexual roles. In this line from her third novel, she conveys a sense of hope won through struggle.

1974   GIL SCOTT-HERON

"The Revolution Will Not Be Televised"

There will be no pictures of pigs shooting down
brothers in the instant replay.
There will be no pictures of Whitney Young being
run out of Harlem on a rail with a brand new process.
There will be no slow motion or still life of Roy
Wilkins strolling through Watts in a Red, Black and
Green liberation jumpsuit that he had been saving
For just the proper occasion.

Green Acres, The Beverly Hillbillies, and Hooterville
Junction will no longer be so damned relevant, and
women will not care if Dick finally gets down with
Jane on Search for Tomorrow because Black people
will be in the street looking for a brighter day.
The revolution will not be televised.

In this song, American musician Scott-Heron, who has written songs about the danger of nuclear power and apartheid in South Africa among many other subjects, also references Richard Nixon, Spiro Agnew, Attorney General John Mitchell, and Creigton Abrams, the general who led the US incursion into Cambodia during the Vietnam War. This was the B-side to a record whose A-side was "Home Is Where the Hatred Is."

URSULA LE GUIN   **1974**

The Dispossessed

You cannot buy the Revolution. You cannot make the Revolution. You can only be the Revolution. It is in your spirit, or it is nowhere.

An American writer of science fiction and fantasy for both adult and young adult audiences, Le Guin often explores the sociology and anthropology of human coexistence in her work. The Dispossessed, her most famous work, describes a fictional society on the planet Urras that is free of government or coercive institutions; it has become an anarchist classic since its publication.

CARLOS MEJÍA GODOY   **1975**

"Peasants' Mass"

I believe in you, comrade,
Christ man, Christ worker,
victor over death.
With your great sacrifice
you made new people
for liberation.
You are risen
in every arm outstretched
to defend the people
against the exploitation of rulers;
you are alive and present in the hut,
in the factory, in the school.

I believe in your ceaseless struggle,
I believe in your resurrection.

Godoy, a Nicaraguan folk singer allied with the Sandinistas, began his career performing on a popular radio show that ridiculed politicians through humorous songs. "Peasants' Mass" was banned within days of its composition; its first performance was broken up by the National Guard.

1975

PETER SINGER

Animal Liberation

Animal liberation will require greater altruism on the part of human beings than any other liberation movement. The animals themselves are incapable of demanding their own liberation, or of protesting against their condition with votes, demonstrations, or boycotts. Human beings have the power to continue to oppress other species forever, or until we make this planet unsuitable for living beings. Will our tyranny continue, proving that morality counts for nothing when it clashes with self-interest, as the most cynical of poets and philosophers have always said? Or will we rise to the challenge and prove our capacity for genuine altruism by ending our ruthless exploitation of other species in our power, not because we are forced to do so by rebels or terrorists, but because we recognize that our position is morally indefensible?

The way in which we answer this question depends on the way in which each one of us, individually, answers it.

Australian philosopher Singer's book popularized the term "speciesism" and became the founding philosophical statement of the animal liberation movement.

1976

BEI DAO

"The Answer"

Debasement is the password of the base,
Nobility the epitaph of the noble.

See how the gilded sky is covered
With the drifting twisted shadows of the dead.

The Ice Age is over now,
Why is there ice everywhere?
The Cape of Good Hope has been discovered,
Why do a thousand sails contest the Dead Sea?

I came into this world
Bringing only paper, rope, a shadow,
To proclaim before the judgment
The voice that has been judged:

Let me tell you, world,
I—do—not—believe!
If a thousand challengers lie beneath your feet,
Count me as number thousand and one.

Written during the 1976 Tiananmen demonstrations, "The Answer" was adopted as an anthem of the pro-democracy movement and appeared on many posters during the 1989 protests. Bei Dao, a renowned Chinese poet, was sent into exile not long after.

NGUGI WA THIONG'O AND NGUGI WA MIRII 1976

I Will Marry when I Want

It was soon after this
That the colonial government
Forbade the people to sing or dance,
It forbade a gathering of more than five.
But we went on meeting clandestinely.
We the workers in factories and plantations said in one voice:
We reject slave wages!
Do you remember the 1948 general strike?

Leftist Kenyan writer and playwright Ngugi wa Thiong'o was arrested for the blatant political message contained in his play I Will Marry When I Want, *which portrayed the hardships of workers and peasants under the capitalist, neo-colonial regime. Having been developed with Kikuyu villagers, it was first performed in open air with local workers and peasants playing all its roles. While in jail, he wrote his novel* Devil on the Cross *on a roll of toilet paper.*

1977

CZECH ACTIVISTS
Charter 77

Responsibility for the observance of civil rights in the country naturally falls, in the first place, on the political and state power. But not on it alone. Each and every one of us has a share of responsibility for the general situation and thus, too, for the observance of the pacts which have been enacted and are binding not only for the government but for all citizens . . .

We believe that Charter 77 will contribute towards all citizens in Czechoslovakia working and living as free people.

Initially signed by 242 individuals including Václav Havel, Charter 77 grew out of opposition to the violent suppression of the Prague Spring of 1968 by the Soviet regime—euphemistically referred to as "normalization." The Charter, which criticized the government for its human rights record, was itself violently suppressed. This text is taken from the first draft of the Charter.

1977

FELA KUTI
"Zombie"

Zombie no go go, unless you tell am to go
Zombie no go stop, unless you tell am to stop
Zombie no go turn, unless you tell am to turn
Zombie no go think, unless you tell am to think

Tell am to go straight—Joro, Jara, Joro
No break, no job, no sense—Joro, Jara, Joro
Tell am to go kill—Joro, Jara, Joro
No break, no job, no sense—Joro, Jara, Joro
Tell am to go quench—Joro, Jara, Joro

No break, no job, no sense—Joro, Jara, Joro

Go and kill
Go and die
Go and quench
Put am for reverse.

Fela was the father of Afrobeat, founder of the political party Movement of the People and a frequent target of attacks by the Nigerian government; "Zombie" describes the army and police. Fela caused riots when he performed it in Accra, Ghana, in 1978, and was subsequently barred from entering the country. A year later, he campaigned for president but was denied.

SAIDA MENEBHI   1977

"Untitled"

The prison is ugly
you draw it my child
with black marks
for the bars and grills
You imagine that it's a place without lights
that scares little ones
also, to show it
you say that it's over there
and you gesture with your little finger
to a point, a lost place
that you don't see.
Maybe the teacher talked to you about it
the hideous prison
the correctional facility
where mean people are put
who steal children.
In your little head you asked the question
how and why
me, who was full of love for you
and all other children

Am I over there
Because tomorrow I want
the prison to no longer be there.

Menebhi was a Moroccan political prisoner under Hassan II's repressive regime; she was tortured and died in prison in 1977 from complications related to a hunger strike. Her poetry has been central in the nationwide attempt to recover the history of the thousands of people who were "disappeared" in the 1970s and 1980s. "Untitled" was written from prison just months before she died.

1977 JULIUS KAMBARAGE NYERERE

"*Ujamaa*, the Basis of African Socialism"

African socialism . . . did not start from the existence of conflicting "classes" in society. Indeed I doubt if the equivalent for the word "class" exists in any indigenous African language; for language describes the ideas of those who speak it, and the idea of "class" or "caste" was nonexistent in African society . . .

We, in Africa, have no more need of being "converted" to socialism than we have of being "taught" democracy. Both are rooted in our own past—in the traditional society which produced us. Modern African socialism can draw from its traditional heritage the recognition of "society" as an extension of the basic family unit. But it can no longer confine the idea of the social family within the limits of the tribe, nor, indeed, of the nation. For no true African socialist can look at a line drawn on a map and say, "The people on this side of that line are my brothers, but those who happen to live on the other side of it can have no claim on me." Every individual on this continent is his brother.

Socialist, democrat and nationalist Julius Nyerere fought to free East Africa from British rule, becoming Tanzania's first president after independence. This essay articulates the concept of ujamaa, *or "familyhood," a socialist political vision drawing on communal African traditions.*

"People Can Cry Much Easier Than They Can Change"

It's no credit to this enormously rich country that there are more oppressive, less decent governments elsewhere. We claim superiority of our institutions. We ought to live up to our own standards, not use misery elsewhere as an endless source of self-gratification and justification. Of course, people tell me all the time in the West that they are trying, they are trying hard. Some have tears in their eyes and let me know how awful they feel about the way our poor live, our blacks, or those in dozens of other countries. People can cry much easier than they can change, a rule of psychology people like me picked up as kids on the street.

Baldwin barnstormed for the civil rights movement across the southern US and published his famous essays on race in America—later collected as The Fire Next Time—*in 1963. But he soon returned to self-imposed exile in France, where he had moved at the age of twenty-four. He returned to the US permanently in 1977, but remained a critic.*

"Open Letter to the Military Junta"

Fifteen thousand people missing without a trace (*desaparecidos*), 10,000 prisoners, 4,000 dead, and tens of thousands of exiles are the statistical bones of this terror.

. . . Many of them are trade unionists, intellectuals, relatives of known guerrillas, unarmed political dissidents, or simply suspicious in the eyes of those who detained them. They are the victims of a doctrine of collective guilt, which long ago disappeared from the norms of justice in any civilized community. They are utterly incapable of influencing the political developments which give rise to the events for which they are murdered. They are killed to balance the number of dead on either side, in accordance with the body count principle first employed by the Nazi Germans in occupied countries in Europe, and afterwards refined by the American invaders in Vietnam.

... These are the thoughts which I wished to share with the members of the Junta on this first anniversary of your disreputable government, without hope of being listened to, in the certainty of persecution, but faithful to the commitment I made a long time ago to bear witness in difficult times.

Walsh was an Argentine investigative journalist and a founder of the Prensa Latina news agency. The day after he published this letter in March 1977, he was abducted and murdered by a group of soldiers.

1978   SUBHAS MUKHOPADHYAY

"For a Poem"

A poem is being written for him.
A poem will be written. For that
Who are those who fasten on the walls
The manifesto of an unborn day?
Leaving the fear of death on the hangman's noose,
He marches forward,
The air and the sky resound
In his booming voice,
On his fingertips is drawn
The face of the new earth, its endless happiness and love
A poem is being written for him.

Bengali poet Mukhopadhyay was also a novelist, essayist, travel writer, and journalist, and edited a children's periodical with the filmmaker Satyajit Ray. A political activist and a member of the Communist Party for many decades, he was briefly a political prisoner in the 1960s. This poem is his tribute to the immortal rebel.

Let Me Speak!

[The] miner is doubly exploited, no? Because, with such a small wage, the woman has to do much more in the home. And really that's unpaid work that we're doing for the boss, isn't it? . . .

In my case, for example, my husband works, I work, I make my children work, so there are several of us working to support the family. And the bosses get richer and richer and the workers' conditions get worse and worse.

But in spite of everything we do, there's still the idea that women don't work, because they don't contribute economically to the home, that only the husband works because he gets a wage. We've often come across that difficulty.

One day I got the idea of making a chart. We put as an example the price of washing clothes per dozen pieces and we figured out how many dozens of times we washed a month. Then the cook's wage, the babysitter's, the servant's. We figured out everything that we miners' wives do every day. Adding it all up, the wage needed to pay us for what we do in the home, compared to the wages of a cook, a washer-woman, a babysitter, a servant, was much higher than what the men earned in the mine for a month. So that way we made our compañeros understand that we really work, and even more than they do in a certain sense. And that we contribute more to the household with what we save. So, even though the state doesn't recognize what we do in the home, the country benefits from it, because we don't receive a single penny for this work

And as long as we continue in the present system, things will always be like this. That's why I think it's so important for us revolutionaries to win that first battle in the home. And the first battle to be won is to let the woman, the man, the children participate in the struggle of the working class, so that the home can become a stronghold that the enemy can't overcome. Because if you have the enemy inside your own house, then it's just one more weapon that our common enemy can use toward a dangerous end. That's why it's really necessary that we have very clear ideas about the whole situation and that we throw out forever that bourgeois idea that the woman should stay home and not get involved in other things, in union or political matters, for example. Because, even if she's at home, she's part of the whole system of exploitation that her compañero lives in anyway, working in the mine or in the factory or wherever—isn't that true?

The wife of a miner and mother of seven children, Barrios de Chungara rose to prominence as an activist with the militant Bolivian labor group Housewives' Committee. She fought for the liberation of women, which she viewed as inseparable from socioeconomic, political, and cultural liberation.

1978

OSCAR ROMERO

"We Are Your People"

We are your people. The peasants you kill are your own brothers and sisters. When you hear the voice of the man commanding you to kill, remember instead the voice of God. Thou Shalt Not Kill . . . In the name of God, in the name of our tormented people whose cries rise up to heaven, I beseech you, I beg you, I command you, stop the repression.

Romero, the archbishop of San Salvador, spoke these words a day before he was assassinated while celebrating Mass. Romero, once a conservative, had spoken out against the social injustice and violence that prevailed in El Salvador. The orders to kill were given by Roberto D'Aubuisson, organizer of death squads— and later, president of El Salvador's Constituent Assembly—who was trained at the School of the Americas in the United States.

1978

WEI JINGSHENG

"The Fifth Modernization"

In ancient China, there were such maxims as "A cake in the picture can appease hunger" and "Watching the plums can quench the thirst."

... For several decades, Chinese people have closely followed the Great Helmsman. Communist ideology has provided "the cake in the picture," and the Great Leap Forward and Three Red Banners have served as "plums for quenching thirst." People tightened their belts and bravely forged ahead. Thirty years soon passed and they have learned a lesson from experience. For thirty years people were like "monkeys reaching out for the moon and feeling only emptiness." ...

Someone has now given you a way out. Take the Four Modernizations as the key link and follow the principle of stability and unity and be brave, to serve the revolution, as an old ox does. Then you will find your way to paradise, namely the prosperity of communism and the Four Modernizations ...

I advise everyone not to believe such political swindlers anymore. Knowing that we are being deceived, we should implicitly believe in ourselves. We have been tempered in the Cultural Revolution and cannot be that ignorant now. Let us find out for ourselves what should be done.

During the Beijing Spring of 1978–9 (a period of political liberalization named to evoke the Prague Spring), many activists and intellectuals posted political critiques on a brick wall in the Xidan district of Beijing, which came to be known as the Democracy Wall. This manifesto was one such posting, targeting the top leaders of the Communist Party. Wei was imprisoned for fifteen years as a result. The "Four Modernizations" were a set of reforms designed to make China an economic powerhouse; they signify modernization in agriculture, industry, national defense, and science and technology.

YOLANDA LOPEZ   1978
Poster

Who's the illegal alien, PILGRIM?

Lopez, a Mexican-American painter, educator and film producer whose work challenges ethnic stereotypes, is most well known for this political poster of an angry youth wearing an Aztec headdress and holding a crumpled piece of paper labeled "Immigration Plans."

1978 MICHELE WALLACE

Black Macho and the Myth of the Superwoman

The white man had offered white women privilege and prestige as accompaniments to his power. Black women were offered no such deal, just the same old hard labor, a new silence, and more loneliness. The patriarchal black macho of Malcolm X might have proven functional—black women might have suffered their oppression for years in comparative bliss—but black men were blinded by their resentment of black women, their envy of white men, and their irresistible urge to bring white women down a peg. With patriarchal macho it would have taken black men years to avenge themselves. With the narcissistic macho of the Black Movement, the results were immediate.

And when the black man went as far as the adoration of his own genitals could carry him, his revolution stopped. A big Afro, a rifle, and a penis in good working order were not enough to lick the white man's world after all.

Published when Wallace was only twenty-seven, Black Macho *quickly found a wide audience—and much controversy—for its argument that black male revolutionaries asserted their manhood by pushing black women into domestic and submissive roles, and for its skewering of the US Labor Department* Moynihan Report, *which blamed "aggressive" black women for the disintegration of black families and communities.*

1978 AUDRE LORDE

"A Litany for Survival"

For those of us
who were imprinted with fear
like a faint line in the center of our foreheads
learning to be afraid with our mother's milk

for by this weapon
this illusion of some safety to be found
the heavy-footed hoped to silence us.
For all of us
this instant and this triumph
We were never meant to survive.

Black lesbian poet Lorde was a member of the American communist youth group the Labor Youth League in the 1950s and an activist in the civil rights, feminist and anti-war movements.

STEVE BIKO — 1978

"The Quest for a True Humanity"

Black Consciousness is an attitude of the mind and a way of life, the most positive call to emanate from the black world for a long time. Its essence is the realization by the black man of the need to rally together with his brothers around the cause of their oppression—the blackness of their skin—and to operate as a group to rid themselves of the shackles that bind them to perpetual servitude.

Biko, the South African anti-apartheid activist and founder of the Black Consciousness Movement, coined the phrase "black is beautiful." He died in police custody in 1977.

EDWARD SAID — 1978

Orientalism

Orientalism is not only a positive doctrine about the Orient that exists at any one time; in the West it is also an influential academic tradition ... as well as an area of concern defined by travelers, commercial enterprises, governments, military expeditions, readers of novels and accounts of exotic adventure, natural historians, and pilgrims to whom the Orient is a specific kind of knowledge about specific places, peoples, and civilizations. For the Orient idioms became frequent, and these idioms took firm hold in European discourse. Beneath the idioms there was a layer of doctrine about the Orient; this doctrine was fashioned out of the experiences of many Europeans, all of them converging upon such essential aspects of the Orient as the Oriental character, Oriental despotism, Oriental sensuality, and the like. For any European during the 1800s—and I think one can say this almost without qualification—Orientalism was such a system of truths, truths in Nietzsche's sense of the word. It is therefore correct that every European, in what he could say about the Orient, was consequently a racist, an imperialist, and almost totally ethnocentric . . .

The Palestinian-American literary and cultural critic Said was a member of the Palestine National Council and an outspoken critic of US foreign policy. He was the author of dozens of books, lectures, and essays, and via Orientalism *and other books, he spurred the development of postcolonial studies and other fields.*

1979

LING BING ("ICICLE")

"For You"

My friend,
Parting time is pending.
Farewell—Democracy Wall.
What can I briefly say to you?
Should I speak of spring's frigidity?
Should I say that you are like the withered wintersweet?

No, I ought instead to talk of happiness,
Tomorrow's happiness,
Of pure orchid skies,
Of golden wild flowers,
Of a child's bright eyes.
In sum, we ought
To part with dignity,
Don't you agree?

On April 1, 1979, the Communist Party banned the hanging of wall posters in public spaces as part of its crackdown on the democracy movement. After the ban was announced, a young man approached the Democracy Wall and posted this poem—now a forbidden act—then promptly walked away without saying a word.

ANONYMOUS   1980s
Joke

What is socialism?
—The painful transition from capitalism to capitalism.

This was one of a large collection of jokes, collected in the winter and spring of 1991 by students at the Vysoka škola strojni a elektroteknicka (VŠSE) v Plzni, now the University of West Bohemia, Plzen, Czech Republic.

CONGREGATION FOR THE
DEMOCRATIZATION OF CHONNAM PROVINCE   1980
"Song We Sang All Together"

The day when the pepper fog and tear gas stopped.
People came from the Mujin plain.
All democratic citizens: intellectuals, laborers, farmers.

People gathered in front of the fountain of the provincial capital.
People tried to touch the fountain.
Sitting on the lawn, hugging each other
Exchanging smiles with each other

There is no song as beautiful as this,
The song we sang all together.

For ten days in May 1980, the citizens of Kwangju, South Korea, took control of the city, making demands for democratization, an end to martial law and an increase in the minimum wage. Citizens passed out meals and voluntarily cleaned the streets as they waited for the counterattack. This poem was written two days before the Kwangju Uprising broke out, at the site where rallies had been occurring and which the protesters renamed Democracy Square.

1981

ANDREA DWORKIN

Pornography: Men Possessing Women

The boys are betting on our compliance, our ignorance, our fear. We have always refused to face the worst that men have done to us. The boys count on it. The boys are betting that we cannot face the horror of their sexual system and survive. The boys are betting that their depictions of us as whores will beat us down and stop our hearts. The boys are betting that their penises and fists and knives and fucks and rapes will turn us into what they say we are—the compliant women of sex, the voracious cunts of pornography, the masochistic sluts who resist because we really want more. The boys are betting. The boys are wrong.

Dworkin was an antiwar activist and anarchist in the late 1960s. In the 1970s and 1980s, she wrote ten books of radical feminist analysis.

1980s

ALFREDO NAVARRO SALANGA

"5 February [1899]"

Find no
symbol in
the capture
of the reservoir:
water can
do no sculpting.

The laws
of physics
tell us
that water
takes the shape
of its
every container.

The North
Americans have
captured nothing
but a vessel
of water,
nothing that
our sun
will find difficult
to empty with its rage.

On February 4, 1899, American forces opened fire at San Juan del Monte in Manila and captured the reservoir, setting into motion what would become known as the Battle of Manila and eventually the Philippine-American War. Salanga's work has often dealt with martial law under the Marcos regime.

MAURICE BISHOP   1981

"Fraternal Love"

This is the true meaning of revolutionary democracy. It is a growth in the confidence in the power of ordinary people to transform their country, and thus transform themselves. It is the growth in the appreciation of people organizing, deciding, creating together. It is a growth of fraternal love.

Bishop was the inspirational leader of the Grenada Revolution of 1979, the first armed socialist revolution to occur in a predominantly black state outside of Africa. Bishop's New Jewel Movement overthrew the government and Bishop became prime minister; just four years later, a faction of the NJM staged a coup, executing Bishop and other cabinet members. One week later the US followed by invading Grenada and ending the revolution.

1982

SANRIZUKA-SHIBAYAMA FARMERS' LEAGUE AGAINST THE NEW TOKYO INTERNATIONAL AIRPORT

Statement

The whole world faces now a great crisis of imminent war—nuclear war; the human being is thus threatened with holocaust and total annihilation. An urgent demand for peace expressed in antiwar, anti-nuclear protest is becoming more and more common not only among the Japanese people but also among people all over the world.

We, members of the opposition league and those who are rallying around it, have been fighting for seventeen years against the construction of Sanrizuka military airport under the banner of "Stop war! Fight for peace!"—in diametrical, violent confrontation with state power.

Now that antiwar, antinuclear struggle is gaining momentum anew, we feel it our duty, as ones fighting in Sanrizuka—a fortress of people's struggle of the whole of Japan—to fill responsible positions in this struggle.

In the late 1960s, student activists, left-wing parties and residents of Sanrizuka and Shibayama villages in Japan, not far from where a new international airport was slated to be built, began protesting against the plan and all that it represented. For twenty years, the movement made popular appeals, filed lawsuits and utilized guerrilla warfare and direct action tactics to hinder its construction. This statement was read at a mass rally five years after the airport had opened, yet it would be another three years before the last anti-airport riot finally ended.

1983

ERNESTO CARDENAL

"Salmo 43"

The people will enjoy themselves in the exclusive clubs
they will take possession of the private enterprises
the just man shall be joyful before the Popular Tribunals

We shall celebrate in the great squares the anniversary of the Revolution
The God that does exist is the god of the workers.

*A Liberation Theology priest and poet aligned with the Sandinistas, becoming
the country's first minister of culture after the revolution in 1979, Cardenal
was once publicly admonished by the pope for his political work. Psalm
("Salmo") 43 of the Bible is a plea to God for vindication and rescue "from
deceitful and wicked men."*

GREAT MINERS' STRIKE 1984–85

Picket-line slogan

I'd rather be a picket than a scab.

*The miners' strike, the decisive British class struggle of the Thatcher era, was
the longest mass strike in history. The police had their own chant—"Arthur
Scargill pays our mortgage"—a reference to the leader of the National Union of
Miners and the overtime pay that police officers received for battling miners.*

RIGOBERTA MENCHÚ 1984

I, Rigoberta Menchú

[My cause] wasn't born out of something good, it was born out of
wretchedness and bitterness. It has been radicalized by the poverty in
which my people live. It has been radicalized by the malnutrition
which I, as an Indian, have seen and experienced. And by the exploitation and discrimination that I've felt in the flesh. And by the oppression
which prevents us from performing our ceremonies, and shows no
respect for our way of life, the way we are. At the same time, they've
killed the people dearest to me, and here I include my neighbors from
my village among my loved ones. Therefore, my commitment to our
struggle knows no boundaries nor limits. This is why I've traveled to
many places where I've had the opportunity to talk about my people.
Of course, I'd need a lot of time to tell you all about my people,
because it's not easy to understand just like that.

And I think I've given some idea of that in my account. Neverthe-less, I'm still keeping my Indian identity a secret. I'm still keeping secret what I think no-one should know. Not even anthropologists or intellectuals, no matter how many books they have, can find out all our secrets.

Menchú's memoir, about her life as an indigenous Guatemalan who lived through the Guatemalan Civil War, drew global attention to the massacres carried out by the Guatemalan armed forces. 200,000 people were killed and 40,000 to 50,000 "disappeared" during the thirty-six-year war. In 1992 Menchú was awarded the Nobel Peace Prize. Greg Grandin's Who Is Rigoberta Menchú? *addresses the controversy surrounding some aspects of her account.*

1984

PARK NO-HAE

"Maybe"

Maybe
Maybe I'm a machine
Absorbed in soldering subassemblies
Swarming down the conveyor,
Like a robot repeating,
The same motions forever,
Maybe I've become a machine . . .
Those gentle smiles,
That refined beauty and culture,
That rich and dazzling opulence,
Maybe all of that is ours.

Korean poet Park, whose poems were often recited within the democracy move-ment of the 1980s and 1990s, was also a leading figure in the Socialist Workers' League. In 1991 he was arrested, beaten and sentenced to death for "violating the National Security Law" through his labor organizing activities. His sentence was commuted to a life sentence, and he was quickly released.

DAVE FOREMAN **1985**

"Strategic Monkeywrenching"

John Muir said that if it ever came to a war between the races, he would side with the bears. That day has arrived.

Foreman, American environmentalist, founded the activist group Earth First!, whose motto is "No Compromise in the Defense of Mother Earth!" Foreman called for "monkeywrenching"—the sabotage of machinery that damages the earth.

THOMAS SANKARA **1985**

"I Want to Be One of Those Madmen"

I would like to leave behind me the conviction that if we maintain a certain amount of caution and organization we deserve victory . . . You cannot carry out fundamental change without a certain amount of madness. In this case, it comes from nonconformity, the courage to turn your back on the old formulas, the courage to invent the future. It took the madmen of yesterday for us to be able to act with extreme clarity today. I want to be one of those madmen. We must dare to invent the future.

Sankara was the Marxist-Leninist leader of the Burkinabé Revolution, which nationalized mineral wealth and redistributed land. The revolution built earth dams and public houses; began literacy and immunization programs; and fought the oppression of women by promoting contraception and condemning polygamy. He was assassinated in 1987, just four years after taking power, by an alliance that included Liberian warlord Charles Taylor and Blaise Compaoré, who has ruled Burkina Faso ever since.

1986

ANONYMOUS

Shanghai Posters

"When will the people be in charge?"
"If you want to know what freedom is, just go and ask Wei Jingsheng."
"To hell with Marxism–Leninism–Mao Zedong Thought."

On December 20, 1986, more than 30,000 students marched through Shanghai, a sign that the democracy movement was growing. These slogans are just some of those that were scrawled on the city's walls. See p. 268 for Wei Jingsheng.

1986

WIJI THUKUL

"Warning"

If the people leave
while the rulers deliver their speeches
we must be careful
perhaps they have lost hope
If the people hide
and whisper
when talking over their own problems
rulers should be aware and learn to listen
If the people don't dare complain
then the situation is dangerous
and if what the rulers' chatter
may not be rebutted
truth is surely menaced
When proposals are rejected without consideration,
voices silenced, criticisms forbidden without reason,
accused of subversion and of disturbing security
then there are only two words: fight back!

Wiji Thukul was an Indonesian poet, trishaw driver, carpenter and labor activist who disappeared in 1998—likely kidnapped and murdered by government forces for participating in anti-government protests. "Warning" was extremely popular in the Suharto years, its last line becoming a slogan for the anti-Suharto movement.

EDUARDO GALEANO   **1986**

Memory of Fire

With a few shots from their guns the English bring down the flag that waves over the fortress and seize the island of Manhattan from the Dutch, who had bought it from the Delaware Indians for sixty florins.

Recalling the arrival of the Dutch over half a century ago, the Delawares say:

"The great man wanted only a little, little land, on which to raise greens for his soup, just as much as a bullock's hide would cover. Here we first might have observed their deceitful spirit."

New Amsterdam, the most important slave market in North America, now becomes New York; and Wall Street is named after the wall built to stop blacks from escaping.

Galeano was imprisoned after a 1973 military coup in his native Uruguay. He fled to Argentina, then had to flee again after his name was added to death squad lists following that country's 1976 military coup. He wrote his classic Memory of Fire, *a history of the Americas, while in exile. He wanted, as he put it, "to rescue the kidnapped memory of all America, but above all of Latin America, that despised and beloved land," from the military dictators, their masters in Washington and their lackeys at home.*

1987

Logo

Silence = Death

In 1987, six gay activists in New York created a graphic of a pink triangle accompanied by this slogan, to protest the inaction of the Reagan administration in the face of the AIDS epidemic, which was then mainly killing gay men (an upside-down pink triangle was used to mark gays in Nazi concentration camps). The activists soon joined the AIDS Coalition to Unleash Power, which adopted the logo, and would go on to stage raucous protests at government offices, media outlets, Wall Street, and elsewhere.

1988

DAISY ZAMORA

"Let Me Talk about My Women"

This whole land knows their names by heart:
El Chipote, La Chispa, the cave at Tunagualan
remember their names and sometimes entrust them to the
wind . . .

Who could forget any of our women.
Without them, the war would have been impossible,
my army's invisible column;
they have spread love between ambushes
and extended their love to the boys.

No single book would suffice to recount their deeds
nor would all the stars in this Segovian sky suffice
for comparison,
but the wind of this earth knows their names, echoes
their names,
speaks their names, while it plays the pine groves as if
strumming a deep dark guitar.

Nicaraguan poet, editor, translator, and teacher Zamora was a member of the Sandinista National Liberation Front, participated in an armed assault on the National Palace, and became the voice of Radio Sandino as well as vice minister of culture in the new Sandinista government.

MAHMOUD DARWISH
1988

"Those Who Pass Between Fleeting Words"

O those who pass between fleeting words
From you the sword—from us the blood
From you steel and fire—from us our flesh
From you yet another tank—from us stones,
From you tear gas—from us rain
Above us, as above you, are sky and air
So take your share of our blood—and be gone
Go to a dancing party—and be gone
As for us, we have to water the martyrs' flowers
As for us, we have to live as we see fit.

O those who pass between fleeting words
Pile your illusions in a deserted pit, and be gone
Return the hand of time to the law of the golden calf
Or to the time of the revolver's music!
For we have that which does not please you here, so be gone
And we have what you lack
A bleeding homeland of a bleeding people
A homeland fit for oblivion or memory.

The poems of Darwish, Palestine's national poet, speak of dispossession, exile and the loss of homeland in terms of the fall from Eden. Shortly after its publication, "Those Who Pass Between Fleeting Words" was denounced in the Knesset for demanding that Jews leave Israel; in fact, Darwish was writing of the West Bank and Gaza, and commentators have claimed that his accusers simply misinterpreted the poem. Darwish joined the Palestine Liberation Organization in 1973 and has become a symbol of Arab resistance against Israel.

1989

E. M. S. NAMBOODIRIPAD

History, Society, and Land Relations

The dark age of all-round backwardness has slowly been coming to an end; hard knocks have already been given to the socio-political forces which kept the mass of toilers under subjection; the alien rulers who did this job of destroying the old have been forced to quit India; democratic forces have been rising as a united army fighting for freedom; India's freedom movement came to be linked with the forces of the international revolution for peace, freedom, democracy, and socialism.

Marxist theoretician and politician Namboodiripad was the head of the socialist wing of the Indian Independence Movement. In Kerala state in 1957, he became the first democratically elected communist minister in the world.

1989

HOU DEJIAN

"Heirs of the Dragon"

In the far-off East flows a river called the Yangtze.
In the far-off East flows the Yellow River, too.
I've never seen the beauty of the Yangtze
though often have I sailed it in my dreams.
And while I've never heard the roar of the Yellow River,
It pounds against its shores in my dreams.

In the ancient East there is a dragon;
China is its name.
In the ancient East there lives a people,
The dragon's heirs every one.
Under the claws of this mighty dragon I grew up
And its heir I have become.
Like it or not—
Once and forever, an heir of the dragon.

It was a hundred years ago on a quiet night,
the deep dark night before the great changes,
A quiet night shattered by gunfire,
Enemies on all sides, the sword of the dictator.
For how many years did those gunshots resound?
So many years and so many years more.
Mighty dragon, open your eyes
For ever and ever, open your eyes.

A runaway pop hit in Hong Kong and Taiwan when it was first released in the 1980s, "Heirs of the Dragon" was later adopted by the Tiananmen protesters, who were singing it as the square was being surrounded on June 4. The Taiwan-born Hou defected to China in 1983 and was one of the leading activists at Tiananmen. He was one of the last remaining hunger strikers in early June.

ADAM MICHNIK   **1989**

Interview with *UNESCO Courier*

For my generation, the road to freedom began in 1968. While students in Paris and Berkeley were rejecting bourgeois democracy, we in Prague or Warsaw were fighting for a freedom that only the bourgeois order could guarantee. In appearance, everything divided us.

But something brought us together: the need to rebel stemming from the conviction that, as long as the world is the way it is, it's worth not dying a peaceful death in your bed. Here, we were the first generation able to build projects for the future and those projects were not groundless, as subsequent events showed. The situation did change after a few years. Many factors came into play at the same time. Poland was going through a deep economic crisis. The changes taking place in the Soviet Union also had an impact. Lastly, the communist nomenklatura itself was evolving, becoming more pragmatic. It was the end of the utopian dream, and it enabled us to dismantle the dictatorship by negotiation.

The Polish activist Michnik was jailed following student protests in 1968, worked with the opposition group Workers' Defence Committee, edited illegal underground newspapers through the 1980s, and advised the union federation Solidarity, which organized a series of strikes in 1988 that brought Poland to a standstill and helped precipitate the fall of the Polish communist regime. The collapse of socialist states throughout Eastern Europe would follow not long after. In this 2001 interview, Michnik reflects on the strikes.

1989

PUBLIC ENEMY

"Fight the Power"

Most of my heroes don't appear on no stamps
Sample a look back you look and find
Nothing but rednecks for 400 years if you check
"Don't worry be happy"
Was a number one jam
Damn if I say it, you can slap me right here
Let's get this party started right
Right on, c'mon
What we got to say
Power to the people, no delay
To make everybody see
In order to fight the powers that be.

"Fight the Power" was first released on the soundtrack for Spike Lee's film Do the Right Thing. *The song's chorus is drawn from a 1975 protest song by the Isley Brothers—"Fight the Power (Part 1 and 2)."*

1989 BEIJING WORKERS' AUTONOMOUS FEDERATION

"Ten Strange Things about China These Days"

The Third Plenum said get rich faster, but the people's pockets have not swelled, and cats black and white have gotten fatter.

Opening to the outside world, importing foreign capital, foreign debts have gotten larger, private bank accounts have prospered.

Bank notes and treasury bonds bear interest, and food subsidies are 7.50, but prices shoot upward like a rocket.

The reforms are doing fine, we won't give up the policy, but foreigners don't move to China, while the burned-out flee overseas.

New hotels have gone up and changed the city's face, but the people still lack decent housing space.

This satirical rhyming handbill, which took aim at China's reforms under Deng Xiaoping, was issued by the workers' federation leading up to the Tiananmen protests. The federation was established by a small group of workers on April 20, just five days after groups began gathering in Tiananmen Square, and soon became the organizing center for the workers' movement. Two days later, 100,000 people gathered in the square and one million marched in the streets for the funeral of Hu Yaobang.

MICHEL FOUCAULT　　1990

The History of Sexuality, Vol. 1

Power operated as a mechanism of attraction; it drew out those peculiarities over which it kept watch. Pleasure spread to the power that harried it; power anchored the pleasure it uncovered.

The medical examination, the psychiatric investigation, the pedagogical report, the family controls may have the overall and apparent objective of saying no to all wayward or unproductive sexualities, but the fact is that they function as mechanisms with a double impetus: pleasure and power. The pleasure that comes of exercising a power that questions, monitors, watches, spies, searches out, palpates, brings to light; and on the other hand, the pleasure that kindles at having to evade this power, flee from it, fool it, or travesty it. The power that lets itself be invaded by the pleasure it is pursuing; and opposite it, power asserting it in the pleasure of showing off, scandalizing, or resisting. Capture and seduction, confrontation and mutual reinforcement: parents and children, adults and adolescents, educator and students, doctors and patients, the psychiatrist with his hysteric and his perverts, all have played this game continually since the nineteenth century. These attractions, these evasions, these circular incitements have traced around bodies and sexes, not boundaries not to be crossed, but *perpetual spirals of power and pleasure.*

The political activist and historian-philosopher Foucault was at one time a member of the French Communist Party; co-founded the Prison Information Group, a venue for prisoners to articulate their needs and concerns; and reported in Iran for the Italian newspaper Corriere della Sera *following the revolution in 1979. He conceptualized knowledge and discourse as expressions of power, tracing the origins and evolution of modern discipline and punishment, and of sexuality. He died from AIDS in 1984.*

1990   AUNG SAN SUU KYI

"Freedom from Fear"

It is not power that corrupts but fear. Fear of losing power corrupts those who wield it and fear of the scourge of power corrupts those who are subject to it . . .

The people of Burma had wearied of a precarious state of passive apprehension where they were "as water in the cupped hands" of the powers that be.

> Emerald cool we may be
> As water in cupped hands
> But oh that we might be
> As splinters of glass
> In cupped hands . . .

Saints, it has been said, are the sinners who go on trying. So free men are the oppressed who go on trying and who in the process make themselves fit to bear the responsibilities and to uphold the disciplines which will maintain a free society . . .

Within a system which denies the existence of basic human rights, fear tends to be the order of the day. Fear of imprisonment, fear of torture, fear of death, fear of losing friends, family, property or means of livelihood, fear of poverty, fear of isolation, fear of failure . . . Yet even under the most crushing state machinery courage rises up again and again, for fear is not the natural state of civilized man . . .

Aung San Suu Kyi, Nobel Prize winner and leader of the Burmese democracy movement, has spent much of the past twenty years under house arrest. She is the daughter of Burmese nationalist revolutionary Aung San and was propelled to fame during the 8888 Uprising—a series of mass riots and protests that began on August 8, 1988—after calling openly for democracy. The uprising was violently crushed by government troops, who some have estimated killed 10,000 people.

PAUL FOOT **1990**

"The Thatcher Bubble Has Burst"

The Thatcher Bubble has burst . . . The polls reflect a deep and angry shift of mood. The anger has flared up over the hated poll tax, which attacks everyone except the rich and has succeeded in uniting opposition to the Thatcher government for the first time. From the north of Scotland to the Isle of Wight, the biggest movement of civil disobedience in Britain this century has persuaded hundreds of thousands of people to resist the tax by not paying it. Their mood was summed up by a woman who defied a court summons for not paying her tax in terms which echoed the great protests of the poor, homeless and unemployed a hundred years ago:

You are asking us for more money—us, the scum or rebels as you call us, who work hard for every penny. I want food in my stomach and clothes on my child's back.

. . . But the new anger does not stop at the poll tax. It has become the symbol of all the other Tory plans and policies.

Foot was a prominent campaigning journalist and a well-known member of the Socialist Workers Party. His assessment of the prospects for socialists at the end of the "Thatcher decade" is characteristically optimistic.

1991

"Until You Dig a Hole"

Until you dig a hole, you plant a tree, you water it and make it survive, you haven't done a thing. You are just talking.

In 1977, Kenyan activist Maathai founded the Green Belt Movement, a non-profit organization promoting environmental conservation and empowering poor, rural women—and she has been building this movement ever since. Maathai has been jailed twice and badly beaten by police, and the Green Belt offices have been shut down by the government. She won the Nobel Peace Prize in 2004.

1991

MARIA ELENA MOYANO

"The Terror of the Shining Path"

The revolution is an affirmation of life and of individual and collective dignity. It is our ethic. Revolution is not death, nor imposition, nor submission, nor fanaticism. Revolution is new life—the belief in and struggle for a just and dignified society—in support of the organizations the people have created, respecting their internal democracies, sowing new seeds of power in a new Peru. I will continue to stand with my people, with the women, youth, and children; I will continue to fight for peace with social justice.

Moyano, a Peruvian community organizer of Afro-Peruvian descent, led a federation of women in Villa El Salvador, a vast shantytown on the outskirts of Lima. In 1992, she was gunned down and her body blown up by the Shining Path, the Maoist guerrilla group, which was at that time targeting women's groups (for their "reformism").

"Plan for the Reconstruction of Los Angeles"

The Los Angeles communities are demanding that they are policed and patrolled by individuals who live in the community and the commanding officers by ten-year residents of the community in which they serve. Former gang members shall be given a chance to be patrol buddies in assisting the protection of the neighborhoods. These former gang members will be required to go through police training and must comply with all of the laws instituted by our established authorities. Uniforms will be issued to each and every member of the "buddy system"; however, no weapons will be issued. All patrol units must have a buddy patrol notified and present in the event of a police matter. Each buddy patrol will be supplied with a video camera and will tape each event and the officers handling the police matter. The buddy patrol will not interfere with any police matter, unless instructed by a commanding officer . . .

Meet these demands and the targeting of police officers will stop!

You have seventy-two hours for a response and a commitment, in writing, to support these demands. Additionally, you have thirty days to begin implementation. And, finally, you have four years to complete the projects of construction of the major hospitals and restorations.

Give us the hammer and the nails, we will rebuild the city.

Following the acquittal of the LAPD officers who beat Rodney King, which set off some of the worst urban rioting in US history, rival Los Angeles gangs the Crips and the Bloods formed a truce and issued this plan, which also included provisions for neighborhood upkeep; improving health, welfare and education in economically deprived areas; economic development; and commitments from the Bloods and Crips to match government funds for construction efforts and building a minority-run AIDS awareness center.

1993 GRACE LEE BOGGS

Living for Change

Rebellion is a stage in the development of revolution but it is not revolution. It is an important stage because it represents the standing up of the oppressed. Rebellions break the threads that have been holding the system together and throw into question its legitimacy and the supposed permanence of existing institutions. A rebellion disrupts the society but it does not provide what is necessary to make a revolution and establish a new social order. To make a revolution, people must not only struggle against existing institutions. They must make a philosophical/spiritual leap and become more *human* human beings. In order to change/transform the world, they must change/transform themselves.

Chinese American Boggs worked with C. L. R. James and Raya Dunayevskaya—once Trotsky's secretary and later the founder of what she called Marxist humanism—in a group called the Johnson-Forest Tendency. She married the black radical James Boggs and became so identified with black Detroit that, after riots in the city in 1967, she was described by the FBI as Afro-Chinese.

1993 GENERAL UNION OF PALESTINIAN WOMEN

"Palestinian Declaration of Women's Rights"

We, the women of Palestine, from all social categories and various faiths, including workers, farmers, housewives, students, professionals and politicians, promulgate our determination to proceed with our struggle to abolish all forms of discrimination and inequality against women, which were propagated by the different forms of colonialism on our land, ending with the Israeli occupation, and which were reinforced by the conglomeration of customs and traditions prejudiced against women, embodied in a number of existing laws and legislation.

Released by a coalition of women's organizations just as the Palestine Liberation Organization was drafting its constitution, this declaration was meant to highlight the importance of including provisions guaranteeing women's rights.

ZAPATISTA ARMY OF NATIONAL LIBERATION 1994

"First Declaration of the Lacandon Jungle"

Today we say: ENOUGH IS ENOUGH!

. . . We are millions, the dispossessed who call upon our brothers and sisters to join this struggle as the only path, so that we will not die of hunger due to the insatiable ambition of a seventy-year dictatorship led by a clique of traitors who represent the most conservative and sellout groups. They are the same ones that opposed Hidalgo and Morelos, the same ones that betrayed Vicente Guerrero, the same ones that sold half our country to the foreign invader, the same ones that imported a European prince to rule our country, the same ones that formed the "scientific" Porfirista dictatorship, the same ones that opposed the Petroleum Expropriation, the same ones that massacred the railroad workers in 1958 and the students in 1968, the same ones that today take everything from us, absolutely everything.

To prevent the continuation of the above and as our last hope, after having tried to utilize all legal means based on our Magna Carta, we go to our constitution, to apply Article 39, which says:

National Sovereignty essentially and originally resides in the people. All political power emanates from the people and its purpose is to help the people. The people have, at all times, the inalienable right to alter or modify their form of government.

Therefore, according to our Constitution, we declare the following [war on] the Mexican federal army, the pillar of the Mexican dictatorship from which we suffer, monopolized by a one-party system and led by Carlos Salinas de Gortari, the maximum and illegitimate federal executive that today holds power.

When three thousand armed Zapatista guerrillas seized a series of towns in Chiapas on January 1, 1994, their goal was to instigate revolution in Mexico and to protest that same day's implementation of the North American Free Trade Agreement, which had recently been signed by presidents Carlos Salinas and Bill Clinton.

1994 SUBCOMANDANTE MARCOS

"In Our Dreams We Have Seen Another World"

In our dreams we have seen another world, an honest world, a world decidedly more fair than the one in which we now live. We saw that in this world there was no need for armies; peace, justice and liberty were so common that no one talked about them as far-off concepts, but as things such as bread, birds, air, water, like book and voice. This is how the good things were named in this world. And in this world there was reason and goodwill in the government, and the leaders were clear-thinking people; they ruled by obeying. This world was not a dream from the past, it was not something that came to us from our ancestors. It came from ahead, from the next step we were going to take. And so we started to move forward to attain this dream, make it come down and sit at our tables, light our homes, grow in our corn-fields, fill the hearts of our children, wipe our sweat, heal our history. And it was for all. This is what we want. Nothing more, nothing less. Now we follow our path toward our true heart to ask it what we must do. We will return to our mountains to speak in our own tongue and in our own time. Thank you to the brothers and sisters who looked after us all these days. May your footsteps follow our path.

Marcos, spokesperson and "anti-leader" of the Zapatistas, has become an icon of the global anti-capitalist struggle—a "postmodern Che Guevara," as one journalist put it. He's refused to disclose his identity, though the Mexican government says he is Rafael Sebastián Guillén Vicente, formerly a professor in Mexico City. He has written more than two hundred essays and stories and published more than twenty books.

Statement of the Ogoni People to the Tenth Session of the Working Group in Indigenous Populations

This time last year, the Nigerian military invaded our land, clamped our leaders into jail and muddled all our planned activities—all in an attempt to frighten our truth into the care of despair. Yet we danced in celebration of our new power, in defiance of their abuse of power. In the last year, Nigeria's military leaders have stumbled from one Ogoni ditch into another.

From passing a decree (The Treason and Treasonable Felony Decree in 1993) aimed specifically at the Ogoni nation, to the detention and torture of our leaders; from the devastation of our peaceful villages to the declaration of war on Ogoni babies, pregnant women and unarmed men; from the use of armed troops to stop our representation at the National Constitutional Conference, to the extortion of money from the poor citizens of our Shell-shocked land.

Yet they have not succeeded in destroying our truth, our morale. The Ogoni is a plain of agony, the disgrace of the Nigerian military . . . a people, no matter how few, who are aware of their rights and determined to reclaim them in a nonviolent manner, cannot be crushed by military might. Ogoni is on the map of the world.

Therefore, my brothers and sisters, my beloved children, dance, dance, dance, this 4 January 1995, as we inaugurate the United Nations Decade of the World's Indigenous Peoples. Dance your anger and your joys; dance the military guns to silence; dance their dumb laws to the dump; dance oppression and injustice to death; dance the end of Shell's ecological war of thirty years . . .

As the power of our truth finds wing and spreads over Nigeria, the oppressors shall flee . . . and a new, restructured Nigeria emerge [sic], wherein every ethnic group shall be allowed to develop at its own pace, using its intellectual and material resources. Ogoni is the plain of hope.

*Saro-Wiwa was a Nigerian environmental activist and writer who led the Move-
ment for the Survival of the Ogoni People in a prolonged nonviolent campaign
against Shell Oil. In November 1995, Saro-Wiwa was executed by hanging
along with eight other members of MOSOP. This statement was smuggled out
of his prison cell and was read to a crowd of 200,000 on January 4, 1995, in
celebration of Ogoni Day.*

1996   **JOHN PERRY BARLOW**

"A Cyberspace Independence Declaration"

Governments of the Industrial World, you weary giants of flesh and
steel, I come from Cyberspace, the new home of Mind. On behalf of
the future, I ask you of the past to leave us alone. You are not welcome
among us. You have no sovereignty where we gather . . .

We will create a civilization of the Mind in Cyberspace. May it be
more humane and fair than the world your governments have made
before.

*Barlow's declaration was written in response to the Communications Decency
Act, passed by the US Congress and signed by president Bill Clinton in 1996.
The law was supposed to regulate pornography on the Internet, but was widely
seen as threatening to chill online speech dramatically, and was partially struck
down by the Supreme Court the following year.*

1997   **ANTI-SUHARTO MOVEMENT**

Anthem during May 1997 Elections

This is our country
Where rice is piled in abundance
Its oceans seething with wealth
Our land made fertile by God

In this jewel of a country
Millions upon millions of the people are covered with wounds

Hungry children unschooled
Village youth with no work . . .

Their rights have been stolen
Thrown out of their homes and hungry
Mother bless us if our blood is spilled in struggle
We take a vow to you, mother.

Rumored to have been written by two students at Gajah Mada University, John Tobing and Dadang Juliantara, this song became the anthem of the anti-Suharto protest movement ahead of the 1997 election and was sung at many protests, gatherings and strikes. Beginning in the late 1980s, anti-Suharto activists had begun to revive tactics such as street protests, factory strikes and land occupations, which had been banned since 1965; eventually, the movement grew to become a million strong and toppled the Suharto dictatorship in 1998.

MUSA ABU MARZUQ   1997
"The Oslo Agreement Will Not Work"

From the outset, Hamas has said that this type of agreement will not work. The Oslo agreement is a very obscure document which, because of its special nature, will never be able to free Palestine from Israeli occupation. It will not put the Palestinians on the road to an independent state. Declarations in Oslo will always be made by the stronger party, which in this instance is Israel. The Palestinians will achieve nothing from the Oslo agreement, and we told Yasir Arafat so from the outset.

Abu Marzuq, who lives in exile, is a leading figure in Hamas's political wing. Hamas opposed the Oslo accords and the "peace process" that was initiated in secret between Israel and the Palestine Liberation Organization in 1993, and continues to wage armed struggle against Israel throughout the 1990s, partially in response to the inadequacies of the accords.

1997

HASSAN NASRALLAH

"We Take Pride in Our Sons"

In the past, we used to take pride—and still do and forever will—in the fact that ours is a forward march, a resistance force and a jihadi movement, some of whose leaders and great men, like the martyr Sheikh Ragheb Harb, have been martyred. We used to hold our heads high for the fact that our leader, master, and beloved secretary-general, Sayyed Abbas Mussawi, his wife, and his child were among our martyrs. Today, however, we wish to tell this enemy: we are not a resistance movement whose leaders want to enjoy their private lives and fight you through the sons of their loyal followers and their good and true supporters from among the ordinary citizens. The martyr Hadi's martyrdom is the proof that we in Hezbollah's leadership do not spare our own sons; we take pride in them when they go to the front lines, and hold our heads high when they fall as martyrs.

In 1993, nine Hezbollah supporters died at the hands of the Lebanese army. Four years later, and just hours before giving this speech to commemorate those deaths, Nasrallah, the leader of Hezbollah, received news that his son and two friends had been killed by the Israeli army. Hezbollah, a Lebanese Islamist political organization, is widely considered to be a resistance movement in the Arab and Muslim world and, apart from its military actions, also provides social services to thousands of Lebanese Shi'ites. The US considers it a terrorist organization.

1998

ABDULLAH ÖCALAN

"We Shall Achieve a State"

Our history has shown the following: by leaving Ankara we became a party; by going into the Middle East, we became an army; when we go out into the world, we shall achieve a state.

Öcalan is a revolutionary socialist and founder of the Kurdistan Workers Party (PKK) in Turkey, which aims to create an independent Kurdish state and has been waging an armed campaign against Turkey for the past forty years. Turkey has responded with a scorched-earth policy of counterinsurgency in the Kurdish region. Öcalan was captured in 1999 by Turkey and sentenced to death; his sentence was subsequently commuted to life in prison.

2PAC   1998

"Changes"

And still I see no changes can't a brother get a little peace
It's war on the streets and the war in the Middle East
Instead of war on poverty they got a war on drugs
so the police can bother me
And I ain't never did a crime I ain't have to do
But now I'm back with the facts givin' it back to you.

Tupac Shakur released five albums before being fatally shot in Las Vegas at the age of twenty-five. The personification of street violence and police brutality, Shakur was also a convicted sex offender. In 1991, he filed a $10 million dollar lawsuit against the Oakland Police for allegedly beating him for jaywalking.

ANGELA DAVIS   1998

"Masked Racism"

Prisons do not disappear problems, they disappear human beings. And the practice of disappearing vast numbers of people from poor, immigrant, and racially marginalized communities has literally become big business.

Davis—former member of the Student Nonviolent Coordinating Committee, the Communist Party, and the Black Panthers—was also the third woman to make it onto the FBI's Ten Most Wanted Fugitives List for the kidnapping, conspiracy and murder of a judge (charges of which she was later acquitted). She was a founder of Critical Resistance, the grassroots organization aimed at dismantling the prison-industrial complex; and twice ran as a vice-presidential candidate for the Communist Party.

AHARON SHABTAI

"The New Jew"

The new Jew,
Der neue Jude,
Rises at night,
Puts his uniform on,
Kisses his wife and child,
And, in two or three hours, destroys
A quarter in one of Gaza's ghettos.
He manages to make it back
In time for coffee and rolls.
In the paper,
The fresh picture of women and children
Picking through islands of rubble,
Like frightened hens,
Pales beside
The shuttle within
That professional gesture.

All the while, above, a helicopter
Observes the grounded humanity
Of those who laugh
When they are tickled,
And bleed when they
Are shot by snipers,
And, in memory's skies—
Packed with clichés
And plays on words—
It outlines a lazy spiral,
Enclosing once and for all
Identity within parenthesis.
Whether it be with a barbed-wire fence
Or with a ring of outposts:

Identity becomes the ghetto,
And the ghetto becomes identity.

Israeli poet Shabtai is one of the Hebrew language's leading poets and transla-
tors of Greek drama. He was born in Tel Aviv during the British Mandate of
Palestine and remains fiercely critical of Israeli political and social policy.

ACME COLLECTIVE   # 1999

"On the Violence of Property"

When we smash a window, we aim to destroy the thin veneer of
legitimacy that surrounds private property rights . . .

A storefront window becomes a vent to let some fresh air into the
oppressive atmosphere of a retail outlet (at least until the police
decide to tear-gas a nearby road blockade). A newspaper box
becomes a tool for creating such vents or a small blockade for the
reclamation of public space or an object to improve one's vantage
point by standing on it. A dumpster becomes an obstruction to a
phalanx of rioting cops and a source of heat and light. A building
facade becomes a message board to record brainstorm ideas for a
better world.

The number of broken windows pales in comparison to the number
of broken spells—spells cast by a corporate hegemony to lull us into
forgetfulness of all the violence committed in the name of private
property rights and of all the potential of a society without them.
Broken windows can be boarded up (with yet more waste of our
forests) and eventually replaced, but the shattering of assumptions will
hopefully persist for some time to come.

In November 1999, tens of thousands of activists converged on the World
Trade Organization meeting in Seattle to protest neoliberal trade policies. After
numerous clashes with police and security forces, the ACME Collective, with
ties to the N30 Black Bloc, released this communiqué.

SERGIO RAMÍREZ

Adiós muchachos

Doctor Emilio Alvarez Montalván, Nicaragua's most respected conservative ideologue, once said—when we had already been defeated in the 1990 elections—that Sandinismo had brought to Nicaraguan political culture for the very first time a sense of responsibility towards the poor.

This is, in truth, one of the irreversible legacies of the Revolution, beyond the ideological illusions that confused us at the time—beyond, too, the bureaucratic excesses and deficiencies of Marxism in practice, beyond the inexperience and the improvisations, the poses, the cheap imitations, the rhetoric. The poor continued to be the humanist frame of references of the project that came apart, piece by piece, on the road . . .

In identifying itself with the poor, the Revolution was radical in the purest sense of the term, and under the rubric of a search for justice, capable of being repeatedly naïve or arbitrary, many times losing a proper perspective of what was possible, or even what was just and desirable . . .

The arcadia of our first months in power was marked by an unlimited innocence, and our collective sentiment alternated between delirium and dreams, between anxiety and hope, an emotion that acquired political weight and would never be repeated. The operative emotion was one of feeling oneself firmly oriented on the path towards change, determined to pursue matters to their ultimate logic.

And to the very end that meant all or nothing. No one had picked up a rifle to make a revolution half-way. To dethrone Somoza required as its necessary antecedent a violent revolution, not a peaceful transition to which other sectors of society might aspire. And a program of radical change required a radical power capable of defending itself and freeing itself from risks and constraints. It was, evidently, to be power in perpetuity, for one does not prevail in war to acquire power for the short term, when one is determined to sweep history aside.

Nicaraguan writer and politician Ramírez was a key member of the Group of Twelve—members of the Nicaraguan elite who provided critical support and legitimacy to the Sandinista struggle against Somoza. Adios Muchachos, written ten years after the Revolution emerged victorious, records his memories of the struggle.

MIGUEL ALVES DOS SANTOS   2000s

"To Overcome"

To learn respect, to be young until you're one hundred years old—skin color, black or white, doesn't matter. We're all equal. That is important. The MST has that spark—it has that character of freedom. So this is why I have joined the MST, with a destiny—destined for something that was to come again, destined to go back to that old process, that struggle together, to commit to that common alliance; this is what I've always wanted: "to overcome, to overcome." Fighting to overcome. To see our children, our grandchildren, our comrades, laughing. To have a home, a home of plenty, of full bellies, in good health and with education. It is very important that you go around and see old people having fun.

A rural and industrial worker who was tortured and imprisoned for being an alleged communist and spent two years homeless in the streets of São Paulo, Alves dos Santos has since become a leader of Brazil's Rural Landless Workers Movement (MST). The organization has roughly 1.5 million members; currently, 1.6% of Brazil's landowners control nearly half of all arable land.

LEONARD PELTIER   2000

Prison Writings

I don't know how to save the world. I don't have the answers or The Answer. I hold no secret knowledge as to how to fix the mistakes of generations past and present. I only know that without compassion and respect for all of Earth's inhabitants, none of us will survive—nor will we deserve to.

*One of the leaders of the American Indian Movement, Ojibwa-Sioux activist
Peltier was convicted and imprisoned in 1977 for the murder of two FBI
agents. The trial has been widely criticized for improper handling of evidence
and various inconsistencies in the FBI's case—the Dalai Lama, Nelson
Mandela, Jesse Jackson, Rigoberta Menchú, and the UN High Commissioner
for Human Rights have all spoken in his favor—but all appeals have failed,
and he remains one of America's most famous political prisoners.*

2001

NAOMI KLEIN

"Reclaiming the Commons"

What is now the anti-globalization movement must turn into thousands of local movements, fighting the way neoliberal politics are
playing out on the ground: homelessness, wage stagnation, rent escala-
tion, police violence, prison explosion, criminalization of migrant
workers, and on and on. These are also struggles about all kinds of
prosaic issues: the right to decide where the local garbage goes, to
have good public schools, to be supplied with clean water. At the
same time, the local movements fighting privatization and deregula-
tion on the ground need to link their campaigns into one large global
movement, which can show where their particular issues fit into an
international economic agenda being enforced around the world . . .
But the goal should not be better faraway rules and rulers, it should
be close-up democracy on the ground.

The Zapatistas have a phrase for this. They call it "one world with
many worlds in it." Some have criticized this as a New Age non-
answer. They want a plan. "We know what the market wants to do
with those spaces, what do you want to do? Where's your scheme?"
I think we shouldn't be afraid to say: "That's not up to us." We need
to have some trust in people's ability to rule themselves, to make the
decisions that are best for them. We need to show some humility
where now there is so much arrogance and paternalism. To believe
in human diversity and local democracy is anything but wishy-
washy. Everything in McGovernment conspires against them.
Neoliberal economics is biased at every level towards centralization,

consolidation, homogenization. It is a war waged on diversity. Against it, we need a movement of radical change, committed to a single world with many worlds in it, that stands for "the one no and the many yeses."

Klein, a Canadian journalist and activist, gained renown with her book No Logo, *which was published one year after the Seattle demonstrations against the WTO in 1999 and quickly became a manifesto for the anti-corporate and global justice movements that prompted that protest and followed in its wake.*

ASSATA SHAKUR   2001

"Love Is Contraband in Hell"

Love is contraband in Hell,
cause love is a acid
that eats away bars. But you, me, and tomorrow
hold hands and make vows
that struggle will multiply.
The hacksaw has two blades.
The shotgun has two barrels.
We are pregnant with freedom.
We are a conspiracy.
It is our duty to fight for our freedom
It is our duty to win.
We must love each other and support each other.
We have nothing to lose but our chains.

Shakur was a member of the Black Panther Party and the Black Liberation Army, an underground black nationalist–Marxist organization of the 1970s—and was convicted of killing a New Jersey State Trooper in 1973. She escaped from prison in 1979 and fled to Cuba, where she has lived for the past twenty-five years.

2003

NOAM CHOMSKY

Media Control

So we need something to tame the bewildered herd, and that something is this new revolution in the art of democracy; the manufactured consent. The media, the schools, and popular culture have to be divided. For the political class and the decision makers they have to provide them some tolerable sense of reality, although they also have to instill the proper beliefs . . .

In what is nowadays called a totalitarian state, or a military state, it's easy. You just hold a bludgeon over their heads, and if they get out of line you smash them over the head. But as society has become more free and democratic, you lose that capacity. Therefore you have to turn to the techniques of propaganda. The logic is clear. Propaganda is to a democracy what the bludgeon is to a totalitarian state.

Chomsky, the celebrated theorist of linguistics, rose to public fame in the 1960s as a voice of dissent with his critiques of US foreign policy and opposition to the Vietnam War. Since then, his targets have ranged from corporate mass media to the Israeli government, and from state capitalism and wage slavery to the Iraq War. He in turn has been on the receiving end of many death threats, even appearing on the Unabomber's planned target list.

2003

OMAR LITTLE

"It's All in the Game"

Levy: You are amoral, are you not? You are feeding off the violence and the despair of the drug trade. You're stealing from those who themselves are stealing the lifeblood from our city. You are a parasite who leeches off—
Omar: Just like you, man.
Levy: —the culture of drugs . . . Excuse me, what?

Omar: I got the shotgun. You got the briefcase. It's all in the game, though, right?

Omar is the principled gay vigilante who sticks up drug kingpins on The Wire, *the HBO series about the drug trade, politics, business, the media and life in Baltimore. Maurice Levy, lawyer for the drug dealer Bird, regularly advises and defends the members of the Barksdale drug-trafficking crew; here he questions Omar on the witness stand during Bird's trial.*

TREVOR NGWANE   **2003**
"Sparks in the Township"

The point is, we have to build where we are. We have had workshops on the World Bank, the IMF, the WTO and we've got strong people working on those issues. We've set up structures for the Campaign Against Neoliberalism in Southern Africa. But in the end we had to get down to the most basic questions: what are the problems facing people on the ground that unite us most? In Soweto, it's electricity. In another area, it is water. We've learned that you have to actually organize—to talk to people, door to door; to connect with the masses. But you have to build with a vision. From Day One we argued that electricity cuts are the result of privatization. Privatization is the result of GEAR. GEAR reflects the demands of global capital, which the ANC are bent on pushing through. We cannot finally win this immediate struggle unless we win that greater one. But still, connecting with what touches people on a daily basis, in a direct fashion, is the way to move history forward.

Ngwane is a South African activist and founder of the Anti-Privatisation Forum and the Soweto Electricity Crisis, and a former member of the ANC until his expulsion in 1999. GEAR stands for "Growth, Employment and Redistribution," a neoliberal economic strategy adopted by the government of South Africa in 1996 to increase jobs and GDP through foreign investment.

SAADI YOUSSEF

"The Jackals' Wedding"

O, Mudhaffar al-Nawab—
today isn't yesterday
(truth is as evanescent as the dream of a child)—
truth is, this time we're at their wedding reception,
yes, the jackals' wedding
you've read their invitation:

For tho' we trudge past Dahna empty-handed
We depart Dareen our purses lined with gold.
"While the townsfolk attend to their affairs
Now, Zuraik, fleece them, quick as a fox!"
. . .
O, Mudhaffar al-Nawab,
let's make a deal:

I'll go in your place
(Damascus is too far away from that secret hotel . . .)
I'll spit in the jackals' faces,
I'll spit on their lists,
I'll declare that we are the people of Iraq—
we are the ancestral trees of this land,
proud beneath our modest roof of bamboo.

The Iraqi poet-in-exile Youssef composed "The Jackals' Wedding" on the eve of the 2003 invasion by coalition forces. The poem's title refers to the unpleasant noise and stench caused by jackals congregating at night, which local Iraqis sarcastically refer to as a "wedding"; Mudhaffar al-Nawab, whom he addresses, is a fellow poet-in-exile, living in Damascus.

Public Power in the Age of Empire

When language has been butchered and bled of meaning, how do we understand "public power"? When freedom means occupation, when democracy means neoliberal capitalism, when reform means repression, when words like "empowerment" and "peacekeeping" make your blood run cold—why, then, "public power" could mean whatever you want it to mean. A biceps building machine, or a Community Power Shower. So, I'll just have to define "public power" as I go along, in my own self-serving sort of way.

In India, the word *public* is now a Hindi word. It means people. In Hindi, we have *sarkar* and public, the government and the people. Inherent in this use is the underlying assumption that the government is quite separate from "the people." This distinction has to do with the fact that India's freedom struggle, though magnificent, was by no means revolutionary. The Indian elite stepped easily and elegantly into the shoes of the British imperialists. A deeply impoverished, essentially feudal society became a modern, independent nation state. Even today, fifty-seven years on to the day, the truly vanquished still look upon the government as *mai-baap*, the parent and provider. The somewhat more radical, those who still have fire in their bellies, see it as *chor*, the thief, the snatcher-away of all things . . .

The question is: is "democracy" still democratic?

Are democratic governments accountable to the people who elected them? And, critically, is the public in democratic countries responsible for the actions of its *sarkar*?

The crisis in modern democracy is a profound one . . .

The thing to understand is that modern democracy is safely premised on an almost religious acceptance of the nation state. But corporate globalization is not. Liquid capital is not. So, even though capital needs the coercive powers of the nation state to put down revolts in the servants' quarters, this setup ensures that no individual nation can oppose corporate globalization on its own.

Radical change cannot and will not be negotiated by governments; it can only be enforced by people. By the public. A public who can link hands across national borders.

Since winning the Booker Prize in 1997 for her novel The God of Small Things, *Roy has has championed grassroots anti-dam activists and international global justice campaigners, while denouncing corporate exploitation of India, US warmongering, and her own Indian government's crackdown on Naxalite-Maoist insurgents. In 2002, she was jailed for a day by the Indian Supreme Court for criticizing it.*

2004

TINARIWEN

"Amassakoul"

I am a traveler in the lone desert
It's nothing special
I can stand the wind
I can stand the thirst
And the sun
I know how to go and walk
Until the setting of the sun
In the desert, flat and empty,
where nothing is given
My head is alert, awake
I have climbed up and climbed down
The mountains where I was born
I know in which caves the water is hidden
These worries are my friends
I'm always on familiar
terms with them and that
Gives birth to the stories of my life
You who are organized
assembled, walking together
Hand in hand, you're living
A path which is empty of meaning
In truth, you're all alone.

The members of Tinariwen, a band from Northern Mali, were once rebel soldiers who trained with Colonel Gadaffi in Libya, seeking to preserve the Tuareg way of life and its people's access to basic resources. In the past century, four prolonged Tuareg guerrilla rebellions against the governments of Mali and Niger have broken out, most recently in 2007. The Niger region, which is home to many Tuareg clans, contains some of the largest uranium deposits in the world; the Tuareg people see very little of the profits reaped from the mines.

HAROLD PINTER   2005

Nobel Prize Speech

As every single person here knows, the justification for the invasion of Iraq was that Saddam Hussein possessed a highly dangerous body of weapons of mass destruction, some of which could be fired in forty-five minutes, bringing about appalling devastation. We were assured that was true. It was not true. We were told that Iraq had a relationship with al Qaeda and shared responsibility for the atrocity in New York of September 11, 2001. We were assured that this was true. It was not true. We were told that Iraq threatened the security of the world. We were assured it was true. It was not true.

The truth is something entirely different. The truth is to do with how the United States understands its role in the world and how it chooses to embody it.

. . . The United States supported and in many cases engendered every right-wing military dictatorship in the world after the end of the Second World War. I refer to Indonesia, Greece, Uruguay, Brazil, Paraguay, Haiti, Turkey, the Philippines, Guatemala, El Salvador, and, of course, Chile. The horror the United States inflicted upon Chile in 1973 can never be purged and can never be forgiven.

Hundreds of thousands of deaths took place throughout these countries. Did they take place? And are they in all cases attributable to US foreign policy? The answer is yes, they did take place and they are attributable to American foreign policy. But you wouldn't know it.

It never happened. Nothing ever happened. Even while it was happening it wasn't happening. It didn't matter. It was of no interest.

The crimes of the United States have been systematic, constant, vicious, remorseless, but very few people have actually talked about them. You have to hand it to America. It has exercised a quite clinical manipulation of power worldwide while masquerading as a force for universal good. It's a brilliant, even witty, highly successful act of hypnosis.

I put to you that the United States is without doubt the greatest show on the road.

British writer, director, and actor Pinter—author of twenty-nine plays and twenty-seven screenplays—called his acceptance speech for the Nobel Prize in Literature "Art, Truth, and Politics." He was accused of anti-Americanism, but he replied that his critique was of American policy, while many Americans were "demonstrably sickened, shamed and angered by their government's actions." As a young man, Pinter was a conscientious objector, an early member of the Campaign for Nuclear Disarmament and supported the anti-apartheid fight, and he continued to be politically active all his life.

2005   EVO MORALES

"Our Struggle Is against US Imperialism"

What happened these past days in Bolivia was a great revolt by those who have been oppressed for more than 500 years. The will of the people was imposed this September and October, and has begun to overcome the empire's cannons. We have lived for so many years through the confrontation of two cultures: the culture of life represented by the indigenous people, and the culture of death represented by the West.

I believe only in the power of the people. That was my experience in my own region, a single province—the importance of local power. And now, with all that has happened in Bolivia, I have seen the importance of the power of a whole people, of a whole nation . . . We may have differences among our popular leaders—and it's true that we have them in Bolivia. But when the people are conscious, when the people know what needs to be done, any difference among the different local leaders ends. We've been making progress in this for a long time, so that our people are finally able to rise up, together.

In 2006, Morales became the first elected indigenous president of Bolivia. Formerly a leader of a coca farmers' union and the Movement for Socialism party, Morales has been an outspoken advocate of indigenous rights and a sharp critic of neoliberalism.

PALESTINIAN CIVIL SOCIETY ORGANIZATIONS 2005
"Call for Boycott, Divestment and Sanctions against Israel"

In light of Israel's persistent violations of international law; and . . . given that all forms of international intervention and peace-making have until now failed to convince or force Israel to comply with humanitarian law, to respect fundamental human rights and to end its occupation and oppression of the people of Palestine; and . . . inspired by the struggle of South Africans against apartheid and in the spirit of international solidarity, moral consistency and resistance to injustice and oppression;

We, representatives of Palestinian civil society, call upon international civil society organizations and people of conscience all over the world to impose broad boycotts and implement divestment initiatives against Israel similar to those applied to South Africa in the apartheid era. We appeal to you to pressure your respective states to impose embargoes and sanctions against Israel. We also invite conscientious Israelis to support this Call, for the sake of justice and genuine peace.

This call, which helped spur an international movement for boycott, divestment and sanctions, was endorsed by over 170 Palestinian civil society organizations—trade unions, political parties and other associations—representing Palestinian refugees, Palestinians in the occupied West Bank and Gaza Strip, and Palestinian citizens of Israel.

"We Are the Third Force"

The shack dwellers' movement that has given hope to thousands of people in Durban is always being accused of being part of the Third Force . . . What is it and who is part of the Third Force? Well, I am Third Force myself. The Third Force is all the pain and the suffering that the poor are subjected to every second in our lives . . .

The 16th of February 2005 was the dawn of our struggle. On that day the Kennedy Road committee . . . promised us the vacant land on the Clare Estate for housing . . . But then we were betrayed by the most trusted people in our city. Just one month later, without any warning or explanation, bulldozers began digging the land. People were excited. They went to see what was happening and were shocked to be told that a brick factory was being built there. More people went down to see. There were so many of us that we were blocking the road. The man building the factory called the police and our local councillor, a man put into power by our votes and holding our trust and hopes. The councillor told the police, "Arrest these people, they are criminals." The police beat us, their dogs bit us and they arrested fourteen of us. We asked what happened to the promised land. We were told, "Who the hell are you people to demand this land?" This betrayal mobilized the people. The people who betrayed us are responsible for this movement. Those people are the Second Force . . .

We are driven by the Third Force, the suffering of the poor. Our betrayers are the Second Force. The First Force was our struggle against apartheid. The Third Force will stop when the Fourth Force comes. The Fourth Force is land, housing, water, electricity, health care, education and work. We are only asking what is basic—not what is luxurious. This is the struggle of the poor.

S'bu Zikode is a leader of the Abahlali baseMjondolo ("Shack dwellers") movement. In the later years of apartheid, "Third Force" was a pejorative term used by the ANC to describe black security agents fomenting violence against them, the implication being that these black Africans were victims of white manipulation. An estimated twelve million South Africans live in shack dwellings or "informal settlements."

ALEJANDRO QUIROGA   2006
"Zanon Is No Longer a Laboratory"

Zanon is not an isolated experience or crazy idea, it is a concrete experience that a group of workers have put into action. Many people talk about Zanon as a laboratory for experimenting with workers' dreams. After five years, this is no longer a laboratory: we are demonstrating an economic alternative to what the capitalist model proposes.

When the 2001 financial crisis destroyed the Argentinian economy, leading many factories and businesses to shut down, a wave of workers reoccupied their workplaces and formed worker's cooperatives; their slogan was "Occupy, Resist, Produce!" Zanon Ceramics was one such factory; today, it operates under the name FASINPAT—"Factory Without a Boss"—and Quiroga is one of its workers. As of 2007, 10,000 Argentinians were employed in self-managed businesses.

HUGO CHÁVEZ   2006
Address to the UN General Assembly

The Devil came here yesterday, right here. It still smells of sulfur today. Yesterday on this rostrum the president of the United States, whom I refer to as the Devil, talked as if he owned the world. It would be appropriate to have a psychiatrist analyse yesterday's address by the president of the United States. As the spokesman of imperialism he came to share his prescriptions for preserving the current pattern of domination, exploitation and pillage of the peoples of the world. It was like an Alfred Hitchcock movie. I would even propose a title: "The Devil's Recipe" . . .

American imperialism is doing all it can to consolidate its hegemonistic system of domination. We cannot allow it to do that. We cannot allow the establishment and consolidation of world dictatorship. The address of the world tyrant, cynical and full of hypocrisy, shows the imperialists' intention to control everything. They say that they want to impose a democratic model, but it is the democratic model of their own conception: the false democracy of elites, and furthermore an original democratic model imposed by bombs, bombardments and invasions. What a strange democracy! It would be necessary to revise the ideas of Aristotle and the other Greek pioneers of democracy in the face of this model, imposed by marines, invasions, aggression and bombs.

. . .

It is not that we are extremists. What is happening is that the world is waking up and people everywhere are rising up. I tell the world dictator, "I have a feeling that the rest of your days will be a living nightmare, because everywhere you will see us rising up against American imperialism, demanding freedom, equality of peoples and respect for the sovereignty of nations." Yes, we may be described as extremists, but we are rising against the empire, against the model of domination . . .

Now we must define the future of the world. The dawn is breaking all over: Latin America, Africa, Europe and Oceania. I want to emphasize that optimistic vision, so that we may strengthen our will and our readiness to fight to save the world and build a new and better world.

Venezuelan president Chávez, who describes his movement as the Bolivarian Revolution, addressed the General Assembly the day after president George W. Bush spoke. Chavez's attempted coup of 1992 failed, but he was elected president in 1998 (reelected in 2000 and 2006) and prevailed over a US-backed coup in 2002.

"Spread This Number"

09 F9 11 02 9D 74 E3 5B D8 41 56 C5 63 56 88 C0

*When the Motion Picture Association of America and the Advanced Access
Content System Licensing Administrator tried to prevent the spread of a propri-
etary DVD encryption code on the Internet—the code for Blu-Ray and HD
DVD discs—Internet geeks reposted it over 700,000 times, peppering the
Internet in what has been described as a "digital riot." Considered the first
instance of Internet geeks using social networking to defeat major corporations,
the code has since become code—among Internet activists—for the idea that
information should be free.*

"Death Poem"

Take my blood.
Take my death shroud and
The remnants of my body.
Take photographs of my corpse at the grave, lonely.
Send them to the world,
To the judges and
To the people of conscience,
Send them to the principled men and the fair-minded.
And let them bear the guilty burden before the world,
Of this innocent soul.
Let them bear the burden before their children and before history,
Of this wasted, sinless soul,
Of this soul which has suffered at the hands of the "protectors of peace."

*Al-Dossari is a Bahraini citizen who was captured in Pakistan and handed
over to US troops as bounty, falsely accused of terrorist activity, held in detention at Guantánamo Bay for five years, and subjected to torture. He spent three*

and a half of those years in solitary confinement; during the five years, he appears to have made at least ten suicide attempts. Since his release, he has spoken publicly about the conditions in Guantánamo.

2008   **SAMPAT PAL DEVI**

Interview

I am the commander of the Gulabi Gang . . . I visit numerous villages every day and meet the various members of the gang. We have gang meetings where we decide the plan of action if we hear of something that we oppose going on. First we go to the police and request that they do something. But since the administration is against the poor people of our country, we often end up taking matters into our own hands. We first speak to the husband who is beating his wife. If he doesn't understand then we ask his wife to join us while we beat him with *lathis*. Our missions have a 100 percent success rate. We have never failed in bringing justice when it comes to domestic problems. Dealing with the administration is the tricky part since we cannot always take the law in our hands—especially with such corrupt lawmakers. We did beat up some corrupt officials but we were ultimately helpless. The goons of the corrupt officials and the political parties constantly threaten me. Once, a few goons came and threatened to shoot me down, but the women came to my rescue and threw bricks at them and they ran away. They haven't come back since.

Sampat Pal is the founder of the Gulabi Gang (Pink Sari Gang), a group of women from one of the poorest districts of the Uttar Pradesh province of India, who, armed with sticks, battle against those who abuse women, and seek to empower the poor, the underprivileged, and the lower castes.

Charter 08

China has many laws but no rule of law; it has a constitution but no constitutional government. The ruling elite continues to cling to its authoritarian power and fights off any move toward political change. The stultifying results are endemic official corruption, an undermining of the rule of law, weak human rights, decay in public ethics, crony capitalism, growing inequality between the wealthy and the poor, pillage of the natural environment as well as of the human and historical environments, and the exacerbation of a long list of social conflicts, especially, in recent times, a sharpening animosity between officials and ordinary people.

As these conflicts and crises grow ever more intense, and as the ruling elite continues with impunity to crush and to strip away the rights of citizens to freedom, to property, and to the pursuit of happiness, we see the powerless in our society—the vulnerable groups, the people who have been suppressed and monitored, who have suffered cruelty and even torture, and who have had no adequate avenues for their protests, no courts to hear their pleas—becoming more militant and raising the possibility of a violent conflict of disastrous proportions. The decline of the current system has reached the point where change is no longer optional.

Initially signed by 303 Chinese writers, Charter 08 promotes greater reform and democratization. It was released on the sixtieth anniversary of the Universal Declaration of Human Rights and just a few months before the tenth anniversary of the Tiananmen Square protests, and was named after Charter 77, signed by Czechoslovakian dissidents fighting for human rights. Its signatories include Woeser and Liu Xiaobo.

**ATHENS SCHOOL OF ECONOMICS AND
BUSINESS STUDENTS**

Occupation Statement

We are here / we are everywhere / we are an image from the future

For in the destroyed and pillaged streets of our cities of light we see not only the obvious results of our rage, but the possibility of starting to live. We have no longer anything to do than to install ourselves in this possibility, transforming it into a living experience: by grounding on the field of everyday life, our creativity, our power to materialize our desires, our power not to contemplate but to construct the real. This is our vital space. All the rest is death.

Those who want to understand will understand. Now is the time to break the invisible cells that chain each and everyone to his or her pathetic little life. And this does not require solely or necessarily one to attack police stations and torch malls and banks. The time that one deserts his or her couch and the passive contemplation of his or her own life and takes to the streets to talk and to listen, leaving behind anything private, involves in the field of social relations the destabilizing force of a nuclear bomb. And this is precisely because the (till now) fixation of everyone on his or her microcosm is tied to the traction forces of the atom. Those forces that make the (capitalist) world turn. This is the dilemma: with the insurgents or alone. And this is one of the really few times that a dilemma can be at the same time so absolute and real.

The shooting of a fifteen-year-old boy by a police officer on December 6 set off protests and rioting in Athens, which would last for three weeks, spread throughout Greece, result in a paralyzing one-day general strike, and lead students at several universities to occupy university buildings. Not just a reaction against police brutality, these actions were also expressions of frustration and protest against government corruption, economic and educational policies.

"The Fear in"

A hurried farewell to Lhasa,
Now a city of fear.

A hurried farewell to Lhasa,
Where the fear is greater than all the dear after '59, '69, and '89 put
together.

A hurried farewell to Lhasa,
Where the fear is in your breathing, in the beating of your heart,
In the silence when you want to speak but don't,
In the catch in your throat.

A hurried farewell to Lhasa,
Where constant fear has been wrought by legions with their guns,
By countless police with their guns,
By plainclothesmen beyond counting,
And still more by the colossal machinery of the State that stands
behind them night and day;
But you mustn't point a camera at them or you'll get a gun pointed
at you,
maybe hauled off into some corner and no one will know.

A hurried farewell to Lhasa,
Where the fear is now minutely scanned by the cameras that stud
avenues and alleys and offices, and every monastery and temple
hall;
All those cameras,
Taking it all in,
Swiveling from the outer world to peer inside your mind.
"*Zap zap jé!* They're watching us"—among Tibetans this has become
a byword, furtively whispered.

A hurried farewell to Lhasa:
The fear in Lhasa breaks my heart. Got to write it down.

Woeser, a prominent Tibetan poet and blogger, was placed under house arrest after speaking to reporters during the 2008 Tibet uprisings, which began with demonstrations to commemorate the failed 1959 uprising against Chinese rule. Both were suppressed by Beijing. Woeser writes in Chinese.

2009

MUNTAZER AL-ZAIDI

"Why I Threw the Shoe"

I am free. But my country is still a prisoner of war. There has been a lot of talk about the action and about the person who took it, and about the hero and the heroic act, and the symbol and the symbolic act. But, simply, I answer: what compelled me to act is the injustice that befell my people, and how the occupation wanted to humiliate my homeland by putting it under its boot . . .

I say to those who reproach me: do you know how many broken homes that shoe which I threw had entered? How many times it had trodden over the blood of innocent victims? Maybe that shoe was the appropriate response when all values were violated.

When I threw the shoe in the face of the criminal, George Bush, I wanted to express my rejection of his lies, his occupation of my country, my rejection of his killing my people. My rejection of his plundering the wealth of my country, and destroying its infrastructure. And casting out its sons into a diaspora.

Al-Zaidi is an Iraqi journalist whose act has since inspired many others to launch their shoes in political protest around the world; ironically, one such act, performed by a reporter in Paris, was aimed at Al-Zaidi himself. The number of violent civilian deaths due to the occupation of Iraq has been estimated at between several hundred thousand and over one million between 2003 and 2010.

"My Dear School Friend"

My dear school friend,
You are with me on the same road.
The wooden stick is held over our heads.
My unbearable grief, you are my memory of pain.
Carved are our names, mine and yours,
on the body of this blackboard.
The wounds of the whip of oppression and injustice
still remain on our flesh.
Our field, deserted for lack of principle,
is corrupted everywhere with weeds.
Good if good, bad if bad,
in this field the heart of the people has died.
Your hands and mine
must destroy these curtains.
For if not you and I,
who will be able to heal our pain?

"My Dear School Friend," a Persian pop song written and performed by Mansour Tehrani from the 1980s, has been adopted by Iranian anti-regime movements of all strips and became the anthem of Iran's pro-democracy Green Movement in 2009, when protesters sang it loudly while marching through the streets. The June 15 protest in Tehran, which opposed the allegedly fraudulent presidential election results that gave Mahmoud Ahmadinejad a landslide victory, drew an estimated two to three million people.

2009

"My Self-Defense"

Whether in China or elsewhere in the world, in antiquity or in the modern and contemporary era, literary inquisition through the criminalization of speech is an act against humanity and human rights . . . The first emperor of the Qin dynasty achieved the unification of China, but the tyranny of his "burning books and burying Confucius scholars alive" lived on in infamy. Emperor Wu of the Han dynasty was a man of great talent and vision, but his decision to have the Grand Historian Sima Qian castrated brought him blame and shame

In terms of objective effect, it is more dangerous to stop people's mouths than to dam a river. The tall prison walls cannot hold back free expression. A regime cannot establish its legitimacy by suppressing different political views, nor can it maintain lasting peace and stability through literary inquisition. For the problems that come from the barrel of a pen can only be resolved by the barrel of a pen.

A participant in the Tiananmen Square protests who has campaigned for human rights in China ever since, Liu Xiaobo was sentenced in 2009 to eleven years' imprisonment for organizing and signing Charter 08.

2010

HENNING MANKELL

"It's the Action that Proves the Word"

The Gaza Strip has been transformed into the biggest open prison in the world and it was obvious we had to do something. We thought maybe we should try to break that whole blockade and the only way to do it is with a convoy of ships. When I first heard about it I thought it's a good idea, I'd like to be on board. I believe so strongly in solidarity as an instrument to change the world, and I believe in dialogue, but it's the action that proves the word.

Mankell, the Swedish mystery writer, was on a boat in the aid flotilla that tried to break the Israeli embargo of the Gaza strip. Israeli armed forces boarded the boats on May 13, 2010, killing nine people. Having visited Palestine the previous year, Mankell—who has written extensively about Africa—said "it was like seeing the apartheid system again." Israel has restricted movement in Gaza since 1989, and the current blockade, enacted in 2007, allows in a very limited amount of aid. Gaza has been described by UK Prime Minister David Cameron as a "prison camp."

SOURCES

Anonymous. "Colombian Folk Song," quoted in Michael F. Jimenez, "Class, Gender, and Peasant Resistance in Central Colombia, 1900–1930," in Forrest D. Colburn, ed., *Everyday Forms of Peasant Resistance*, M.E. Sharpe Inc., 1989.

Anonymous. "Congolese folksong," quoted in Adam Hochschild, *King Leopold's Ghost*, Houghton Mifflin, 1998.

Anonymous. "Judgments of Karakash," quoted in J. E. Hanauer, *Folklore of the Holy Land: Moslem, Christian and Jewish*, Dover Publications, 2002.

Anonymous. "Paris graffiti," quoted in Marc Rohan, *Paris '68: Graffiti, Posters, Newspapers and Poems of the May 1968 Events*, Impact Books, 1988.

Anonymous. "Pattinappaalai," quoted in Kallidaikurichi Aiyah Nilakanta Sastri, *The Colas*, University of Madras, 1955.

Anonymous. "Poem by Korean Elementary-School Student," quoted in George Katsiaficas, *Deliver Us From Evil: South Korean Social Movements in the Twentieth Century*, forthcoming.

Anonymous. "Poem in Blood," quoted in Sheila Rowbotham, *Women, Resistance and Revolution*, Allen Lane, 1972.

Anonymous. "Shanghai Posters," quoted in Orville Schell, *Discos and Democracy: China in the Throes of Reform*, Anchor, 1989.

Anonymous. "The Tale of the Eloquent Peasant," quoted in R. B. Parkinson, ed., *The Tale of Sinuhe and Other Ancient Egyptian Poems 1940–1640 BC*, Oxford University Press, 1997.

Anonymous. "Woe on us Wingate," quoted in George Young, *Egypt*, Ernest Benn, 1927.

Anonymous, "Joke," quoted in Nathan Rosenberg, *Exploring the Black Box: Technology, Economics, and History*, Cambridge University Press, 1994.

Abd al-Qadir al Jaza'iri. Quoted in Raphael Danziger, *Abd al-Qadir and the Algerians: Resistance to the French and Internal Consolidation*, Holmes and Meier, 1977.

Abd al-Rahim Mahmud. Quoted in Salma Khadra Jayyusi, *Anthology of Modern Palestinian Literature*, Columbia University Press, 1992.

Abdukhaliq "Uyghur." Quoted in Justin Rudelson, *Oasis Identities*, Columbia University Press, 1997.

Abou Deeb, Mahmoud. Quoted in Zeina B. Ghandour, *A Discourse on Domination in Mandate Palestine: Imperialism, Property, and Insurgency*, Routledge, 2010.

Abu ala al-Ma'ari. Adapted from Reynold A. Nicholson, *Studies in Islamic Poetry*, Cambridge University Press, 1921.

Abu Marzuq, Musa. Quoted in Glenn E. Robinson, "Hamas as a social movement" in Quintan Wiktorowicz, ed., *Islamic Activism: A Social Movement Theory Approach*, Indiana University Press, 2004.

Abu Salma. Quoted in Salma Khadra Jayyusi, *Anthology of Modern Palestinian Literature*, Columbia University Press, 1992.

Acme Collective. Quoted in David Graeber, *Possibilities*, AK Press, 2007.

ACT UP. Quoted in Gabrielle Griffin, *Representations of HIV and AIDS: Visibility Blue/s*, Manchester University Press, 2000.

Adams, Abigail. Quoted in John Rhodehamel, ed., *The American Revolution: Writings from the War for Independence*, Library of America, 2001.

Adorno, Theodor. "Messages in a Bottle," *New Left Review* I/200 (July–August 1993).

Albizu Campos, Pedro. Quoted in Stevens Arroyo and Antonio M., *The Political Philosophy of Pedro Albizu Campos: Its Theory and Practice*, New York University, Ibero-American Language and Area Center, 1974.

Al-Bustani, Wadi. Quoted in Ghassan Kanafani, *The 1936–1939 Revolt in Palestine*, Committee for Democratic Palestine, 1972.

Al-Dossari, Jumah. Quoted in Marc Falkoff, ed., *Poems from Guantánamo: The Detainees Speak*, University of Iowa Press, 2007.

Al-e-Ahmad, Jalal. *Occidentosis: A Plague From The West*, trans. R. Campbell, Mizan Press, 1984.

Al-Jawahiri, Muhammad Mahdi. Quoted in Robert A. Fernea and W. Roger Louis, eds, *The Iraqi Revolution of 1958: The Old Social Classes Revisited*, I. B. Tauris Publishers, 1991.

Al-Kinana. Quoted in James Gelvin, *Divided Loyalties: Nationalism and Mass Politics in Syria at the Close of Empire*, University of California Press, 1998.

Al-Zaidi, Muntazer. Quoted in *The Guardian* (September 23, 2009).

Ali ibn Muhammad. Quoted in Abu Ja'far Muhammad Bin Jarir al-Tabari, *The History of al-Tabari, Vol. 36: The Revolt of the Zanj*, trans. David Waines, SUNY Press, 1991.

Ali, Muhammed. Quoted in Jeffrey Haas, *The Assassination of Fred Hampton: How the FBI and the Chicago Police Murdered a Black Panther*, Lawrence Hill Books, 2009.

Ali, Tariq. *Street Fighting Years: An Autobiography of the Sixties*, Verso, 2005.

Allende, Salvador."Overthrow of Salvador Allende in Chile," *Monthly Review*, September 2006.

Alves dos Santos, Miguel. Quoted in Boaventura de Sousa Santos, *Voices of the World*, Verso, 2010.

Ambedkar, B. R. *Annihilation of Caste*, Critical Quest, 2007.

American Jewish Intellectuals. Quoted in Hannah Arendt, *The Jewish Writings*, Schocken Books, 2007.

Anthony, Susan B. Quoted in Phillip S. Foner, *We, The Other People: Alternative Declarations of Independence*, University of Illinois Press, 1976. Cited in Timothy Patrick McCarthy and John McMillan, eds., *The Radical Reader: A Documentary History of the American Radical Tradition*, New Press, 2003.

Anti-Suharto Movement. Quoted in Max Lane, *Unfinished Nation: Indonesia Before and After Suharto*, Verso, 2008.

Apess, William. *A Son of the Forest and Other Writings*, ed. Barry O'Connell, University of Massachusetts Press, 1997.

Arévalo, Juan José. Quoted in Stephen C. Schlesinger and Stephen Kinzer, *Bitter Fruit*, expanded edn, Harvard University Press, 1999.

Asturias, Miguel Ángel. Quoted in *Dictionary of Literary Biography DLB 329: Nobel Prize Laureates in Literature: Aganon-eucken Part 1*, Gale, 2006.

Athens School of Economics and Business Students. "We are here / we are everywhere / we are an image from the future," *Occupied London* 4 (February 2009).

Aung San Suu Kyi. *Freedom From Fear*, Penguin, 2010.

Awolowo, Obafemi. *Adventures in Power, Book One: My March Through Prison*, Macmillan Nigeria Publishers, 1985.

Bakunin, Mikhail. Quoted in Brian Morris, *Bakunin: The Philosophy of Freedom*, Black Rose Books, 1993.

Baldwin, James. Quoted in Robert Coles, "James Baldwin Back Home," *New York Times*, July 31, 1977.

Ball, John. Quoted in David Preest, trans., *The Chronica Maiora of Thomas Walsingham, 1376–1422*, Boydell Press, 2005.

Bardacke, Frank. Quoted in Philip J. Deloria, *Playing Indian*, Yale University Press, 1999.

Barlow, John Perry. Quoted in Martin Gay, *The New Information Revolution: A Reference Handbook*, University of Michigan Press, 1996.

Barrios de Chungara, Domitila. *Let Me Speak! Testimony of Domitila, a Woman of the Bolivian Mines*, Monthly Review Press, 1978.

Basil of Caesaria. Quoted in Michael Rosen and David Widgery, eds, *Vintage Book of Dissent*, Vintage, 1996.

de Beauvoir, Simone. *The Second Sex*, Knopf, 1953.

Bei Dao. *The Rose of Time: New and Selected Poems*, ed. Eliot Weinberger, New Directions, 2010.

Beijing Workers' Autonomous Federation. Quoted in Andrew G. Walder and Gong Xiaoxia, "Workers in the Tiananmen Protests: The Politics of the Beijing Workers' Autonomous Federation," *Australian Journal of China Affairs* 29 (1993).

Benjamin, Walter. *Illuminations*, ed. Hannah Arendt, trans. Harry Zohn, Schocken 1969.

Bestes, Peter, et al. Quoted in Herbert Aptheker, ed., *A Documentary History of the Negro People in the United States, Volume One*, Carol Publishing Group, 1990.

Biko, Steve. Quoted in Aelred Stubbs, ed., *I Write What I Like: The Selected Writings of Steve Biko*, University of Chicago Press, 2002.

Bishop, Maurice. Quoted in Manning Marable, *African and Caribbean Politics*, Verso, 1987.

Black Women's Protest. Quoted in Donald Crummey, *Banditry, Rebellion and Social Protest in Africa*, Heinemann, 1986.

Blanc, Louis. Quoted in Branko Horvak, Mihailo Marković and Rudi Supec, eds, *Self-Governing Socialism: A Reader*, M. E. Sharpe, 1975.

Blanchot, Lanzmann, Sartre et al. "Manifesto of the 121," *International Socialist Review*, vol. 22, no. 1 (Winter 1961).

Blake, William. *Milton*, Shambhala, 1978.

Blanco, Hugo. *Land or Death: The Peasant Struggle in Peru*, Pathfinder Press, 1972.

Blanqui, Louis–Auguste. *Textes Choisis*, trans. Andy Blunden, Editions Social, 1971.

Boerne, Ludwig. Quoted in Eric Hobsbawm, *The Age of Revolution*, Abacus, 2008.

Boggs, Grace Lee. *Living for Change: An Autobiography*, University of Minnesota Press, 1998.

Bolívar, Simón. Quoted in Matthew Brown, ed., *Hugo Chávez Presents Simón Bolívar: The Bolivarian Revolution*, Verso, 2009.

Bouhired, Djamila. Quoted in *The Arab Human Development Report 2005: Towards the Rise of Women in the Arab World*, UNDP, Stanford University Press, 2006.

Bourne, Randolph. Quoted in Lillian Schlissel, ed., *The World of Randolph Bourne*, E. P. Dutton & Co., Inc., 1965.

Boxers, The. Quoted in Jonathan Spence, *The Search for Modern China*, W. W. Norton, 1999.

Brecht, Bertolt. *Brecht on Theatre,* trans. John Willett, Hill and Wang, 1984.

Brecht, Bertolt. *Poems 1913–1956*, trans. John Willett, Routledge, 1997.

Brown, H. Rap. Quoted in Jamil Al-Amin and H. Rap Brown, *Die Nigger Die!*, Lawrence Hill Books, 2002.

Brutus, Dennis. Quoted in Aquino De Braganca and Immanuel Wallerstein, *The African Liberation Reader*, Vol. 2, St. Martin's Press, 1982.

Bryan, Alfred. Quoted in Mark W. Van Wienen, *Rendezvous With Death: American Poems of the Great War*, University of Illinois Press, 2002.

Bulosan, Carlos. Quoted in E. San Juan, Jr., ed., *On Becoming Filipino: Selected Writings of Carlos Bulosan*, Temple University Press, 1995.

Byron, Lord. Quoted in John Nichols and John Cordy Jeaffreson, eds, *The Complete Poetical and Dramatic Works of Lord Byron*, D. McKay, 1883.

Cabral, Amilcar. Quoted in William H. Worger, Nancy L. Clark and Edward A. Alpers, *Africa and the West: A Documentary History: Volume 2: From Colonialism to Independence, 1875 to the Present*, Oxford University Press, 2010.

Cade, Jack. Quoted in James Gairdner, *Three Fifteenth-Century Chronicles, with Historical Memoranda by John Stowe*, BiblioBazaar, 2009.

Câmara, Dom Hélder. Quoted in Francis McDonagh, ed., *Dom Hélder Câmara: Essential Writings*, Orbis Books, 2009.

Cardenal, Ernesto. Quoted in Mike Gonzales and David Treece, *The Gathering of Voices: The Twentieth-Century Poetry of Latin America*, Verso, 1996.

Carmichael, Stokely. Quoted in James Robertson Andrews and David Zarefsky, *Contemporary American Voices: Significant Speeches in American History: 1945–Present*, Longman, 1992.

Carpenter, Edward. Quoted in Chris White, *Nineteenth-Century Writings on Homosexuality*, Routledge, 1999.

Castro, Fidel. Quoted in Tariq Ali, ed., *Castro: The Declarations of Havana*, Verso, 2008.

Chartists, The. Quoted in G. D. H. Cole and A. W. Filson, eds, *British Working Class Movements: Select Documents 1789–1875*, Macmillan, 1951.

Chávez, César. "Letter from Delano," *Christian Century*, April 23, 1969.

Chávez, Hugo. Quoted in Peter H. Smith, *Talons of the Eagle: Latin America, the United States and the World*, Oxford University Press, 2007.

Chen Duxiu. Quoted in J. Mason Gentzler, *Changing China: Readings in the History of China from the Opium War to the Present*, Praeger, 1977.

Chibas, Eduardo. Quoted in James Dunkerley, *Political Suicide in Latin America*, Verso, 1992.

Chinese Writers (Charter 08). Quoted in *New York Review of Books* (January 15, 2009), trans. Perry Link.

Chomsky, Noam. *Media Control: The Spectacular Achievements of Propaganda*, Open Media, 2003.

Civavakkiyar. Quoted in Sanford B. Seever, "Civavakkiyar's Abecedarium Naturae," *Journal of the American Oriental Society* 114:3, 1994.

Clarkson, Laurence. Quoted in B. Manning, *The Far Left in the English Revolution, 1640 to 1660*, Bookmarks, 1999.

Clyde Workers' Committee. Quoted in Tony Cliff, *Marxism and Trade Union Struggle: The General Strike of 1926*, Bookmarks, 1986.

Cohn-Bendit, Daniel and Gabriel. *Obsolete Communism: The Left-Wing Alternative*, AK Press, 2000.

Columbia Student Demonstrations. Quoted in Stefan M. Bradley,

Harlem Vs Columbia University: Black Student Power in the Late 1960s, University of Illinois Press, 2009.

Comfort, Alex. Quoted in David Widgery, *The Left in Britain, 1956–1968*, Penguin, 1976.

Congregation for the Democratization of Chonnam Province. Quoted in George Katsiaficas, "Remembering the Kwangju Uprising," *Socialism and Democracy*, vol. 14 issue 1 (January 2000).

Conrad, Joseph. *Heart of Darkness*, Penguin Books, 1995.

Cooke, Sam. *Sam Cooke: Portrait of a Legend: 1951–1964*, Abkco Records, 2003.

Cooper, Anna Julia. Quoted in Henry Louis Gates, Jr., and Nellie McKay, eds, *The Norton Anthology of African American Literature*, W. W. Norton, 1997.

Connolly, James. *Collected Works*, University of Michigan Press, 1987.

Crips and Bloods. "Plan for the Reconstruction of Los Angeles," *Z Magazine 5: Issues 7–12*, Institute for Social and Cultural Communications, 1992.

Czech Activists. "Declaration of Charter 77," http://libpro.cts.cuni.cz/charta/docs/declaration_of_charter_77.pdf (accessed August 10, 2010).

Dacus, Joseph A. Quoted in Albert Fried, ed., *Except to Walk Free: Documents and Notes in the History of American Labor*, Anchor Books, 1974. Cited in Timothy Patrick McCarthy and John McMillan, eds, *The Radical Reader: A Documentary History of the American Radical Tradition*, New Press, 2003.

Darwish, Mahmoud. Quoted in Zachary Lockman and Joel Beinin, eds, *Intifada: The Palestinian Uprising Against Israeli Occupation*, MERIP, 1999.

Davis, Angela. "Masked Racism," *ColorLines* (Fall 1998).

Debord, Guy. Quoted in Tom McDonough, ed., *Guy Debord and the Situationist International: Texts and Documents*, MIT Press, 2004.

Debray, Régis. *Strategy for Revolution*, Monthly Review Press, 1970.

Debs, Eugene V. *Eugene V. Debs Speaks*, Pathfinder Press, 1994.

Deutscher, Isaac. "Roots of Bureaucracy," *Socialist Register*, vol. 6, 1969.

Digg & Internet Geeks. Quoted in Charlene Li and Josh Bernoff, *Groundswell: Winning in a World Transformed by Social Technologies*, Harvard Business Press, 2008.

Domingo, Charles. Quoted in George Shepperson and Thomas Price, *Independent African*, Edinburgh University Press, 1958.

Domingo, W. A. "The New Negro—What Is He?" cited in Timothy Patrick McCarthy and John McMillian, eds, *The Radical Reader: A Documentary History of the American Radical Tradition*, New Press, 2003.

Donghak Rebellion. Quoted in Bruce Cumings, *Korea's Place in the Sun: A Modern History*, W. W. Norton, 1997.

Dos Passos, John. *USA*, Library of America, 1996.

Douglass, Frederick. *Selected Addresses of Frederick Douglass (An African American Heritage Book)*, Wilder Publications, 2008.

Du Bois, W. E. B. *Reconstruction in America: 1860–1880*, Free Press, 1998.

Du Wenxiu. Quoted in Li Shujiang and Karl W. Luckert, *Mythology and Folklore of the Hui: A Muslim Chinese People*, State University of New York Press, 1994.

Durruti, Buenaventura. Quoted in Albert Meltzer, *A New World In Our Hearts: The Faces of Spanish Anarchism*, Cienfuegos, 1978.

Dworkin, Andrea. *Pornography: Men Possessing Women*, Putnam, 1981.

Easter Rising. Quoted in Charles Townshend, *Easter 1916: The Irish Rebellion*, Penguin, 2006.

Edelman, Marek. *The Warsaw Ghetto: The 45th Anniversary of the Uprising*, Interpress Publishers, 1989.

Einstein, Albert. "Why Socialism?" *Monthly Review* 1: 1 (1949).

Ellsberg, Daniel. *Secrets: A Memoir of Vietnam and the Pentagon Papers*, Viking, 2002.

Engels, Friedrich. *The Condition of the Working Class in England*, Panther Books, 1969.

Evans, George Henry. Philip S. Foner, ed., *We, The Other People: Alternative Declarations of Independence*, University of Illinois Press, 1976. Cited in Timothy Patrick McCarthy and John McMillan, eds, *The Radical Reader: A Documentary History of the American Radical Tradition*, New Press, 2003.

Faiz, Faiz Ahmed. *The Rebel's Silhouette: Selected Poems*, trans. Agha Shahid Ali, University of Massachusetts Press, 1995.

Fakhr al-Din II, Quoted in A. J. Abraham, *Lebanon in Modern Times*, University Press of America, 2008.

Fanon, Frantz. *The Wretched of the Earth*, Grove Press, 1966.

Farrokhzad, Forugh. Quoted in Michael C. Hillmann, *Iranian Culture: A Persianist View*, University Press of America, 1990.

Federation of South African Women. Quoted in Helen Joseph, *Side by Side*, Zed Books, 1986.

Fifth Pan-African Congress. Quoted in Roland Oliver, *Africa Since 1800*, Cambridge University Press, 2008.

Figner, Vera. Quoted in Barbara Alpern Engel and Clifford N. Rosenthal, eds, *Five Sisters: Women Against the Tsar—The Memoirs of Five Young Anarchist Women of the 1870s*, Routledge, 1992.

Fonseca, Carlos. Quoted in Matilde Zimmermann, *Sandinista: Carlos Fonseca and the Nicaraguan Revolution*, Duke University Press, 2000.

Foot, Paul. *The Case for Socialism*, Bookmarks, 1990.

Foreman, Dave. Quoted in Dave Foreman and Bill Haywood, eds, *Ecodefense: A Field Guide to Monkeywrenching*, Ned Ludd Books, 1985.

Foucault, Michel. *The History of Sexuality, Vol. I*, Vintage, 1990.

Fourier, Charles. *The Utopian Vision of Charles Fourier: Selected Texts on Work, Love, and Passionate Attraction*, trans. Jonathan Beecher and Richard Bienvenu, Jonathan Cape, 1972.

Freire, Paulo. *Pedagogy of the Oppressed*, trans. Myra Bergman Ramos, Continuum, 1970.

Fried, Erich. Quoted in Erich Fried and Stuart Clink Hood, eds, *100 Poems Without A Country*, Red Dust, 1980.

Friedan, Betty. *The Feminine Mystique*, W. W. Norton, 1963.

Gaitán, Jorge Eliécer. Quoted in Bert Ruiz, *The Colombian Civil War*, McFarland, 2001.

Galeano, Eduardo. *Genesis (Memory of Fire Trilogy, Part 1)*, trans. Cedric Belfrage, W. W. Norton, 1998.

Gandhi, Mohandas K. Quoted in R. L. Khipple, ed., *Famous Letters of Mahatma Gandhi*, Indian Printing Works, 1947.

Garibaldi, Giuseppe. Quoted in Lewis Copeland, Lawrence W. Lamm and Stephen J. McKenna, eds, *The World's Great Speeches*, Dover Publications, 1999.

Garrison, William Lloyd. Quoted in William E. Cain, ed., *William Lloyd Garrison and the Fight against Slavery: Selections from the Liberator*, Bedford Books, 1995.

Gay Cheerleaders. Quoted in Lucian Truscott IV, "Gay Power Comes to Sheridan Square," *Village Voice* (June 31, 1969).

General Union of Palestinian Woman. Quoted in Abida Samiuddin and R. Hanam, eds, *Muslim Feminism and Feminist Movement, Volume II*, Global Vision, 2002.

Ginsberg, Allen. *Howl and Other Poems*, City Lights Books, 1956.

Gold, Mike. *New Masses* 21 (November 5, 1935). Cited in Alan Wald, *Exiles from the Future*, University of North Carolina Press, 2001.

Goldman, Emma. *Anarchism and Other Essays*, Mother Earth Publishing Association, 1911.

Gonzales, Rodolfo "Corky." Quoted in Carlos Muñoz, Jr., *Youth, Identity, Power: The Chicano Movement*, Verso, 2007.

de Gouges, Olympe. Quoted in Daline Gay Levy, Harriet Branson Applewhite, and Mary Durham Johnson, eds, *Women in Revolutionary Paris 1789–1795: Selected Documents*, University of Illinois, 1979.

Gramsci, Antonio. *Selections from the Prison Notebooks*, International Publishers, 1971.

Great Miners' Strike. Quoted in Alex Callinocos and Mike Simon, *The Great Miners' Strike*, Bookmarks, 1985.

Green Movement. Trans. Puya Gerami.

Grimke, Angelina. *An Appeal to the Christian Women of the South*, Arno Press, 1969.

Grimke, Sarah. *Letters on the Equality of the Sexes and the Condition of Woman*, Lenox Hill, 1970.

Guaman Poma de Ayala. Quoted in Orin Starn, Carlos Iván Degregori and Robin Kirk, eds, *The Peru Reader: History, Culture, Politics*, Duke University Press, 1995.

Guevara, Ernesto "Che." *The Che Reader*, ed. David Deutschmann, Ocean Press, 2003.

Guthrie, Woody. Quoted in Mark Allan Jackson, *Prophet Singer: The Voice and Vision of Woodie Guthrie*, University Press of Mississippi, 2008.

Hagos, Bahta. Quoted in Richard Caulk, "'Black Snake, White Snake': Bahta Hagos and his revolt against the Italian overrule in Eritrea, 1894," cited in Donald Crummey, *Banditry, Rebellion and Social Protest in Africa*, Heinemann, 1986.

Hamer, Fannie Lou. Quoted in Davis W. Wouck and David E. Dixon, eds, *Women and the Civil Rights Movement 1954–1965*, University Press of Mississippi, 2009.

Hampton, Fred. "Power Anywhere Where There's People," http://

www.historyisaweapon.com/defcon1/fhamptonspeech.html (accessed August 10, 2010).

Hancock, John, et al. *The Declaration of Independence and Other Great Documents of American History 1775–1865*, Dover Thrift Editions, 2000.

Har Dayal, Lala. Quoted in Dharmavira, *Lala Har Dayal and Revolutionary Moments of His Times*, Indian Book Company, 1970.

Harrison, Hubert R. "Two Negro Radicalisms," *New Negro* (October 1919).

Hassan, Mohammed Abdulla. Quoted in D. Jardine, *The Mad Mullah of Somaliland*, Greenwood Press, 1923.

Hatuey. Quoted in Bartolomé de Las Casas, *Short Account of the Destruction of the Indies*, trans. Nigel Griffin, Penguin, 1999.

Hayford, Adelaide Casely. Quoted in Adelaide M. Cromwell, *An African Victorian Feminist: The Life and Times of Adelaide Smith Casely Hayford, 1868–1960*, Howard University Press, 1992.

Haywood, William. Quoted in Joyce L. Kornbluh, ed., *Rebel Voices: An IWW Anthology*, revised edition, Charles H. Kerr, 1988.

Head, Bessie. *A Question of Power*, Heinemann, 1987.

Heine, Heinrich. *Germany: A Winter's Tale*, trans. Edgar Alfred Bowring, Mondial, 2007.

Heinmot Tooyalaket. Quoted in Chief Joseph, "An Indian's Views of Indian Affairs," *North American Review* 128 (1879). Cited in Dee Brown, *Bury My Heart at Wounded Knee: An Indian History of the American West*, Holt Paperbacks, 2007.

Heraud, Javier. Quoted in Orin Starn, Carlos Iván Degregori and Robin Kirk, eds, *The Peru Reader: History, Culture, Politics*, Duke University Press, 1995.

Herbst, Josephine. *Rope of Gold*, Harcourt, Brace & Co., 1939.

Hellman, Lillian. *Scoundrel Time*, Back Bay Books, 2000.

Henry, Patrick. Quoted in James Albert Woodburn, ed., *American Orations: Studies in American Political History*, G. P. Putnam's Sons, 1896.

Herero Man. Quoted in Thomas Pakenham, *Scramble for Africa*, Random House, 1991.

Herndon, Angelo. *You Cannot Kill the Working Class*, International Labor Defense and League of Struggle for Negro Rights, 1937.

Herodotus. *Histories Book III*, trans. A. D. Godley, Nabu Press, 2010.

Hesiod. *Theogony* and *Works and Days*, trans. H. G. Evelyn-White, Filiquarian Publishing, 2007.

Herzen, Alexander. Quoted in Isaiah Berlin, "Herzen and Bakunin on Individual Liberty," in *Russian Thinkers*, Penguin, 2002.

Hidalgo, Miguel. Quoted in Michael Meyer, *The Course of Mexican History,* Oxford University Press, 1979.

Hikmet, Nâzım. Quoted in Talat S. Halman, *The Turkish Muse: Views And Reviews, 1960s–1990s,* ed. Jayne L. Warner, Syracuse University Press, 2006.

Hill, Joe. Quoted in Irwin Silber and Earl Robinson, eds, *Songs of the Great American West*, Dover Publications, 1995.

Ho Chi Minh. *On Revolution: Selected Writings, 1920–66*, Bernard B. Fall, ed., Praeger, 1967.

Ho Xuan Hong, *Spring Essence: The Poetry of Ho Xuan Huong,* trans. John Balaban, Copper Canyon Press, 2000.

Hou Dejian. Quoted in Geremie Barmé and Linda Jaivin, *New Ghosts, Old Dreams*, Times Books, 1992.

Howe, Julia Ward. Quoted in Laura E. Richards and Maud Howe Elliott, *Julia Ward Howe, 1819–1910*, Vol. 1, Houghton Mifflin, 1916.

Hughes, Langston. Quoted in Arnold Rampersad, ed., *The Collected Poems of Langston Hughes*, Knopf, 1995.

Indians of All Tribes. Quoted in Paul Chaat Smith and Robert Allen Warrior, *Like a Hurricane*, New Press, 1996.

Ingersoll, Robert. *Some Mistakes of Moses*, C. P. Farrell, 1880.

International African Service Bureau. Quoted in Jonathan Derrick, *Africa's "Agitators,"* Columbia University Press, 2008.

Irish Saying. Quoted in Thomas Pakenham, *The Year of Liberty: The Story of the Great Irish Rebellion of 1798*, Hodder & Stoughton, 1969.

Ito Noe. Quoted in Mikiso Hane, *Peasants, Rebels, Women, and Outcastes: The Underside of Modern Japan,* 2nd edn, Rowman & Littlefield, 2003.

Industrial Workers of the World, The. Quoted in Mari Jo Buhle, Paul Buhle and Dan Georgakas, eds, *Encyclopedia of the American Left*, Oxford University Press, 1998.

Jackson, Aunt Molly. Quoted in Shelly Romalis, *Pistol Packin' Mama: Aunt Molly Jackson and the Politics of Folksong*, University of Illinois Press, 1999.

James, C. L. R. *A History of Pan-African Revolt*, Charles Kerr, 1995.

Jara, Victor. Quoted in Pilar Aguilera and Ricardo Fredes, eds, *Chile: The Other September 11: An Anthology of Reflections on the 1973 Coup*, Ocean Press, 2006.

Jefferson, Thomas. Quoted in *Diplomatic Correspondence of the United States of America*, Vol. 2, BiblioLife, 2009.

Jit Poumisak. Quoted in Craig J. Reynolds, *Thai Radical Discourse: The Real Face of Thai Feudalism Today*, Cornell Southeast Asia Program, 1987.

João, Mutimati Barnabé. Quoted in Georg M. Gugelberger, ed., *Marxism and African Literature*, Africa World Press, 1986.

Juana Inés de la Cruz. Quoted in Silvia Evangelisti, *Nuns: A History of Convent Life*, Oxford University Press, 2007.

Kanno Suga. Quoted in Kaneko Fumiko, *The Prison Memoirs of a Japanese Woman*, trans. Jean Inglis, M. E. Sharpe, 1991.

Kartini, R. A. Quoted in Joost Coté, ed., *Realizing the Dream of R. A. Kartini*, Ohio University Press, 2008.

Katayama Sen. *The Communist Review*, 3: 3 (July 1922).

Keller, Helen. *Selected Writings*, ed. Kim E. Nielsen, NYU Press, 2005.

Kimathi, Dedan. S.M. Shamsul Alam, *Rethinking Mau Mau in Colonial Kenya*, Palgrave, 2007.

King, Martin Luther, Jr. Quoted in James M. Washington, ed., *A Testament of Hope: The Essential Writings and Speeches of Martin Luther King, Jr.*, HarperCollins, 1990.

Kitahara Taisaku. Quoted in Mikiso Hane, *Peasants, Rebels, Women and Outcastes: The Underside of Modern Japan*, 2nd edn, Rowman & Littlefield Publishers, Inc., 2003.

Klein, Naomi. Quoted in Tom Mertes, ed., *A Movement of Movements*, Verso, 2004.

Kochiyama, Yuri. Quoted in Howard Zinn and Anthony Arnove, eds, *Voices of a People's History of the United States*, 2nd edn, Seven Stories Press, 2009.

Kollontai, Alexandra. *Selected Writings of Alexandra Kollontai*, trans. Alix Holt, W. W. Norton, 1980.

Kronstadt Rebels. Quoted in Israel Getzler, *Kronstadt 1917–1921: The Fate of a Soviet Democracy*, Cambridge University Press, 1983.

Kurihara Sadako. Quoted in John H. Dower, *Embracing Defeat: Japan in the Wake of World War II*, W. W. Norton, 2000.

Kuti, Fela. *Zombie*, Wrasse Records, 1977.

de La Boétie, Étienne. Quoted in Paul Bonnefon, *The Politics of Obedience and Étienne de La Boétie: The Discourse of Voluntary Servitude*, Black Rose Books, 2006.

La Pasionaria. Quoted in Ronald Fraser, *Blood of Spain*, Pantheon, 1979.

Lakshmibai (Rani of Jhansi). Quoted in M. L. Bhargava, *Freedom Struggle in Uttar Pradesh, Vol. 3*, Publications Bureau, 1957.

Lawrence Strikers. Quoted in Kim Bobo, Jackie Kendall, and Steve Max, *Organizing For Social Change*, Anmol Publications, 2003.

Lead Belly. *Lead Belly Legacy, Vol. 2*, Smithsonian Folkways, 1997.

Le Guin, Ursula. *The Dispossessed*, Harper & Row, 1974.

Le Loi. Quoted in Robert Goldston, *The Vietnamese Revolution*, Bobbs-Merrill Co., 1972.

Lease, Mary Elizabeth. Quoted in O. Gene Clanton, *A Common Humanity: Kansas Populism and the Battle for Justice and Equality, 1854–1903*, Sunflower University Press, 2004.

Lebrón, Lolita. Quoted in Irene Vilar, *The Ladies' Gallery: A Memoir of Family Secrets*, Vintage Books, 1998.

Lenin, V. I. *State and Revolution*, Kessinger Publishing, 2004.

Lennon, John. *Power to the People*, Apple Records, 1971.

Leopald, Aldo. *Sand County Almanac*, Oxford University Press, 1949.

Levellers, The. *Geoffrey Robertson presents The Levellers: The Putney Debates*, Verso, 2007.

Leviné, Eugen. Quoted in Rosa Leviné-Meyer, *Leviné, the Spartacist*, Gordon and Cremonesi, 1978.

Li Dazhao. Quoted in Maurice J. Meisner, *Li Ta-chao and the Origins of Chinese Marxism*, Atheneum, 1977.

Lili'uokalani (Queen). *Hawaii's Story by Hawaii's Queen*, Lee & Shepard, 1898.

Ling Bing. Quoted in David S. G. Goodman, *Beijing Street Voices: The Poetry and Politics of China's Democracy Movement*, Marion Boyars, 1984.

Lingg, Louis. Quoted in John Peter Altgeld, *The Chicago Martyrs: The Famous Speeches of the Eight Anarchists in Judge Gary's Court*, Kessinger Publishing, 2009.

Little, Omar. *The Wire*, Season 2, Episode 6, "All Prologue," HBO, original airdate July 6, 2003.

Liu Xiaobo. "My Self-Defense," *China Rights Forum 2010, no. 1: Freedom of Expression on Trial in China.*

López Pérez, Rigoberto. Quoted in John Brentlinger, *The Best of What We Are: Reflections On the Nicaraguan Revolution*, University of Massachusetts Press, 1995.

Lopez, Yolanda. Quoted in George Lipsitz, *American Studies in a Moment of Danger*, University of Minnesota Press, 2001.

Lorde, Audre. *Unicorn: Poems*, W. W. Norton, 1978.

Lu Xun. *Selected Stories of Lu Hsun*, Foreign Languages Press, 1972.

Luddites. Quoted in E. P. Thompson, *The Making of the English Working Class*, Vintage, 1966.

Lumumba, Patrice. Quoted in Wilfred G. Cartey and Martin Kilson, eds, *The Africa Reader: Independent Africa*, Random House, 1970.

Luther, Martin. Quoted in Adolph Spaeth, L. D. Reed, Henry Eyster Jacobs et al., eds and trans., *Works of Martin Luther, Vol. 1*, A. J. Holman Company, 1915.

Luxemburg, Rosa. Quoted in Spencer Tucker, ed., *Encyclopedia of World War I*, ABC-CLIO, 2005.

Maathai, Wangari. Quoted in Priscilla Sears, "Wangari Maathai: 'You Strike The Woman . . .'," *In Context* #28 (Spring 1991).

Maceo, Antonio. Quoted in Fidel Castro, "We Will Never Lower Our Guard," *In Defense of Socialism: Four Speeches on the 30th Anniversary of the Cuban Revolution*, Pathfinder, 1989.

Machel, Samora. *Mozambique: Sowing the Seeds of Revolution*, Zimbabwe Publishing House, 1981.

MacLean, John. Quoted in Thomas Bell, *John MacLean, A Fighter for Freedom*, Communist Party Scottish Committee, 1944.

Mainardi, Pat. Quoted in Barbara Crow, ed., *Radical Feminism: A Documentary Reader*, NYU Press, 2000.

Maji-Maji Rebellion. Quoted in Thomas Pakenham, *The Scramble for Africa*, Random House, 1991.

Malcolm X. Quoted in George Breitman, ed., *Malcolm X Speaks: Selected Speeches and Statements*, Merit Publishers, 1965.

Mandela, Nelson. Quoted in Brian MacArthur, ed., *The Penguin Book of Twentieth-Century Speeches*, Penguin, 2000.

Mandelstam, Osip. Quoted in Carolyn Forché, ed., *Against Forgetting*, trans. W. S. Merwin and Clarence Brown, W. W. Norton, 1993.

Mankell, Henning. Quoted in Kate Connolly, "Henning Mankell on Gaza Flotilla Attack," *Guardian*, June 3, 2010, http://www.guardian.co.uk/world/2010/jun/03/gaza-flotilla-attack-henning-mankell (accessed August 10, 2010).

Marcos, Subcomandante. *Our Word Is Our Weapon: Selected Writings*, Seven Stories Press, 2001.

Manjok. Quoted in Bok-Rae Kim, "Korean Nobi Resistance under the Chosun Dynasty (1392–1910)," *Slavery & Abolition* 25:2 (2004).

Mao Zedong. Quoted in J. Mason Gentzler, *Changing China: Readings in the History of China from the Opium War to the Present*, Praeger, 1977.

Marcuse, Herbert. *One-Dimensional Man: Studies in the Ideology of Advanced Industrial Society*, Beacon Press, 1964.

Maréchal, Sylvain. Quoted in Brian Tierny and Joan Scott, *Western Societies: A Documentary History*, McGraw-Hill, 1984.

Mariátegui, José Carlos. Quoted in Michael Pearlman, ed. and trans., *The Heroic and Creative Meaning of Socialism: Selected Essays of José Carlos Mariátegui*, Humanities Press, 1996.

Marti, José. *Our America: Writings on Latin America and the Struggle for Cuban Independence*, ed. Philip S. Foner, Monthly Review Press, 1977.

Marvell, Andrew. *An Account of the Growth of Popery and Arbitrary Government in England*, Gregg International Publishers Limited, 1971.

Marx, Karl and Engels, Friedrich. *Manifesto of the Communist Party*, Verso, 1998.

Matsushima Shotaro. Quoted in John H. Dower, *Embracing Defeat: Japan in the Wake of World War II*, W. W. Norton, 2000.

Mayakovsky, Vladimir. *Poems*, trans. Dorian Rottenberg, Progress Publishers, 1972.

McCarthy and John McMillan, eds, *The Radical Reader: A Documentary History of the American Radical Tradition*, New Press, 2003.

McKay, Claude. Quoted in Arnold Adoff and Benny Andrews, eds, *I Am the Darker Brother: An Anthology of Modern Poems by Negro-Americans*, Simon & Schuster, 1997.

Meeropol, Abel. Quoted in Billie Holiday, *20th Century Masters: Millennium Collection*, Hip-O Records, 2002.

Mejía Godoy, Carlos. Quoted in Dorothee Sölle, *Thinking About God: An Introduction to Theology*, SCM Press, 1990.

Mekatilili Wa Menza. Quoted in Cynthia Brantley, "Mekatilili and the Role of Women in Giriama Resistance," in Donald Crummey, ed., *Banditry, Rebellion and Social Protest in Africa*, Heinemann, 1986.

Menchú, Rigoberta. *I, Rigoberta Menchú*, Verso, 2009.

Menehbi, Saida. Quoted in Valerie Orlando, *Francophone Voices of the "New" Morocco in Film and Print*, Palgrave MacMillan, 2009.

Michnik, Adam. Quoted in Phillipe Demenet, "Adam Michnik: The Sisyphus of Democracy." *The UNESCO Courier*, September 2001, http://www.unesco.org/courier/2001_09/uk/dires.htm (accessed August 10, 2010).

Mills, C. Wright. *The Power Elite*, Oxford University Press, 1956.

Milton, John. *Paradise Lost*, Modern Library, 2008.

Min Sheng Pao. Quoted in Anthony Short, *The Communist Insurrection in Malaya, 1948–1960*, Muller, 1975.

Morales, Evo. "Speech given at the 'In Defense of Humanity' conference," December 24, 2005, http://www.counterpunch.org/morales 12302005.html (accessed August 10, 2010).

Morris, William. *Nowhere and Other Writings*, Penguin, 1993.

Mossadegh, Mohammad. "Biography," http://www.mohammadmossadegh.com/biography (accessed August 10, 2010).

Mother Jones. Quoted in Philip S. Foner, *Mother Jones Speaks*, Monad Press, 1983.

Moyano, Maria Elena. Quoted in Diana Miloslavich Tupac, ed., *The Autobiography of Maria Elena Moyano: The Life and Death of a Peruvian Activist*, trans. Patricia S. Taylor Edmisten, University Press of Florida, 2000.

Muir, John. *Our National Parks*, Cosimo Classics, 2006.

Mukhopadhyay, Subhas. Quoted in K. M. George, ed., *Modern Indian Literature: An Anthology, Vol. II: Fiction*, Sahitya Akademi, 1992.

Muktabai. Quoted in Susie Tharu and K. Lalita, eds, *Women Writing in India: 600 B.C. to the Present, Vol. 1: 600 B.C. to the Early 20th Century*, The Feminist Press at CUNY, 1991.

Müntzer, Thomas. *Wu Ming presents Thomas Müntzer: Sermon to the Princes*, Verso, 2010.

Murrow, Edward. Quoted in Anthony R. Fellow, ed., *American Media History*, Wadsworth Publishing, 2009.

Namboodiripad, E. M. S. *History, Society and Land Relations: Selected Essays*, LeftWord Books, 2010.

Nasrallah, Hassan. Quoted in Nicholas Noe and Nicholas Blanford, eds, *Voice of Hezbollah: The Statements of Sayyed Hassan Nasrallah*, Verso, 2007.

Nasser, Gamal Abdel. Quoted in Dan Hofstadter, *Egypt and Nasser, Volume 1*, Facts on File, 1973.

National Constituent Assembly. Quoted in Hutton Webster, ed., *Historical Sourcebook*, D.C. Heath & Co., 1920.

Naylor, James. Quoted in Douglas Van Steere, ed. *Quaker Spirituality: Selected Writings*, Paulist Press, 1984.

Nazrul Islam, Kazi. *The Rebel and Other Poems*, Sahitya Akademi, 1998.

Nehru, Jawaharlal. Quoted in Salman Rushdie and Elizabeth West, eds, *Mirrorwork: 50 Years of Indian Writing, 1947–1997*, Henry Holt and Co., 1997.

Neruda, Pablo. *Canto General*, trans. Jack Schmitt, University of California Press, 1991.

Neto, Antonio Agostinho. Quoted in Aquino De Braganca and Immanuel Wallerstein, *The African Liberation Reader*, vol. 2, St. Martin's Press, 1982.

Newton, Huey P. Quoted in David Hillard and Donald Weise, eds, *The Huey P. Newton Reader*, Seven Stories Press, 2003.

Ngugi Wa Thiong'o and Ngugi Wa Mirii. *I Will Marry When I Want*, Heinnemann, 1982.

Ngwane, Trevor. "Sparks in the Township: Interview with Trevor Ngwane," *New Left Review* 22 (July/August 2003).

Nkrumah, Kwame. *Revolutionary Path*, International Publishers, 1973.

Ntantala, Phyllis. Quoted in Langston Hughes, ed., *An African Treasury*, Crown, 1960.

Nyo Mya. Quoted in Richard Butwell, *U Nu of Burma*, Stanford University Press, 1969.

Nguyen An Ninh. Quoted in Truong Buu Lam, *Colonialism Experienced: Vietnamese Writings on Colonialism 1900–1931*, Michigan University Press, 2000.

Nguyen Quang Bich. Quoted in David G. Marr, *Vietnamese Anticolonialism 1885–1925*, University of California Press, 1971.

Nguyen Tuong Tam. Quoted in Neil L. Jamieson, *Understanding Vietnam*, University of California Press, 1993.

Nyerere, Julius Kambarage. *Ujamaa: Essays on Socialism*, Oxford University Press, 1973.

Öcalan, Abdullah. Quoted in Paul J. White, *Primitive Rebels or Revolutionary Modernizers?: The Kurdish National Movement in Turkey*, Zed Press, 2000.

Odets, Clifford. *Three Plays*, Random House, 1935.

Odinga, Oginga. *Uhuru: Autobiography of Oginga Odinga*, Heinemann, 1968.

Ohashi Genzaburo. Quoted in Roger W. Bowen, *Rebellion and Democracy in Meiji Japan*, University of California Press, 1980.

Orwell, George. Quoted in Hugh Purcell, *The Last English Revolutionary: Tom Wintringham 1898–1949*, Sutton Publishing, 2004.

Padmore, George. Quoted in Walter Rodney, *How Europe Underdeveloped Africa*, Howard University Press, 1981.

Paine, Thomas. *Political Writings*, ed. Bruce Kuklick, Cambridge University Press, 2000.

Palestinian Civil Society Organizations. Quoted in Kole Kilibarda, "Confronting Apartheid: The BDS Movement in Canada," *Upping the Anti* 7 (October 2008).

Pankhurst, Emmeline. *My Own Story*, Hearst International Library, 1914.

Paris Communards. Quoted in Stewart Edwards, ed., *The Communards of Paris*, Cornell, 1973.

Park No-Hae. Quoted in Hagen Koo, "The State, *Minjung*, and the Working Class in Korea," in Hagen Koo, *State and Society in Contemporary Korea*, trans. Kyung-ja Chun, Cornell University Press, 1993.

Parsons, Lucy. Quoted in Lisa Grunwal, Stephen J. Adler, eds., *Women's Letter's: America from the Revolutionary War to the Present*, Dial Press, 2005.

Pasdermajian, Garegin. *Why Armenia Should Be Free*, Hairenik, 1918.

Pattirakiriyar. Quoted in Kamir Zvelebil, *The Smile of Murugan: On Tamil Literature of South India,* Brill, 1973.

Pederson, Lyn. Quoted in Mark Blasius and Shane Phelan, eds, *We Are Everywhere*, Routledge, 1997.

Peltier, Leonard. *Prison Writings*, Macmillan, 2000

Plato. *Apology*, trans. Benjamin Jowett, Quiet Vision, 2004.

Phan Boi Chau. Quoted in David G. Marr, *Vietnamese Anticolonialism*, University of California Press, 1971.

Pinter, Harold. Quoted in *Nobel Lectures: From the Literature Laureates, 1986 to 2006*, New Press, 2007.

Plough Jogger, Quoted in Howard Zinn, *A People's History of the United States: 1492–Present*, HarperCollins, 2003.

Pontecorvo, Gillo. *Battle of Algiers*, 1966.

Potter, Paul. Quoted in Todd Gitlin, *The Sixties: Years of Hope, Days of Rage*, Bantam Books, 1987.

Proudhon, Pierre-Joseph. *What Is Property?* Dodo Press, 2007

Priestly, J.B. Quoted in Angus Calder, *The People's War*, Pimlico, 1992.

Pullman Workers. Quoted in Albert Fried, ed., *Except to Walk Free: Documents and Notes in the History of American Labor*, Anchor Books, 1974. Cited in Timothy Patrick McCarthy and John McMillan, eds, *The Radical Reader: A Documentary History of the American Radical Tradition*, New Press, 2003.

Qabbani, Nizar. Quoted in Tariq Ali, *Clash of Fundamentalisms*, Verso, 2003.

Qu Yuan. *Li Sao and Other Poems of Qu Yuan*, trans. Yang Xianyi and Gladys Yang, Foreign Language Press, 1980.

Quiroga, Alejandro. Quoted in Chris Spannos, ed., *Real Utopia: Participatory Society in the 21st Century*, AK Press, 2009.

Rabelais, François. Quoted in Stephen Duncombe, ed., *Cultural Resistance Reader*, Verso, 2002.

Radicalesbians. Quoted in Karla Jay and Allen Young, *Out of the Closets: Voices of Gay Liberation*, Douglas Books, 1972.

Rainsborough, Thomas. Quoted in J. P. Kenyon, *The Stuart Constitution, 1603–1688, Documents and Commentary*, Cambridge University Press, 1966.

Pal Devi, Sampat. Quoted in Sanjit Das, "A Flux of Pink Indians," *Vice Magazine* (February 2008).

Ramírez, Sergio. *Adios Muchachos: Una Memoria de la Revolucion Sandinista*, Aguilar, 1999. Translated by Mark Falcoff for http://www.sergioramirez.org (accessed August 10, 2010).

Randolph, A. Philip. "Why Should We March?" *Survey Graphic* 31 (November 1942).

Ranters, The. Quoted in Christopher Hill, *The World Turned Upside Down: Radical Ideas During the English Revolution*, Viking Press, 1972.

Rebelo, Jorge. Quoted in Gerald Moore and Ulli Beier, eds, *The*

Penguin Book of Modern African Poetry, 4th edn, Penguin Classics, 1999.

Redda, Tewolde. Ruth Iyob, *The Eritrean Struggle for Independence: Domination, Resistance, Nationalism*, Cambridge University Press, 1997.

Reed, John. *Ten Days That Shook the World*, Penguin Classics, 2007.

Revolutionary War Council of the Persian Red Army. Quoted in *How the Revolution Armed: The Military Writings and Speeches of Leon Trotsky: Materials and Documents on the History of the Red Army, Volume III: The Year 1920*, New Park Publications, 1981.

Riel, Louis. Quoted in Larry Warwaruk, *Sundog Highway: Writing from Saskatchewan*, Coteau Books, 2000.

Riis, Jacob. *How the Other Half Lives*, W. W. Norton, 2010.

Rizal, José. *Noli Me Tangere*, trans. Harold Augenbraum, Penguin Books, 2006.

Robespierre, Maximilien. *Slavoj Žižek presents Robespierre: Virtue and Terror*, Verso, 2007

Rodney, Walter. *How Europe Underdeveloped Africa*, Howard University Press, 1974.

Rokeya Sakawat Hossein. *Sultana's Dream: A Feminist Utopia and Selections from The Secluded Ones*, ed. Roushan Jahan, Feminist Press, 1988.

Romero, Oscar. Quoted in James R. Brockman, ed. and trans., *The Violence of Love: The Pastoral Wisdom of Archbishop Oscar Romero*, Harper & Row, 1988.

Roy, Arundhati. *Public Power in the Age of Empire*, Seven Stories Press, 2004.

Russell, Bertrand, et al. Quoted in Jussi Hanhimäki and Odd Arne Westad, eds, *The Cold War: A History in Documents and Eyewitness Accounts*, Oxford University Press, 2004.

Sacco, Nicola. *Industrial Worker*, August 20, 1927.

de Sade, Marquis. *Philosophy in the Boudoir*, trans. Joachim Neugroschel, Penguin, 2006.

Saeki Jinzaburo. Quoted in John H. Dower, *Embracing Defeat: Japan in the Wake of World War II*, W. W. Norton, 2000.

Said, Edward W. *Orientalism*, Vintage, 1979.

de Saint-Just, Louis Antoine. Quoted in François René, *The Memoirs of François René*, Freemantle, 1902.

Sakharov, Andrei. Quoted in Robert V. Daniels, ed., *A Documentary History of Communism in Russia: From Lenin to Gorbachev,* 3rd edn, Vermont, 1993.

Sanders, Ed. "Predictions for Yippie Activities," *The Berkeley Barb,* August 2–8, 1968.

Salanga, Alfredo Navarro. Quoted in Angela Velasco Shaw and Luis H. Francia, eds., *Vestiges of War: The Philippine-American War and the Aftermath of an Imperial Dream 1899–1999,* NYU Press, 2002.

Sallust. Quoted in Adrian Goldsworthy, *Caesar: Life of a Colossus,* Yale University Press, 2008.

Sankara, Thomas. *Thomas Sankara Speaks: The Burkina Faso Revolution 1983–87,* Pathfinder, 1988.

Sanrizuka-Shibayama Farmers' League. Quoted in David E. Apter and Nagayo Sawa, *Against the State: Politics and Social Protest in Japan,* Harvard University Press, 1986.

Santhal Rebellion. Quoted in Sumanta Banerjee, *In the Wake of Naxalbari: A History of the Naxalite Movement in India,* Subarnarekha, 1980.

Sappho. *Sappho: Poems, A New Version,* trans. Willis Barnstone, Green Integer, 1999.

Saro-Wiwa, Ken. Quoted in Cameron Duodu, "Jailed Nigerian Writer Pledges Victory," *Observer,* January 8, 1995.

Sartre, Jean-Paul. Quoted in Annie Cohen-Solal, *Sartre: A Life,* Minerva, 1991.

Savio, Mario. Quoted in Robert Cohen, ed., *Freedom's Orator: Mario Savio and the Radical Legacy of the 1960s,* Oxford University Press, 2009.

Schreiner, Olive. Quoted in Carol Barash, ed., *An Olive Schreiner Reader: Writings on Women and South Africa,* Pandora, 1987.

Scott-Heron, Gil. Quoted in Daniel R. Katz, ed., *Why Freedom Matters: The Spirit of the Declaration of Independence in Prose, Poetry, and Song from 1776 to the Present,* Workman Publishing Company, 2003.

Sembène, Ousmane. *God's Bits of Wood,* Heinemann, 1996.

Senghor, Lamine. Quoted in J. Ayo Langley, *Ideologies of Liberation in Black Africa, 1856–1970,* Rex Collings, 1979.

Senghor, Leopald. *The Collected Poetry,* CARAF Books/University of Virginia Press, 1991.

Serge, Victor. *Year One of the Russian Revolution,* Writers & Readers Publishing, 1990.

Shaarawi, Huda. *Harem Years: The Memoirs of an Egyptian Feminist*, trans. Margot Badran, Feminist Press at the City University of New York, 1986.

Shabtai, Aharon. *J'Accuse*, trans. Peter Cole, New Directions, 2001.

Shahin, Tanyus. Quoted in Ussama Makdisi, "Corrupting the Sublime Sultanate: The Revolt of Tanyus Shahin in Nineteenth-Century Ottoman Lebanon," *Comparative Studies in Society and History*, v. 42, n. 2 (January 2000).

Shakur, Assata. *An Autobiography*, Lawrence Hill Books, 2001.

Shakur, Tupac. *Greatest Hits*, Interscope/Def Jam/Amaru, 1998.

Shariati, Ali. *Man and Islam*, trans. Fatollah Marjani, FILINC, 1981.

Sharpe, Samuel. Quoted in Vincent Brown, *The Reaper's Garden: Death and Power in the World of Atlantic Slavery*, Harvard University Press, 2008.

Shelley, Percy Bysshe. Quoted in Carl Woodring and James S. Shapiro, eds, *The Columbia Anthology of British Poetry*, Columbia University Press, 1995.

Sheppard, William. Quoted in Adam Hochschild, *King Leopold's Ghost*, Houghton Mifflin, 1998.

Shinde, Tarabai. Quoted in Rosalind O'Hanlon, *A Comparison Between Men and Women: Tarabai Shinde and the Critique of Gender Relations in Colonial India*, Oxford University Press, 1994.

Singer, Peter. *Animal Liberation*, Avon Books, 1975.

Singh, Bhagat. Quoted in Orin Starn, Carlos Iván Degregori and Robin Kirk, eds, *The Peru Reader: History, Culture, Politics*, Duke University Press, 1995.

Sioux Warriors, Quoted in Hila Gilbert, *Big Bat Pourier*, Wyoming Mills Company, 1968. Cited in Dee Brown, *Bury My Heart at Wounded Knee: An Indian History of the American West*, Holt Paperbacks, 2007.

Sitting Bull. Quoted in Robert M. Utley, *The Lance and the Shield*, Henry Holt and Co., 1993.

Smash the Security Treaty. Quoted in Glenn D. Hook and Gavan McCormack, *Japan's Contested Constitution: Documents and Analysis*, Routledge, 2001.

Smith, Elizabeth Oakes. *Proceedings of the Woman's Rights Convention*, J. E. Masters, 1852.

Sima Qian. Quoted in Cyril Birch, ed., *Anthology of Chinese Literature:*

Volume One: From Early Times to the Fourteenth Century, trans. J. F. Hightower, Grove Press, 1994.

Simone, Nina. *Simone Anthology*, RCA Records, 2003.

Sinclair, Upton. *The Jungle*, Doubleday, 1906.

Skanderbeg. Quoted in Edward Gibbon, *The Decline and Fall of the Roman Empire,* Phoenix, 2005.

Solanas, Valerie. *SCUM Manifesto*, Verso, 2004.

Soyinka, Wole. *Early Poems*, Oxford University Press, 1998.

Spartacus. Quoted in Appian, *The Roman History of Appian of Alexandria, Vol. 2: The Civil Wars*, trans. Horace White, Kessinger Publishing, 2007.

Spence, Thomas. Quoted in Peter Linebaugh, *The London Hanged*, Verso, 2003.

de Spinoza, Benedict. *A Theological-Political Treatise, and a Political Treatise*, trans. R. H. M. Elwes, Cosimo Classics Inc., 2007.

Stephen Junius Brutus. *Vindiciae Contra Tyrannos, or Concerning the Legitimate Power of a Prince Over the People, and of the People Over a Prince*, ed. George Garnett, Cambridge University Press, 1994.

Steward, Ira. Quoted in Albert Fried, ed., *Except to Walk Free: Documents and Notes in the History of American Labor*, Anchor Books, 1974. Cited in Timothy Patrick McCarthy and John McMillan, eds, *The Radical Reader: A Documentary History of the American Radical Tradition*, New Press, 2003.

Stewart, Maria. Quoted in Richard Newman, Patrick Rael and Phillip Lapsansky, eds, *Pamphlets of Protest: An Anthology of Early African-American Protest Literature, 1790–1860*, Routledge, 2001.

Sukarno. Quoted in *Africa-Asia Speaks from Bandung*, Indonesian Ministry of Foreign Affairs, 1955.

Tacitus. Quoted in Alfred John Church and William Jackson Brodribb, eds, *Complete Works of Tacitus*, McGraw-Hill, 1964.

Tagore, Rabindranath. *English Writings of Rabindranath Tagore, Volume Two: Poems*, Atlantic, 2007.

Tan Malaka. Benedict Anderson, trans., from *Gerpolek, gerilya-politik-ekonomi*, Djambatan, 2000.

Taruc, Luis. *Born of the People*, International Publishers, 1953.

Tecumseh. Quoted in Alan R. Velie, ed., *American Indian Literature: An Anthology*, University of Oklahoma, 1991.

Thiruvalluvar. Quoted in W. H. Drew and John Lazarus, *Thirukkural*, trans. S. Shankar, Laurier Books, 2001.

Thoreau, Henry David. Quoted in Nina Baym et al., eds, *The Norton Anthology of American Literature, Vol. 1*, 5th edn, W. W. Norton, 1998.

Three Marias. Quoted in Maria Isabel Barreno, Maria Teresa Horta and Maria Velho da Costa, *The Three Marias: New Portuguese Letters*, trans. Helen R. Lane, Doubleday & Co., 1975.

Thucydides. *The History of the Peloponnesian War*, trans. Richard Crawley, The Echo Library, 2006.

Tilak, Bal Gangadhar. Quoted in Gail Omvedt, *Reinventing Revolution: New Social Movements and the Socialist Tradition in India*, M. E. Sharpe, 1993.

Tinariwen. *Amassakoul*, World Village Records, 2004.

Tone, Wolfe. Quoted in John Mitchel, *The History of Ireland: From the Treaty of Limerick to the Present Time, Volume 1*, James Duffy, 1869.

To Huu. Quoted in Sheila Rowbotham, *Women, Resistance and Revolution*, Allen Lane, 1972.

Tonkin Free School. Quoted in David G. Marr, *Vietnamese Anticolonialism*, University of California Press, 1971.

Toussaint L'Ouverture. Quoted in Nick Nesbitt, ed., *Jean-Bertrand Aristide Presents Toussaint L'Ouverture: The Haitian Revolution*, Verso, 2008.

Trotsky, Leon. Quoted in Isaac Deutscher, *The Prophet Outcast: Trotsky 1929–1940*, Verso, 2003.

Trumbo, Dalton. *Johnny Got His Gun*, J. B. Lippincott Company, 1939.

Truth, Sojourner. Quoted in Carleton Mabee, *Sojourner Truth: Slave, Prophet, Legend*, NYU Press, 1995.

Tupac Amaru II. Quoted in Ronald Wright, *Stolen Continents: 500 Years of Conquest and Resistance in the Americas*, Mariner Books, 2005.

Tupac Katari, Quoted in Jim Shultz and Melissa Crane Draper, eds, *Dignity and Defiance: Stories from Bolivia's Challenge to Globalization*, University of California Press, 2009.

Tuqan, Ibrahim. Quoted in Salma Khadra Jayyusi, *Anthology of Modern Palestinian Literature*, Columbia University Press, 1992.

Turner, Nat. Quoted in Eric Foner, ed., *Nat Turner*, Prentice-Hall, 1971.

Tyler, James. Quoted in Marcus Rediker, *The Slave Ship: A Human History*, Penguin, 2008.

Tzara, Tristan. Quoted in Ann Caws, ed., *Manifesto: A Century of Isms*, University of Nebraska Press, 2000.

Umm Kulthum. Quoted in Vijay Prashad, *The Darker Nations*, New Press, 2008.

Vonnegut, Kurt. *Cat's Cradle*, Dial Press, 2006.

Walker, David. Quoted in Peter P. Hinks, ed., *David Walker's Appeal to the Coloured Citizens of the World*, Pennsylvania State University Press, 2000.

Wallace, Michele. *Black Macho and the Myth of the Superwoman*, Verso, 1999.

Walsh, Rodolfo. "Witness in Difficult Times," *Index on Censorship*, Vol. 6, No. 5, September/October 1977, Writers and Scholars International.

Weather Underground, The. Quoted in Harold Jacobs, ed., *Weatherman*, Ramparts Press, 1970.

Webb, Sidney. Quoted in Tudor Jones, *Remaking the Labour Party: From Gaitskell to Blair*, Routledge, 1996.

Wei Jingsheng. Quoted in James D. Seymour, *The Fifth Modernization: China's Human Rights Movement 1978–1979*, Earl M. Coleman Enterprises, 1980.

Wells-Barnett, Ida B. Quoted in Jacqueline Jones Royster, ed., *Southern Horrors and Other Writings: The Anti-Lynching Campaign of Ida B. Wells, 1892–1900*, Bedford Books, 1997.

Wenya Boatman. Quoted in Thomas Pakenham, *The Scramble for Africa*, Weidenfeld & Nicolson, 1991.

White Rose, The. Quoted in Inge Scholl and Dorothee Sölle, *The White Rose: Munich, 1942–1943*, Wesleyan University Press, 1983.

Whitman, Walt. Quoted in Andrew Lawson, *Walt Whitman and the Class Struggle*, University of Iowa Press, 2006.

Wiji Thukul. Translated by Benedict Anderson.

Wilde, Oscar. *The Soul of Man Under Socialism and Selected Critical Prose*, ed. Linda Dowling, Penguin Classics, 2001.

Williams, Eric. *Capitalism and Slavery*, University of North Carolina Press, 1994.

Williams, Robert F. "Is Violence Necessary to Combat Injustice? For the Positive: Williams Says, 'We Must Fight Back'," *Liberation* (September 1959).

Winstanley, Gerrard. *Tony Benn presents Gerrard Winstanley: A Common Treasury*, Verso, 2010.

Woeser. *Tibet's True Heart: Selected Poems*, Ragged Banner Press, 2009.

Women's Political Council. Quoted in Jo Ann Robinson, *The Montgomery Bus Boycott and the Women Who Made It: The Memoir of Jo Ann Gibson Robinson*, ed. David J. Garrow, University of Tennessee Press, 1987.

Wong Chin Foo. "Why Am I a Heathen?" *North American Review* 145: 369 (August 1887).

Woodhull, Victoria. Quoted in Cari M. Carpenter, ed., *Selected Writings of Victoria Woodhull: Suffrage, Free Love, and Eugenics*, University of Nebraska Press, 2010.

Wright, Frances. *Life, Letters, and Lectures, 1834–1844*, Arno Press, 1972.

Wright, Richard. Quoted in Claire A. Culleton and Karen Leick, eds, *Modernism on File: Writers, Artists, and the FBI 1920–1950*, Palgrave Macmillan, 2008.

Wu Han. Quoted in Clive Ansley, *Heresy of Wu Han: His Play "Hai Jui's Dismissal" and Its Role in China's Cultural Revolution*, University of Toronto Press, 1971.

Yamashiro Tomoe. Quoted in Mikiso Hane, *Peasants, Rebels, Women and Outcastes: The Underside of Modern Japan*, 2nd edn, Rowman & Littlefield Publishers, Inc., 2003.

Youssef, Saadi. Quoted in Tariq Ali, *Bush in Babylon*, Verso, 2003.

Zamora, Daisy. *Riverbed of Memory*, trans. Barbara Paschke, City Lights Publishers, 1988.

Zapata, Emiliano. Quoted in John Womack, Jr., *Zapata and the Mexican Revolution*, Vintage, 1970.

Zapatista Army of National Liberation. Quoted in Subcomandante Insurgente Marcos, *Our Word is Our Weapon: Selected Writings*, ed. Juana Ponce de León, Seven Stories Press, 2001.

Zetkin, Clara. *Selected Writings*, ed. Philip Foner, trans. Kai Schoenhals, International Publishers, 1984.

Zikode, S'bu. "We are the Third Force," *Drum Magazine* (December 1, 2005).

Zola, Émile. Quoted in Alain Pagès, ed., *The Dreyfus Affair: "J'Accuse" and Other Writings*, Yale University Press, 1996.

Zou Rong. Quoted in Jonathan Spence, *The Search for Modern China*, W W. Norton, 1991.

INDEX

Wu Han, 354

Yamashiro Tomoe, 187
Youssef, Saadi, 308

Zamora, Daisy, 282
Zapata, Emiliano, 107
Zapatista Army of National Liberation, 293
Zetkin, Clara, 93
Zikode, S'bu, 314
Zola, Émile, 95
Zou Rong, 100

Africa

Anonymous, "Congolese Folksong," 85
Anonymous, "Tale of the Eloquent Peasant," 1
Anonymous, "Woe on Us Wingate," 115
Abd al-Qadir al-Jaza'iri, 52
Ali ibn Muhammad, 10
Awolowo, Obafemi, 216
Biko, Steve, 271
Black Women's Protest, 112
Bouhired, Djamila, 203
Brutus, Dennis, 236
Cabral, Amilcar, 221
Domingo, Charles, 107
Fanon, Frantz, 213
Federation of South African Woman, 199
Fifth Pan-African Congress, 174
Hagos, Bahta, 92
Hayford, Adelaide Casely, 194
Hassan, Mohammed Abdulla, 121
Head, Bessie, 258
Herero Man, 99
International African Service Bureau, 162
João, Mutimati Barnabé, 246
Kimathi, Dedan, 188
Kuti, Fela, 262
Lumumba, Patrice, 212
Maathai, Wangari, 290
Machel, Samora, 257
Maji-Maji Rebellion, 103
Mandela, Nelson, 219
Mekatilili Wa Menza, 114
Menebhi, Saida, 263
Nasser, Gamel Abdel, 200
Neto, Antonio Agostinho, 251
Ngugi Wa Thiong'o and Ngugi Wa Mirii, 261
Ngwane, Trevor, 307

Nkrumah, Kwame, 230
Ntantala, Phyllis, 212
Nyerere, Julius Kambarage, 264
Odinga, Oginga, 229
Padmore, George, 160
Rebelo, Jorge, 224
Redda, Tewolde, 211
Rodney, Walter, 240
Sankara, Thomas, 279
Saro-Wiwa, Ken, 295
Schreiner, Olive, 105
Sembène, Ousmane, 211
Senghor, Lamine, 143
Senghor, Leopold, 174
Shaarawi, Huda, 349
Sheppard, William, 106
Soyinka, Wole, 228
Tinariwen, 310
Umm Kulthum, 200
Wenya Boatman, 77
Zikode, S'bu, 314

Asia

Anonymous, "Pattinappaalai," 7
Anonymous, "Poem by Korean Elementary-
    School Student," 208
Anonymous, "Poem in Blood," 150
Anonymous, "Shanghai Posters," 280
Abdukhaliq "Uyghur," 137
Ambedkar, B.R., 160
Anti-Suharto Movement, 296
Aung San Suu Kyi, 288
Basil of Caesaria, 10
Bei Dao, 260
Beijing Workers' Autonomous Federation, 286
Boxers ("Righteous Fists of Harmony"), 97
Chen Duxiu, 130
Chinese Writers (Charter 08), 319
Civakkiyar, 11
Congregation for the Democratization of
    Chonnam Province, 273
Donghak Rebellion, 91
Du Wenxiu, 70
Faiz, Faiz Ahmed, 176
Gandhi, Mohandas K., 148
Har Dayal, Lala, 152
Hikmet, Nâzım, 168
Ho Chi Minh, 133
Ho Xuan Hong, 40

Latin America and the Caribbean

363

PERMISSIONS

Thank you to Gorgias Press for permission to reprint "Woe on Us Wingate"; to Roger W. Bowen for permission to reprint his translation of "The Rain Still Falls"; to the University of California Press for permission to reprint "Indictment of Corrupt Customs," "Letter From Abroad Written in Blood" and "United Fruit Company"; to Ragged Banner Press for permission to reprint "The Fear in Lhasa"; to University of Toronto Press for permission to reprint *Hai Ru's Dismissal*; to Continuum Books for permission to reprint "Peasants' Mass"; to Cornell Press for permission to reprint "Maybe"; to Syracuse University Press for permission to reprint "Invitation"; to PM Press (www.pmpress.org) for permission to reprint "Paris Graffiti"; to Peter Singer for permission to reprint an extract from *Animal Liberation*; to University of Minnesota Press for permission to reprint "Living for Change"; to Columbia University Press for permission to reprint "Lest We Lose," "The Aqsa Mosque," "My Country on Partition Day" and "It is Close at Hand"; to Duke University Press for permission to reprint "A Guerrilla's Words"; to the University of Virginia Press for permission to reprint "The Message"; to Atlantic Books for permission to reprint "Walk Alone"; to Canongate Books for permission to reprint "The Revolution Will Not Be Televised"; to Lawrence Hill Books for permission to reprint an excerpt from Assata Shakur's *An Autobiography*; to Jobete Music for permission to reprint "What's Going On"; to Lenono Music for permission to reprint "Power to the People"; and to New Directions for permission to reprint "The Answer" and "The New Jew."

All efforts have been made to contact copyright holders for material reproduced in the book, and all citations are listed in the sources section. But if any have been inadvertently overlooked, we are happy to make the necessary arrangements at the first opportunity.